THE CHRISTIAN MARXIST DIALOGUE

THE
Christian Marxist
Dialogue

AN INTERNATIONAL SYMPOSIUM

EDITED BY

Paul Oestreicher

THE MACMILLAN COMPANY

COLLIER-MACMILLAN LIMITED, London

He hath put down the mighty from their seats and exalted them of low degree.

He hath filled the hungry with good things and the rich he hath sent empty away. LUKE 2, 52–3

Contents

Preface

AT A TIME when relatively few men in East and West wield immense power with cynical pragmatism, ideologies serve as useful smoke-screens to fool the gullible. The American and Russian variants make the largely spurious claim to be on the one hand Christian, on the other Marxist. The successfully indoctrinated, the brainwashed on both sides, really believe it to be so. Luckily for us all, the wielders of power are—by and large—not taken in by their own propaganda. If they were, a holocaust might already have put an end to our era of history. Pascal reminds us that "men never do evil so fully and so happily as when they do it for conscience's sake." When the ruler turns grand inquisitor men have good cause to be afraid. That is why the confrontation of China with both America and the Soviet Union is potentially so horrific. Instead of recognizing it for the power struggle it is, even the rulers may be fooled by their own ideologies into believing that principles are involved. That would be fatal. But even here, cynicism may still come to the rescue.

Against this background men who believe themselves to *be* Christians and to *be* Marxists go on persecuting each other in many places. It suits the wielders of power, it keeps the myths in being, without which the smoke-screens would be blown away. Both sides in this game need an enemy and thrive on martyrs. The real victim is the truth, which, were it to emerge, would destroy the whole charade. It goes without saying that both Christianity and Communism are utterly devalued in the process. To millions of thinking men and women they symbolize rival *reactionary* establishments, incompatible with the new humanity that could be born.

Is it any wonder then that Christian and Communist radicals—those in both camps who reject the ideological clap-trap and who are prepared to reinterpret and reenact old faiths for a new age—are being driven together in their search for fulfilment? That is at least part of the explanation for the Christian Marxist dialogue. Neither *faith* (as opposed to power-structure) is doing well. And so they seek each other. "They" are not the powerful, not the managers, not the wealthy, not the establishments. They are human beings who care. And they care not least for the powerful who can no longer afford to care. They care from within the structures even for the manipulators, the *apparatchiks;* they are a loyal opposition. And they are permanently insecure unless they succumb to the temptation of turning their faith into a rival, anti-establishment ideology. Sectarianism is a constant lure and a fatal trap. It confirms the status quo.

All this is relevant to the Christian Marxist dialogue. Undoubtedly there are some who promote the dialogue for tactical reasons. Most do not. They do it because they believe that either Jesus or Marx was right. They are a minority and they know it. They know too that, however great their differences, there is a connection between Jesus of Nazareth and Marx, the prophet.

The dialogue, then, is part of a reform movement in both "camps." It is orthodox because both the Church and the Party stand in need of constant reformation or perhaps even "permanent revolution." It is in many ways the pretext for impassioned dialogue *within* the Church and *within* the Party—or, more accurately, within the churches and the parties, for "World Communism" is as much of a myth as "Christendom."

There is a sense in which those who are engaged in the encounter between Communism and Christianity find solace in each other's existence. They have more than ideas in common. They have needs in common. They want to replace the opium of ideology with the leaven of faith. That is not the only valid way to explain and to legitimize the dialogue. It is as subjective as one man's apologia for it must be.

Both Christian theologians and Communist theoreticians have gone to great lengths to disprove that their own faith is idealistic—with tragic consequences. The ideals inherent in both faiths can be jettisoned by their practitioners with impunity. Theological and dialectical justification is always at hand. The controllers of the KGB and the CIA can sleep with quiet minds. The ideology will stand *anything*.

The disaster is that men have been persuaded of the impracticability of idealism. To be taken seriously men must be seen to be realists. Fine. But are idealism and realism opposites? Might not the implementation of ethical ideals *be* the only worthwhile form of realism? My terminology may at this point be unconventional. Yet I am stating something fundamental to both Christian and Communist faith. Each affirms not only that man can discern the world but that he has power to

change it; and further, that he is ethically bound to use
that power.

The dialogue cannot long evade the central issue of
the source of that power. On man's perception of its
source will depend how he plans to use his power. And
here there can be no easy Christian-Marxist synthesis. It
may be easy enough to agree on a secular "realized
eschatology," on an ultimately attainable "end" for man
in tomorrow's world. *How* to get there is quite another
matter. The end is not independent of the means but is
in part determined by them. Peace is not made on a
road strewn with corpses. There is no emerging from a
tunnel of half-truths (the *stuff* of propaganda) into the
clear light of truth. Begin to clothe these assertions,
these bare bones, with sociological, political and economic flesh—and the dialogue *in all its spiritual dimensions* is under way.

This symposium does little more than to highlight it
at a few tangential points. The choice of material has
been subjective. It had to be. A completely different set
of essays could have made just as good a book. The
contributors have only this in common, that they are
either Christians or Communists. Their approaches differ
as widely as does their style. There is something here
for most readers. Few will find that everything speaks
to their condition. Some pieces are frankly intellectual;
some are almost demonstratively anti-intellectual. All
strike me as honest. Taken together I hope the whole
symposium stands up to the demands of integrity
without which the dialogue itself would be worse than
meaningless. But because each piece, and the whole, is
part of the dialogue, they are open to correction and
even to refutation. No author, in the light of the dialogue, should want to write the same again six months
or even six weeks later. A living faith is not demon-

strated by the maintenance of positions but by the freedom to abandon them without fear.

If it does not seek to influence events, however indi-
rectly, if its aim is not "to make a difference," it has no
justification. It can then be dismissed as one more
opiate, as an LSD, as a psychological sop to the
dreamers. The dialogue of which I speak must help to
set men free everywhere—spiritually, mentally and phys-
ically—or it will die of its own irrelevance. It is a
tremendous encouragement that in Czechoslovakia
where, in difficult and discouraging times, the dialogue
was carried on with fervor and intensity, the fruits have
become evident. There, those within the Church and
more particularly those within the Party who were
prepared to defy the majority and to seek common
ground have been vindicated. It is no accident that the
number of contributions to this symposium from Czechoslovakia is larger than from anywhere else. It has been
difficult not to make it larger still.

Possibly the most adventurous person on the Communist side has been Dr. Erika Kadlecova who, as head
of the Institute of Sociology in the University of Prague,
was prepared to take Christianity seriously both as an
intellectual and as a sociological phenomenon. Her
research into the Christian presence in Czechoslovak
society has begun to influence religious policy throughout Communist Europe. In 1967 it was due to her
persistence that a major international Christian Marxist
dialogue conference was, for the first time, able to be
held in Eastern Europe. Today Dr. Kadlecova, a charm-
ing and warmhearted young woman as well as an able
scholar, is Secretary of State for Church Affairs in
Prague. She is no longer on the sidelines, but responsible
for policy.

If everything I have written so far suggests that I

place Christianity and Communism on a par, this is true *sociologically*. But I do not pretend to straddle the field. I am bound to come clean: as a Christian I am partisan. I am convinced that it is the power of the living God, working through men, which alone makes a new world possible. He does not lord it over us but is content to be our servant. The pattern of this service suggests that God's revolution in our time is far more radical than either Christians or Communists have yet been prepared to admit.

PAUL OESTREICHER

10 Eaton Gate,
London S.W.1.
May 1968

THE CHRISTIAN MARXIST DIALOGUE

Introduction: Dialogue in Hope

PAUL OESTREICHER

"CHRIST DID NOT die against Karl Marx." In the cool light of reason this must be obvious to every Christian. Yet in the heat of debate this affirmation caused uproar in West Germany's parliament. Social Democrat Dr. Gustav Heinemann, a prominent lay Christian, was making it at the height of the cold war when challenging the foreign policy of Dr. Adenauer's government. This theological declaration was an unexpected rhetorical climax in a political debate. It was strictly orthodox, yet the *Christian* Democratic Party rose to the bait in furious indignation. They could not have been more angry had the speaker suggested that Jesus of Nazareth had been a card-carrying member of the Communist Party. It is, of course, not entirely irrelevant that Jesus was executed as an alleged political troublemaker. Yet all that Dr. Heinemann had implied was that Jesus died *for* Karl Marx, as he died for every other sinner.

Anti-Communism, in its ideological form, is a social disease still prevalent in many parts of the so-called free world. When it has the cloak of the Christian crusader thrown around it, the disease becomes virulent. It is not amenable to rational argument. It has nothing in common with non-Communist beliefs as such. It assumes, for instance, that if Ho Chi Minh really is a Communist, then that settles the argument about Vietnam. All this pinpoints a Western version of the brainwashed personality.

That there is an equally virulent Eastern version does not need to be stressed.

The Christian Marxist dialogue, to which this international symposium is a modest contribution, must primarily have the very practical aim of extending the frontiers of human freedom by radically calling in question the mentality on both sides that presumes that the world can be geographically or ideologically divided into human beings on the one side and some lesser type of mortals on the other. The dialogue must, whatever else it does, affirm the dignity of man. For if the Gospel is true, then *every* man is divine.

That is a sufficient reason for loving Communists. But it is equally applicable to Fascists, racists or any other category of perverted people. Christ *did* die for them all. None of them may be despised. The need to hate sin and to love the sinner has always, in theory, been recognized as a necessary part of Christian living. This is never easy. To know it to be true is one thing. To *love* the man who hates my guts for being a "nigger luvver" is quite another.

The agony, the "cross," of being required to live *for* all other people, regardless of their qualities, is a uniquely Christian problem. It is the fundamental ethical demand of the Gospel. But it is *not* the essential rationale for the dialogue between Christians and Communists which this book exists to promote. If it were, there would be an equally strong case for dialogue with every type of human aberration. While this is arguable, I think it misguided. There are evil realities and perverted ideologies which must be defeated. The ethical difficulty for the Christian lies in his choice of weapons.

Paul has some advice to give on the "warfare of the spirit" but this will not make too much sense to the landless Brazilian peasant whose children are starving and who, in any case, cannot read or write. If the poor in spirit are blessed, they will no doubt be forgiven for believing a hand grenade to be a more effective instrument of change than the "shield of faith." Whether forgiveness operates in quite the same way for the allegedly sophisticated commander of a Polaris submarine, dealing in potential death by the megaton— not to speak of the military chaplain who blesses the death machine—I dare not judge. I only know that both of them have an easier conscience because they believe they are helping to keep the world safe from Communism.

I have said more than enough to give away my assumption that Communism, unlike Fascism, cannot simply be equated with evil. Christian Marxist dialogue is not essentially an activity in which the "goodies" talk to the "baddies." In theory it is a dialogue between two groups of "goodies," each with a particular type of insight into the nature of truth. In practice it is a dialogue between "baddies" who historically have often betrayed their own vision. Commenting on a British consultation between Christians and members of the Communist Party a lead writer in the Anglican *Church Times* wrote: "It is no wonder that many Christians are puzzled . . . at the spectacle of friendly 'dialogue' between systems of thought so opposed as Communism and Christianity. . . . It may be possible for Christians to admire some Communist achievements [but] their hatred of religion is something which no Christian worthy of the name can possibly approve. The only object for Christians of 'dialogue' with sworn enemies of Christianity should be their ultimate conversion."

This statement, with which many Christians would

no doubt agree, is, I believe, *almost* wholly misguided. *Mutatis mutandis,* incidentally, many Communists would also probably give it their assent. The dialogue, however, radically calls into question this assumption that Christianity and Communism are intrinsically opposed systems. In a human context (and there is no other that is relevant) they are strictly comparable systems. Certainly in many essential aspects Communism derives from the Judeo-Christian tradition. The fact that Christians and Communists have been in conflict institutionally proves nothing about their inherent incompatibility. On the contrary, the very bitterness of that conflict suggests that it has something of the quality of a fratricidal war. There is in fact a case for seeing Communism as an early and extreme form of "secular Christianity." Nor is this idea a new one.

Does this allow for the atheism which is so much a part of Communist ideology? I believe it does and at this point the contemporary "God is dead" theology is not irrelevant. Marxist atheism, however it may be presented philosophically, is essentially historic. The God of nineteenth-century European society was found by Marx and Engels to be not only an object of superstitious belief but a reactionary, evil God; or more accurately a God who provided pretexts and alibis for almost everything that was inhuman. And this *was* the God who was offered to those in need of "opium." Marx was relatively unconcerned with fighting religion. It was historically unnecessary. To unmask God was sufficient. Behind this God there lurked man in depravity, man alienated by capitalist society. This God existed to help preserve the status quo. He provided hope to the desperate *in a world to come.* Pie-in-the-sky. This God, who remains to this day the only God known to many Communists and tragically to *many Christians,* is dead. He has always been dead. He is not and never was Christ incarnate, Jesus of Nazareth, the servant of men.

Rejected by Communists, and by many other men, this God of man's making, part social, part psychological must be buried. But "let the dead bury their dead." It is not a function of this dialogue to become part of the God-is-dead syndrome but rather to work for the rehabilitation of God. The God who, incarnate in his people, stands for a radical renewal of this world, is not dead. The God in whose name St. John proclaimed "Behold I make all things new" is a God of revolution. His concern for political and economic justice is made plain in Scripture beyond any shadow of doubt. That is not to jump on any popular political bandwagon. That is not to equate the revolution of the Kingdom of God with any current radical political concept. That is not to make the naive leap, which some Christians have made, which equates the equality of the Kingdom with the classless Marxist paradise. It is to recognize that Christian action intends to change the world. The fact that the "theology of revolution" is now a matter of serious study in the ecumenical movement is an indication that Christians are beginning to respond to the world in a way comparable with the Marxist response to the nineteenth century.

All this is summed up by recognizing that both Christianity and Marxism are rooted in an eschatalogical hope. Christianity and Communism are both fundamentally optimistic. The early Christians indubitably expected the Kingdom of God to become a reality in their lifetime—or very soon thereafter. It is not altogether surprising that now, nearly two thousand years later, Christian hope is a little forlorn. Very similarly in 1917 many Communists believed that the Communist society was imminent. It has taken only half a century to make them talk about the *ultimate* achievement of Communism in terms that are reminiscent of Christians talking "theologically" about the Kingdom.

Both creeds are in danger of being utopian. To counteract this danger both have built-in assurances that they are not idealistic but realistic. The Christian calls "revelation" to witness the fact that his dream will be fulfilled. The Marxist calls in "science." What must be, will be.

Yet neither creed admits to being deterministic. What must be, will be. But only because men cooperate with God or history to make it so.

This is in many ways an age of disillusion. The Church in this as in many past ages has not *really* believed in its own power to enact the Kingdom. It has fallen back on a theology of endless waiting for a *deus ex machina.* The Kingdom will, one day, drop down from the heavens. Meanwhile men can only make the best of a fallen world, using it as a transit camp to "heaven." This is not to say that the churches make no attempt to sweeten the atmosphere of the transit camp. They do, but without urgency.

And Communists? Many have left the Party embittered and disillusioned. The passing of "all power to the Soviets" has produced not a paradise but very often the opposite. The "scientific" analysis has not proved to be accurate. And most others, including those who wield power, have settled for an interim "socialist realism" which relegates Communism to an unreal, dim, distant future. The Bible and the Communist Manifesto remain as ikons, symbolizing great things, revered by a few, bowed down to by many. Church and Party get down to realities.

The parallels go much further than indicated here. A competent social psychologist could well make out a case that as Communism and Christianity go into social decline, they are bound to be driven into each other's arms. Consequently, the dialogue. There is a measure of truth in this. Neither Christians nor Communists should dismiss it lightly. But much more important as a starting point for the dialogue is the very simple fact that the economic and political needs of the world cry out so desperately to be met that Christians and Communists —along with many other people—should be exploring together how they can help to meet them.

I said economic and political needs. But personal, *human* needs are even greater. They are spiritual needs. If the Incarnation is what Christians claim it to be, then the words *human* and *spiritual* can properly be used interchangeably. Christians and Communists are therefore bound to explore together what it means to be human. They both claim to be proponents of genuine humanism. The practical content of that humanism must therefore be a common objective. Erich Fromm's symposium *Socialist Humanism*[1] is an important contribution to that search.

The secular sovereignty of man has been dangerously obscured by a great deal of theology ever since St. Augustine. In the light of the insights of the Jewish prophets and even more so of the assurance by Christ to his disciples that, having faith, they would be able to "move mountains," Christians, of all people, should recognize that the world is in man's power. Heaven and hell are of man's making. This is not to dethrone God. It is merely to topple a superstitious view of "Christ the King" as an absent but absolute ruler over the world. This King has chosen to be man's servant and to abdicate his power to man.

None of this is to belittle the power of evil. It is

[1] New York: Doubleday, 1966.

merely to affirm man's triumph over evil, if he chooses
to accept forgiveness and to accept his restoration to
authority. Man come of age, to use Bonhoeffer's phrase,
is in no sense perfect man, fully mature man or man who
does not sin. He is man accepting responsibility. In all
this I use classical Christian concepts. Demythologize
the language, secularize the thought structures; the
substance remains unaltered. Man is destined to make or
mar tomorrow's world. Now, this is not news to a
Communist. What *is* news is that man is not alone. Man
is not potentate, but *plenipotentiary ambassador*. Like
every metaphor this one is inadequate and has its
dangers. But it makes the point simply.

The misunderstanding of man's role, and more specifically of the Church's role (I suggest that the two
are inseparable), is well illustrated by a story vouched
for by an Episcopal bishop. He was flying across the
Atlantic when his aircraft ran into a series of air pockets
and was violently shaken. A woman thought her last
moments had come and called to a priest, who was
quietly reading his breviary: "Father, is there nothing
you can do?" "I'm sorry, madam," came the cool
reply, "I'm in sales, not management." The woman had
the idea that God could be called in by some magic
procedure to intervene. The priest was *really* powerless.
Only the pilot wielded power at that moment. If the
aircraft had crashed it would not have been an act
of God but a result of the deliberate decision of men
to entrust themselves to an imperfect product of human
technology.

But the misunderstanding goes further. The priest had
also misunderstood his role, and in this he was typical.
God is not a saleable product. The Church through
an act of faith, *is* engaged in management. The Church
shares responsibility for how men direct their affairs.

The Church is meant to be the corporate human expression of God's will in action, the prototype of human community, *not in sales, but effectively in control, in management;* and not merely in a consultant capacity but involved, through every member, in shaping the future. This then should not be a triumphalist institution seeking to dominate society but a servant Church, incognito, putting love into action, sacrificing for men, suffering with men and helping to set men free.

This implies a theology of secular hope, a theology of realized eschatology, a theology that believes in the possibility of freedom and depends for its validity on the assumption of the divinity of man. God becomes real in my neighbor. This is an insight that was common to the early Church and also to the Eastern Fathers. It has largely been obscured in the West by a medieval Catholic and Protestant theology of the primacy *in this world* of sin. This has obscured the kinship between man and God in Christ. The Reformation formula of justification *by faith* was useful to counteract the idea that man could *earn* his passage to heaven. Yet it did not go far enough. We are not justified even by faith. We are restored to the likeness of God *not by our faith, but by his love.* This restoration depends on nothing, not even our response.

But when it comes to entering upon our human heritage, then we shall be known "by our fruits." That is why Pelagius was, in his way, as near to the truth as Augustine. And that is the point at which Christian man and Communist man meet. They both stand judged by their deeds. In historical perspective, for all the good they have each done, they appear to have done as much evil. The Christians, it must be added, have had a lot longer to learn from their betrayal of humanity.

There is hardly a crime that can be attributed to Communists which they have not learned from Christians. Heresy hunts, persecution, censorship, inquisition, brainwashing, violence—the Church has been, and still is in parts of the world, author of or party to them all. Nothing is more sickening today than Christians who deplore the suppression of religion by Communists and who could not care less about the number of Communist or alleged Communists in the prisons of the "free world." When, as I have clearly mentioned, Hitler murdered every active Communist he could lay his hands on, even before he turned on the Jews, there was not a whisper of Christian dissent.

That is not to whitewash Communists or Communist regimes. Quite the contrary. They are guilty of exactly the same hypocrisy in reverse. They remain on shaky ground as long as dissent is suppressed and persecuted in most Communist countries.

I would go further and affirm that world Communism today is extremely vulnerable in a much more absolute sense. Wherever it has power it is, much like the Church, losing the confidence of thinking and responsible people, partly because of its inability to put people before ideology and partly for the opposite reason: the sacrifice of its ideals to personal expediency. Again this has its Christian parallels.[2]

Doctrinaire ideology has no future in a world of starvation, the H-bomb, space-flight and cybernetics. But neither has the cynical pragmatism that so easily usurps the names of Christ and Marx. The only hope is in a new openness which dynamically sets about the creation of human brotherhood. Marxism does provide an economic and political springboard for such

[2] Czechoslovakia is the significant exception that proves this assumption.

development. It also has within it, heavily overlaid with superfluous doctrine, a viable ethic.

And yet I do not believe that a new Marxist vision will, of itself, produce the "new man." It is no doubt a proper part of the dialogue for Marxists to try to persuade me that I am wrong in this and am judging too hastily. For my part, I now return to the one thing said in the *Church Times* critique of the dialogue which I am prepared to accept: the ultimate objective of dialogue *is* the conversion of Communists. This may not be popular, but it is inescapable. It would be evidence of a total disrespect of my partner in dialogue if I were not determined to share with him the experience of faith which alone entitles me to call myself a Christian.

But this needs amplification. Conversion is not what the disciples of Billy Graham would maintain. It is not a psychological process of making a man feel desperately in need of "salvation," not a process of threatening doom and then selling a cheap insurance policy. It is rather a willingness to share one's own very vulnerable personality, of offering one's total friendship, of pretending to no superiority and on the strength of all this to agree to embark with others on the insecure adventure of "making all things new."

That brings me back to revolution. The dialogue must help to clarify what revolution should achieve and, closely linked to that, how it can legitimately be made. The questions both of ends and of means must be considered together and, one way or another, embrace the whole canvas of life.

For the Christian the starting point is divine justice as revealed in the life and teachings of Jesus of Nazareth. Typologically (not just symbolically), *a meal* demonstrates the nature of human community. The

Eucharist, Mass, Holy Communion, Lord's Supper (call it what you will) typifies the politics of the Kingdom. It is not, as the Church has so often made it *seem*, an other-worldly rite, but is a demonstration of the sharing of life, of "Christian Communism." Bread is broken, shared. Wine is drunk, from one cup. In this fellowship which is life-giving (the life of God himself) there is total equality. Every man receives life in its wholeness. This is where the utterly classless society is realized. Not that the Church has cultically operated Communion as though this were true. By making this sharing exclusive to members of a given sect, it obscures the nature of Him who shares *unconditionally*. That is why I believe that the Lord's Table should be open to all men, not just to believers, let alone to selected believers.

Christian community is further typified by the enacted parable of the feeding of the five thousand. This is about the economics of food and about the dynamics of distribution. It is vital for the world today. In brief: there was not much to eat and there were a lot of hungry people. Our world. Jesus commanded: share all that you have! There was enough, and to spare. Miracle? For the superstitious—yes. For the scientist, economist, politician in today's world—no. Take from the earth what it will produce, distribute it totally, share unconditionally, and world poverty could give place to plenty.

This is not utopian. It is scientifically possible, given man's mastery over nature. But men will not obey the command to take all there is and share it. At this point what is often thought to be Marxist wishful thinking becomes highly relevant. "From each according to his ability, to each according to his need" becomes something within the realm of practical politics. It is not just an ethical objective. It is technologically within reach.

But—and here again Marx is right—it will not come about until those are toppled who wield power and who have a vested interest in the status quo. It is more than likely that this now includes even Communist "establishments." The Chinese may not be talking nonsense, even if they fail to notice the beam in their own eye. But certainly Mary's song, the *Magnificat*, is true when turned into the imperative: "He hath put down the mighty from their seat and exalted the humble and meek. He hath filled the hungry with good things and the rich he hath sent empty away."

Yet how can this be done humanely? How can it be done without so violating human personality that the revolution is betrayed before it is completed? These are not so much questions of principle as questions of application in concrete situations. And these are the questions on which, even among those engaged in dialogue, there is no agreement. In its most radical guise the question is: If every man is divine, how does revolutionary man express his love for the oppressor? It is a question Christians have too long shirked. The pacifist answer has too often been a refusal to face the issue itself. The non-pacifist answer has been a refusal to let the question be put at all.

The need to love *all* men (and here love is, as always, also a political term), if affirmed by Christians, may bring a parting of the ways in the dialogue. And yet I am not so sure that the practical answer, when found in concrete situations, will not make equal sense to a Marxist. The parting, when it comes, may cut clean across the Christian-Marxist divide.

The dialogue is bound, if it is to help move the world, to be largely concerned with ethics: by which I mean with action. At this point I believe that Marxism is even more helpless today than Christianity. It has not evolved ethical suppositions valid for both individuals and society today and tomorrow. The ethics of the New Testament—and of the Old—are dynamic and revolutionary and in consequence have been largely rejected by the Church, rejected with a degree of casuistry which Marxist dialectics have not managed to outdo. Marxist morality, on the other hand (and there is an awful lot of it), is no more than a borrowing of bourgeois concepts of virtue. *The Moral Code of the Builder of Communism*[3] would delight the heart of any Western suburban pastor looking for sermon material which could not possibly offend anyone, anyone, that is, in successful suburbia. The Party commends:

1. devotion to the Communist cause; love of the socialist Motherland and of other socialist countries;
2. conscientious labor for the good of society—"He who does not work, neither shall he eat";
3. concern on the part of everyone for the preservation and growth of public wealth;
4. a high sense of public duty, intolerance of actions harmful to the public interest;
5. collectivism and comradely mutual assistance—each for all and all for each;
6. humane relations and mutual respect between people— man is to man a friend, comrade and brother;
7. honesty and truthfulness, moral purity, simplicity and modesty in public and private life;
8. mutual respect in the family, and concern for the upbringing of children;
9. an uncompromising attitude to injustice, favoritism, dishonesty, careerism, and money-grubbing;
10. friendship and brotherhood among all peoples of the U.S.S.R., intolerance of national and racial hatred;

[3] From the program of the Communist Party of the Soviet Union, adopted at the 22nd Congress of the Party, October 31, 1961.

11. an uncompromising attitude to the enemies of Communism, the cause of peace and the freedom of nations;
12. fraternal solidarity with the workers of every country and with all peoples.

The style of this isn't quite adapted to an Anglo-Saxon Sunday school. But only a few word changes, and the trick is done. As for "he who does not work, neither shall he eat," a quote from St. Paul, that's no doubt as good for "labor discipline" in post-revolutionary Russia as it is in the West. But what about the man for whom there *is* no work? That is a *real* problem. Moral generalities will not help. Neither will sets of principles—or doctrines. It is the breakthrough to implementing what is *human* that is so difficult.

It is here that, adapting verses by Paul Potts:

> I want to tell a Communist
> That a worker is only important
> Because he is a man.
> And that a man is important
> Even when he is not a worker.
> (And there are Communists
> Who will believe me.)

That is half the story. Just as fervently:

> I want to tell a Christian
> That to believe in man
> Is one way of worshiping God.
> And that a man is divine
> Even when he denies God.
> (And there are Christians
> Who will believe me.)

Christians and Communists have not suddenly woken up to each other. The way from anathema, through dialogue to cooperation—or, to use an East German theological term, to *pro-existence*—is part of the historic process itself. This volume of essays is no more than a sign of what is being said and written all over the world. The roots of the dialogue go deep. It has always been carried on by a few, even when those in positions of authority did all they could to prevent it. On the Christian side I do not have in mind those fellow-travelers, however great their integrity or idealism, who naively espoused the political cause of international Communism. I mean those who labored tirelessly to cure the psychosis of the cold-war crusaders. I speak of men like—to name only one—Josef Hromádka in Prague who did not fear to be labeled "red," who went more than halfway in love to meet the "other side," who, in hoping almost against hope, made the present dialogue possible. There were other such pioneers both in East and West. But it was Pope John who enabled the banks to burst. It was the peasant Pope who made it clear beyond doubt that he loved Communists, however wrong-headed they might be. And Pope Paul has gone the next step. With John XXIII's *Pacem in Terris* in mind his successor has applied its challenge to the practical issues of world poverty and man's duty to end it. He issued the encyclical *Populorum Progressio* ("On the Progress of Peoples") and thereby made the greatest recent Christian contribution to the dialogue by squarely nailing the heresy that man has an absolute right to private property. This is no place to summarize the encyclical. In one sense it does no more than to restate Christian ortho-doxy, which has always held that when some men are in need, excess property held by others is theft. In any case, New Testament teaching on wealth is not as ambiguous as the rich, institutional churches would like to believe. It was certainly no wonder that the

Wall Street Journal dismissed *Populorum Progressio* as "Marxism warmed up."

The Christian openness to dialogue is now becoming evident all round the world, but it is still far from universal. There are still many warning voices, many who see the need for very long spoons.

And who are the Hromádkas and Pope Johns of world Communism? I have, in asking the question this way, allowed myself to fall into a common error. "World Communism" is a myth, a powerful myth, but not a political reality. Communism, like the Christian Church since its earliest days, is divided. And it is in ferment. The Communist monolithic monster is now as dead as the Roman Catholic one. Inasmuch as these two ever did exist, their existence ended at about the same time.

There are Communist pioneers of the dialogue. Hromádka's counterpart might well be Roger Garaudy, who is looked on by fellow Marxists with the same mixture of respect and disapproval that Hromádka has to contend with from Christians. And Communism's Pope John was surely Palmiro Togliatti. One is tempted, too, to give great credit to Guareschi, the novelist, who, in the creation of Don Camillo and Peppone reduced (or rather lifted) the conflict between two ideologies to the level of human relationships in which there was love and hatred and the liberating effect of laughter.

In a remarkable address on The Destiny of Man[4] Palmiro Togliatti, shortly before his death, in a sense opened the present era of dialogue in the most formal

[4] Delivered in Bergamo, March 20, 1963. Published in English in Foreign Bulletin of the Italian Communist Party, March–April 1963.

of manners, denying at the outset that rapprochement involved a compromise between what he called "the two ideologies." "At times . . . we have been accused of being ourselves a religion and even a Church. This is true, inasmuch as we have a faith, i.e., that the socialist transformation of society for which we are fighting is not merely a need but a task in which the best part of mankind is engaged with sure prospects of success. We believe that man will master nature, which is a biblical task, given to man by God himself in the Genesis story. It was Pope John who, speaking to the Soviet cosmonauts after their wonderful flight in outer space, emphasized this task; his was almost a prayer for progress in the understanding of nature and for its mastery by man . . . who must create a society fit for his freedom. . . . It could be said, if you like, that ours is a complete religion of man."

Togliatti proceeded to acknowledge the difference that arises when the Christian insists on the priority of God. Here, he believes, the "philosophic debate" must begin. Yet he himself carries it beyond this point by saying: "[As for] the development of the religious consciousness, we no longer accept the naive and mistaken view that an increase in knowledge and a change in social structures are enough, by themselves, to bring about a radical change in man. This view, inherited from the Enlightenment of the eighteenth century and the Marxism of the nineteenth has been disproved by history."

Such an admission of error was in itself a major step forward in dialogue. Unless there is in fact readiness on both sides to admit, not only to inhuman actions, but to ideological and theological error, the encounter is likely to be pointless. This in no way implies a false humility which would cave in at the first assault.

The dialogue calls for tough self-confidence. An unwillingness to concede anything, however, is generally a sign of profound insecurity.

And both sides show signs of such insecurity at many points. Perhaps not surprisingly Christian insecurity, both in the West and in the Socialist countries, often centers around the fear that to concede anything at all will lead to the erosion of the whole faith. Communists feel much the same, particularly where they are in power without having won the allegiance of the majority of the people. As for the "card-carrying" Christians and Communists who have no convictions at all, they are the greatest impediments of all to dialogue. By the very nature of things, they are in no position to make a contribution. They are the "hollow men" on both sides of the divide. They are the victims, but not always innocent victims, of ideological conflict.

Without any doubt genuine dialogue demands the humility that springs from assurance. This assurance can never be equated with self-righteousness. Yet *political* power is seldom other than self-righteous. That is why dialogue is generally conducted at several removes from the centers of power. Its liberalizing effects are not, however, likely to by-pass the power centers in the long run. Both Christians and Communists who have learned to trust each other will begin to influence those who directly shape policies. The fruits of this, which can never be predicted with certainty, are in the future. Meanwhile the dialogue leaves power politics unaffected. It may, on the other hand, already be marginally influencing domestic policies.

In the West relatively little pretense is made that political leaders are pursuing specifically Christian policies. Lip-service to this effect is generally recognized as such. But where the Communist Party governs, the

problem is greater. Here power ostensibly serves the
ideology. Does it? Or does it live by its own dynamic?
To put it more simply: Do the Communist rulers really
believe their own ideology? To this there is obviously
no one-word answer, but Erich Fromm's view of the
matter has a good deal to substantiate it:[5] "When we
hear Khrushchev pronounce Marx's or Lenin's words
we believe that he means what they meant, while the
fact is that these ideas are no more real to him than
the wish to save pagan souls was to the European
colonialists. Paradoxically, the only people who take
the Communist ideology seriously are we in the United
States, while the Russian leaders have the greatest
trouble in squaring it up with nationalism, moral teaching and increased material satisfactions."

While such a statement is not easy to substantiate,
the circumstantial evidence for its truth, or at least
its partial truth, is nevertheless convincing. There is,
for instance, overwhelming evidence that nationalism
within what used to be called the "Communist block"
is much stronger than Marxist ideology. Indeed, it
might now be said that—contrary to all theory—capitalism is much more international than socialism. The
quarrel between Russia and China must be seen partly
in this context.

The lip-service mentality in the socialist countries
is widespread. There is often an immense gap between
public profession and private conviction—not least
among young people. There are striking and obvious Christian parallels. It is important therefore
in the context of the dialogue itself to recognize that
it represents no more than significant minorities talking
to each other. One of the tests both of the Church

· [5] *May Man Prevail?* (New York: Doubleday, 1961), p. 128.

and of the Communist Party is whether, in the long run, they will find themselves able to incorporate the results of the dialogue into their systems. Will they have the inner strength and the public self-confidence to break through to such freedom? Will they dare to abandon the rigidities of doctrine which are irrelevant to a faith that is real and not just incanted?

However important dialogue may be, starry-eyed enthusiasm is not likely to change the world for the better. Power remains the fundamental key to tomorrow's world and ideas will not count for much unless their realization is also in the interests of those who wield power. This makes it essential that one element of the discussions (to which this symposium makes insufficient contribution) must be a realistic assessment of political power that is only in part affected by ideology. What is significant in this context is the growing practical cooperation between Christians and Communists where there is a common struggle against oppression. The Spanish situation, dealt with at length in this symposium, is the most striking example, but not the only one. And these struggles are a reminder of the importance of thinking through together the implications of revolutionary action. It may well be at that point that some of the greatest problems of the dialogue will become evident. The Christian obligation to go on loving at all costs may well appear to be a major irrelevance. It is not only a stumbling block to Communists.

The experience of Christians who live in socialist societies demonstrates both the possibilities and limitations of dialogue. Particularly the East German situation highlights the profound problems raised when those who wield power interpret cooperation in such a way that the Christian is hitched to a bandwagon not of

his choosing. He is not given the opportunity to cooperate selectively and critically. He is expected to be
"for or against." Yet this is the very thing that he
is bound to try to avoid in the process of pro-existence—
of living unreservedly *for* other men. The Church as
a whole is still far from sharing that vision and its
implications. Meanwhile Communist atheism remains a
real factor in the situation. But not the simple one
that it is sometimes made out to be. Simone Weil
reminds us that "an atheist . . . capable of pure compassion is as close to God as is a Christian and consequently knows him equally well, although his knowledge
is expressed in other words or remains unspoken. For
'God is Love.'" But that again is not to imply that
Communists outdo others in showing compassion.

If, as indicated above, the "God is dead" theology
has some relevance to the dialogue, it is equally significant that Communists, faced with the hard realities
of life in socialist societies, are increasingly doubtful
whether "pure materialism" is the ultimate measure of
all things. To many questions it simply appears to have
no answer. Death is not the only one. It is significant
in this context that a Marxist equivalent of John Robin-
son's *Honest to God* is about to be published by
Vitezslav Gardavsky in Czechoslovakia. The author is
a young philosopher teaching at the Czechoslovak Military Academy. His title: *God is Not Quite Dead Yet.*
Plainly he means something as intellectually and spiritually challenging as did the London *Observer's* correspondent, reporting from Czechoslovakia that: "God is
not dead, but editing a small, brave party journal in Brati-
slava." That is not the Gardavsky "line," which is, if anything, even more iconoclastic in a Marxist context.
The following extracts appeared in *Literarni Noviny*
(December 24, 1966) and managed to beat the ban

on the publication of revisionist thought which preceded the exhilarating liberation in the spring of 1968.

In this analysis we shall not regard Jesus as a historically
proven personality. Of course, we do not wish thereby to
join those who try to prove that he has never lived. That
simply does not interest us. Jesus exists for us much more
urgently: as a conceptual abbreviation of that Jewish concept
of the world and man in the Jewish world, which appeared
and spread around the beginning of our era and later
in the world of antiquity, and which surpasses its national
determinism. Such a concept makes us free: it offers us an
opportunity to consider Jesus as a personality of the Gospels
and to think of the contents of the challenge which he
personifies and carries.

Our reply to this cannot end with a "rebuttal" of this
legend; it does not depend on our declaration that we do
not believe in God nor in Jesus' divinity and that we are
atheists. The queries presented by original Christianity are
not religious ones. The real answer begins when we regard
these queries as historically justified. . . .

. . . Jesus mobilizes the Jewish masses for a radical decision for the kingdom of God.

What is that kingdom of God? It would be much too
simple to deduce from the Gospels an outline for a socially
just society or a collective project, for the realization of
which Jesus strove. From this viewpoint come the arguments which maintain that Jesus was "really" the first
Communist, that he strove for social justice and that in the
final analysis Marxism is "really" a secularized Christianity.
Such explanation is obviously inadequate. . . .

The call for an opposition against Rome was not inspired
by the ideal of social justice and did not lead to a Utopian
concept of a new social order. Should this be the case,
should this be the deepest level of Christianity, then Christianity would hardly have been able to survive its time.

This concerned a much deeper and much more basic
matter: namely, such an outline of life which could open

a new future by means of a responsible decision after a
merciless inner struggle which reaches to the very bottom;
in that future man becomes worthier than ever before. For
a Jew of Jesus' type this does not sound at all as a path to
an individual improvement and egocentric "moral development" to which he could progress independently from other
people, places and times. . . . A personal death or
catastrophe is not regarded as a terror or a vacuum, but it
has its significance in which the reality is enriched. To
Jesus' Jewishness, i.e., to the original Christianity, as we
can see, the decadent idea of individual salvation through
a provocatively virtuous life which barters for its warm little
spot in the paradise, is completely strange. . . .

. . . Love is one of the eternal themes for which Jesus'
original concept is of extraordinary importance. It does not
contain even a shadow of sentimentality, it is not a moral
commandment, it does not preach a helpless pacifism. Jesus,
to be sure, does not demand from man some specific virtues,
purity, poverty, obedience. He does not create any specific
moral codes. . . .

. . . Jesus' conception of love, so radically prepared, is
always a confrontation of man with death. And where there
is love—and this is the substance of Jesus' challenge—then
death (not only the physical death but death in thousands
of its everyday guises) cannot prevail. Therefore, love is
the most difficult, but also the noblest condition of man: the
fear of death is always its antithesis. To overcome this
limitation means to "rise from the dead," to be alive as a
man. Then everything, even those things which are totally
impossible, become easy. For the man who reaches this far,
this is no more a miracle, but a matter of fact. This seems
to be miraculous only to those who have not yet taken this
decisive step.

Jesus does not preach any all-out love. . . . By his acts
he implies that man is capable of performing miracles.
Miracles happen. In the structure of historical creation they
represent a moment of originality and uniqueness which

cannot be repeated. And love in this concept appears as a spirit of a radical historical subjectivity.

Why should one fear such miracles?

Why should not one rather wish for them?

It seems likely that Gardavsky's thought will prove to be the most challenging East European contribution so far made to the dialogue. It fits no ready-made slot. Neither does the thought of Polish journalist Halina Bortnowska of the Cracow Catholic magazine *Znak*. Commenting in the radical British Catholic monthly *Slant* (Vol. I, No. 5) in 1965 on the Second Vatican Council, she writes: "It is true that Christ rebuked and denounced the sins of the Jewish spiritual and political leaders of his time. He had a right to do so— because they had seen his life and did not want to believe. It is certainly possible that the 'sinners' of today have *not* yet met Christ. We have no right to condemn them as if *to see us* were enough to believe.

"*This problem of abstaining from condemnation is particularly important in relation to atheism.* We ought rather to try to be better theists, and not to denounce atheism *while we profess it in everyday life*. Condemning atheism . . . seems to me like exorcising the devil instead of doing penance. When we say to atheists that their intellectual attitude is contrary to human nature we do not persuade them that they are in error— we insult them, that is all. Would it not be better to help them examine their hearts: maybe what they hate or despise is not what the Christians believe. Perhaps what they love and cherish has its place in God's scheme of things. . . . If the dialogue is essentially a person-to-person relation, then what we must look for is the spiritual good of the persons concerned. . . . Their severe judgment (on us) is a just judgment, even when in individual cases they are not right. Collectively we have to accept their verdict and try to obtain mercy from God. We may be victims of unjust persecution, but at the same time as a community we are co-responsible for all persecution going on in the world, which up till now we have failed to enlighten. It is our duty to plead guilty because each of us has contributed his own share of negligence if not of actual malice. When God gives us an occasion to suffer a little for the faith, we have no right to praise ourselves. . . ."

Such a testimony can only come from within the Communist world. Significantly there are Polish Marxist testimonies from the philosophers Schaff and Kolakowski which are as humble and as challenging. Both men are under a cloud while cold winds from Moscow and East Berlin keep Warsaw in their grip. They are part of the ferment which is giving new life to Eastern Europe and which cannot even be conveniently labeled as "part of the dialogue." Everything is wide open and the more reactionaries on all sides attempt to batten down the hatches for fear of the storm to come, the more will everything blow up in their faces. It is at least partly true, and must therefore be recognized, that unless people have the same experience, logical controversy can degenerate into systematic misunderstanding. The dialogue is always in that danger, but in an undefinable way those who are driven to it by the practical inadequacies of the old orthodoxies *do*, in diverse ways, have the same or at least comparable experiences. Dialogue is simply evidence that ideological self-sufficiency is weaker than human interdependence.

It is necessary too to recognize that for some people, one of whom outlines his reasons in this symposium, the atheist question is not inherent in the dialogue at all. Some Christians have leaped over the hurdle of dialectical materialism and made their personal peace with Communism as providing the most acceptable public expression of their Christian faith. If this is done *without idealizing Communism* and in full recognition of the inhumanity perpetrated in its name (as is also done in the name of Christianity), then this is surely valid. It is an "eccentricity" that has always been acceptable to the Western Communist Parties and more recently to the Yugoslav Party too. Yugoslavia today, Eastern Europe tomorrow? That is too simple. But not nonsense.

I have said little *directly* about the whole question of human rights in Communist and non-Communist societies. It is a sad fact that in varying degrees they are trampled upon almost everywhere in the world. The dialogue would stand condemned as an intellectual luxury if it were not expressly conducted in such a way as to extend human freedom *everywhere*. No Christian who understands what this encounter really signifies should rest, while in the so-called Christian world Marxists are persecuted or at least relegated to the role of social outcasts. Nor should any Communist rest while writers remain behind prison bars or others are turned into social rejects because of their religious beliefs and practice. The dialogue must make practical headway in setting men free. In that context it is a happy thought that this collection of essays should appear in "Human Rights Year."

But the more philosophically minded will not so easily accept that freedom can be won by mere tolerance. *Can* there be any real freedom before the Revolution? Before there are the social prerequisites? To which the answer can only be the question: Is there any real freedom after the Revolution? And then the answer is a two-fold "no." It is also an inescapable "yes." Man *can* be free, *can* have a recognition of necessity (Marxist definition), *can* discern the will of God (Christian definition) independently of his social environment. And in being free he will begin to change that environment.

In *The Good Woman of Szechuan* Bertolt Brecht poses the great human and theological problem of freedom in a dramatic parable worthy of inclusion in the biblical canon. The good woman desperately tries to put love into practice. Society frustrates her. She is forced into moral schizophrenia. She must wear the mask of the scoundrel in order to acquire the means to do good. Society tries to defeat her goodness. The Revolution is not yet. The gods do not bring it. It all ends with a question to the spectator, a challenge to us all to write the end of the play ourselves—an end which can and must vindicate goodness. As in real life, the play is inconclusive. Brecht the critical Marxist and the visionary artist was like Jesus of Nazareth, in no doubt that there is a good end within man's grasp. But between the hope and its realization there stands a Cross. The Christian dialectic insists that death precedes life. "Dying we live" makes Marxist sense, too. But it is at this point that talk ends and action begins.

May 1968

I

Church and Communism

ROBERT ADOLFS

Possibilities of dialogue
That very widespread habit of presenting things as though
Christianity were simply and without remainder opposed to
the Communist ordering of society . . . is extremely dangerous.
PROFESSOR ALBERT DONDEYNE[1]

I. INTRODUCTION

DURING THE LAST hundred years Communism has been
officially anathematized no less than twelve times;[2]
and nobody knows how many *ad hoc*, local condemna-

ROBERT ADOLFS is the prior of the Augustinian House at
Eindhoven in the Netherlands. He is the author of *The
Church Is Different* and of the more recent study on the
Church, *The Grave of God*. This essay assesses in historical
terms the relation between Christianity and Communism. It
is from *The Church Is Different*, copyright © by Amboboeken, Utrecht, 1964; copyright © 1966 in English translation,
The Church Is Different, by Burns & Oates, Ltd., London,
translated from the Dutch, *DeKerk Is Anders*, published
1964 by Amboboeken, Utrecht. Printed in the United States
by Harper & Row, Publishers, Inc.

[1] *Geloof en Wereld* (Bilthoven, 1961), p. 177.
[2] Pius IX in the encyclical *Qui Pluribus* (1846) and in the
Syllabus of 1864; Leo XIII in the encyclical *Quod Apostolici
Muneris* (1878) and in *Rerum Novarum* (1891); Pius XI in the
allocution of 1924; encyclicals *Miserentissimus Redemptor*
(1928); *Quadragesimo Anno* (1931); *Caritate Christi* (1932);
Dilectissimi Nobis (1933); *Divini Redemptoris* (1937); Decree of
the Holy Office (of 1949); condemnation of Chinese Communism
in the encyclical *Ad Apostolorum Pricipis* (1958).

tions have been voiced, in addition, by the Church authorities. As early as 1846 Pius IX declared that Communism contravenes the natural law about as much as anything can *(maxime iuri naturali adversa)*; and Leo XIII called Communism "a mortal plague" *(lethiferam pestem)*. Pius XI, whose condemnations were the most numerous, says that Communism is full of errors and sophisms and in conflict with reason and divine revelation. It is bad through and through; and there is no sphere whatever in which it is permissible to cooperate with it or countenance it.[3]

Against the background of these condemnatory pronouncements it would appear that any form of dialogue with Communism is unwarranted and perilous. This conclusion is reinforced by a whole range of "self-evident facts" entrenched within the collective consciousness of Catholics. Communism, then, came to be regarded as without doubt or dispute the biggest enemy of the Church and of Christianity. Equally self-evident was the fact that Christianity and the atheistic ideology of Communism are two irreconcilable standpoints. What we were told about the conduct of the Communist rulers confirmed yet again the obviously objectionable, nay, damnable, character of a political system that destroyed all who opposed it by means of persecutions, executions, acts of atrocity, arrest and imprisonment, brainwashing and the like. It seemed evident, therefore, that for the Catholic Church to engage in discussion with Communism would be quite absurd. People even went so far as to identify Communism with anti-Christ and the devil—those ancient

---

[3] In the encyclical *Divini Redemptoris, Acta Apostolicae Sedis* 39 (1937), pp. 65–106.

symbols of the arch-enemies of Christianity! Thus, for example, the director of the *Oostpriesterhulp* described discussion with Communism as "a pact with the devil."[4]

"Self-evident facts" are often dangerous, however. They are, as it were, the axioms of people's ordinary, run-of-the-mill thinking—propositions which are *so* evident that nobody thinks of questioning them.

It is not until one puts a question mark against the said propositions that they begin to be troublesome. If we use the expression "self-evident facts" in this connection, this does not mean that the ecclesiastical documents offered no arguments for condemning Communism. We mean only that the mental outlook of the Church and of Catholics in general was firmly wedded to the idea of the total perfidy of Communism, with or without an extensive backing of argument.

During recent years, however, there has been a change in this outlook; and for the first time we hear of a possible dialogue with Communism.[5] This alteration has so far found a response only among a limited circle; for the thought of a possible dialogue meets with fierce resistance, even from an academic quarter.[6]

What follows, therefore, is meant to be an attempt to indicate some of the problematical aspects of the current evidence regarding Communism, and at the same time to explain from what standpoint a dialogue with Communism is possible, not to say necessary.

[4] *Nieuwe Eindhovense Krant* for 12 January 1963. *Cf.* also W. van Straten, *Zij noemen mij Spekpater*, pp. 75–76.

[5] D. Delfgaauw in *De Maand* (August–September 1961); also in *De Jonge Marx* (Baarn, 1962), pp. 119–126.

[6] Professor Zacharian, O.F.M. in *De Bazuin* 46 (1963), 35/1; and in *De Tijd* for 6 September 1963.

II. THE PROBLEMATICAL ASPECTS OF THE CONFLICT
BETWEEN CHRISTIANITY AND COMMUNISM

Current views regarding Communism have been formed, perhaps, too much on the basis of the godless, anti-Church and savage aspect that Communism has presented to the West. The West has let itself be too much governed by its immediate feelings of sympathy with the victims of Communism—a sympathy mixed, understandably enough, with abhorrence and disgust at an inhuman political system. The irksome reality of what Communism was in practice was always obtruding itself and so it became well-nigh impossible to stand aloof and take a detached view. To arrive at a reconstruction of the origin and causes of Communism in the world-process as a whole which would be as objective as possible was therefore extremely difficult.

When as Christians we concern ourselves with the conflict between Christianity and Communism, we are in all honesty bound to view that conflict *in its total aspect*—which is to say that we have to locate it within the history of the Church and Christianity during the last century. If we are candid in our consideration of past events, we shall have to admit that because nineteenth-century Catholicism was so isolated and withdrawn (as were also the main Protestant denominations), and because Christianity remained so aloof from the great issues agitating the world at that time, Christianity in general—and when we say "in general," we allow that there were indeed remarkable exceptions—passed by the human misery which, among other things, resulted from the capitalist system and attended the Industrial Revolution.

Social Blindness

As a consequence of economic stagnation in the seventeenth century, of the Napoleonic Wars and of the existence of an outdated feudal system, there arose in most countries of Europe during the last century an impoverished but ever-growing proletariat. When on top of that came the rise of industry and the introduction within it of the capitalist economy, this already long entrenched penury—until then accepted as one of the facts of life in society—became a problem. The distress was no longer something that the customary forms of charity could alleviate. In some countries the property-less proletariat amounted to a fifth—in a few even to well-nigh a third—of the population being impoverished. Later on, this proletariat in Western Europe was to a considerable degree caught up in a rapidly expanding industrialization, which reduced the majority to a condition of still greater insecurity.

Owing to undernourishment on what came to be recognized as the normal European hunger-diet of potatoes and gin, the workers were stunted and enfeebled; while through hunger, tuberculosis and, above all, their long hours of factory work, the children were even worse off.

The nineteenth century confronts us with a social and economic system that for the greater part of mankind offered little or no scope or prospect. Many children were brought into the world only to be threatened with almost immediate extinction. In England especially—where industrialization set in first—the figures tell a sad story. In Liverpool in 1840 the average expectation of life among the higher classes was thirty-five years, and among manual laborers and day laborers fifteen years. In the County of Rutland, round about 1830, some 28 per cent of the population died before they were five years old; in Essex it was 31 per cent, in the factory town of Preston 49 per cent, and in Leeds as much as 52 per cent. Speaking in the House of Commons in 1863, Ferrand stated that the cotton industry had then been going for ninety years, and in the course of three generations in England as a whole *nine generations* of cotton workers had been swallowed up.[7] Only if one belonged to a certain privileged class did one escape the inhuman threat posed by the socio-economic structure.

What did Christianity and the Christian Churches do in this situation? Here and there the voice of protest was heard.[8] Charitable institutions were spurred on to even greater activity. Natural law was invoked to prove that the existence of master and serf, rich and poor, was prescribed by nature[9] and that the laboring classes must rest content with their lot. In an issue of the Dutch periodical *De Katholiek* in 1880, for instance, we read that "the social question springs from a political conspiracy." The solution to the prevailing unrest lies in *contentedness*, the contented spirits with which the working people must bear their lot, because they are Christians. The last word on the social question is the kindly disposition of the better sort of persons and the charity which their love disposes them to exercise.[10]

[7] A. W. Ijzerman, *Het moderne Kapitalisme* (1930), p. 278.

[8] A particularly biased résumé can be found in *Documentation*, ed. Institut Recherches de l'Europe Centrale (Louvain, April 1963), 2, pp. 21–23.

[9] A. M. Knoll, *Katolische Kirche und scholatisches Naturrecht* (Vienna, 1962).

[10] Cited by Rogier, *In Vrijheid herboren* (Reborn to Freedom), p. 336.

If we now turn to what Karl Marx has to say, we get an exact description of this so-called Christian attitude. In 1847 he writes:

The social principles of Christianity proclaim the necessity for a ruling class and a subject class; and for the latter it merely entertains the pious wish that the former may exercise beneficence towards them. The social principles of Christianity declare that heaven is the place where all injustices will be duly rectified; and therefore these principles justify the continuation of such injustices on earth. The social principles of Christianity explain every outrage perpetrated by the oppressors on the oppressed either as a rightful punishment for original sin, or something of that sort, or as trials visited by the Lord in his infinite wisdom upon his redeemed. The social principles of Christianity encourage dullness, lack of self-respect, submissiveness, self-abasement, in short, all the characteristics of the proletariat.[11]

What we really end up with here is a confrontation of nineteenth-century Christianity and Marxism. Over against the feeble, prevaricating attitude of Christianity towards the great human problem of the time—over against that attitude which rested satisfied with a certain amount of superficial papering over of the cracks—stands the figure of Marx as the thinker who through a piercing analysis of the real condition of society made the discovery that only a radical breakup of the socio-economic structure could put an end to the miseries of the proletariat. Marx applied himself to working out a program that would abolish this inhumane social and economic constellation. The misery was only too real; and his program, forged under the stress of it, was so radical that it falls into another extreme of inhumanity by seeking to eliminate everything and

[11] Marx, in a contribution to the *Deutsch-Brusseler Zeitung* for 12 September 1947; in *Karl Marx/Friedrich Engels, Historisch-Kritische Gesamtausgabe*, 1.6. (Frankfurt/Berlin, 1927), p. 278.

everybody standing in the way of a "new world." This, however, does not altogether preclude there being major positive values in Marxism to which the Christianity of the nineteenth century ought to have been open and to which Christianity must all the while remain receptive today.

There is no getting round it: the Church's isolation gave rise to a grave form of social blindness; and so it was Marx who fathered "social thinking." This is based on the idea that every person in a society has a right to certain minimal opportunities of existence, that an economic and social order must be created that will be worthy of mankind—and thus a world that matches up to the material and mental aspirations of men.

So then, this "social idea" was not the inspiration of a Christian thinker but of the atheistic philosopher Marx (and of a few others with him). It was *not* originally the Christian Churches that broke through with this social idea, but a non-Christian movement: namely, socialism-Communism. It was not, at that time, the Christian Churches who rose up in defense of the most elementary rights of man, but rather the Marxists, socialists and Communists.

The Churches, on the contrary—and their ministers, too—as often as not took the side of the capitalists of the established order that tolerated inhumanity as part of the structure of its society. Of the Catholic Church of the nineteenth century it may be said that it was a Church so out of touch as to have lost all feelings for the mental outlook and temper of the age. Now a Church that in its thinking is not attuned to the fundamental questions of a given moment in history has lost contact with life and is no longer in a position to cope with a social crisis. In the mid-nineteenth century—just when it was most urgently needed, in fact— no Catholic socio-political program had been evolved, let alone a doctrine of property or a Catholic doctrine of labor that would have shown the concept—one so central to the time—in a Christian light. Her closed outlook plunged the Church into a structure crisis from which it was hard for her to extricate herself. On the heels of the French Revolution came the Restoration, eager to welcome the proffered alliance with the Church. This drove the Church, practically speaking, into the arms of the bourgeoisie; and that proved to be the start of a process which alienated the Church from the working class.

Of course, the "social idea" and way of thinking were not wholly absent from the Church; but at the start they were represented only by a few individuals, who often had to wage a heroic fight against a tide of misunderstanding and evil insinuations.

When we look at the climate prevailing in the Rome of the mid-century, it is evident that the social injustice that was rife in the world made little enough impact there. The Church's governing circles at that time saw her as "a religious reserve" (Rogier) or sanctuary amid a world full of errors. Her task was simply to keep the flock together, to shelter and protect it, to signalize the errors and condemn them. In his *Syllabus errorum*—a list of eighty errors, appended to the encyclical *Quanta cura* of 1864—Pope Pius IX took an uncompromising attitude: he roundly condemned all theories and movements not hallowed by centuries-old tradition. Rejected out of hand were: pantheism, naturalism and rationalism; while socialism, Communism and secret societies, Bible Societies and associations of liberal-minded clergy were condemned in a single paragraph. The last error to be censured was the idea that "the Pope of Rome could and should arrive at a conciliation and agreement with progress, liberalism and modern culture."

The Church in her directive capacity here reached the

nadir of her self-isolation. That behind the Communist
and socialist movements there lay a world of social injustice and human misery had so far gone quite unnoticed.
Pius IX's successor was Leo XIII. No sooner had he
succeeded to the papal chair in 1878 than he condemned socialism on theological grounds in the encyclical *Quod Apostolici Muneris.* In after years, however,
through contact with the real situation and with non-
Catholic thought, this Pope grew to be more open-
minded.

Thus there did at last appear the first encyclical to
deal with the social issue: *Rerum Novarum.* The year
was 1891—just forty-three years after the Communist
Manifesto. Even so, almost two decades of the twentieth
century were to elapse before the ideas expressed in this
encyclical had any real effect on Catholic social action.

In a retrospective attempt to create the myth of a
Catholic social movement, *Rerum Novarum* was strongly
idealized, in order to endow Catholic social thought and
action with a history reaching far back into the nineteenth century. In fact *Rerum Novarum* had little
influence, either when it appeared or in the period
immediately after. Furthermore, this encyclical did not
aim at social *reform,* but was rather an attempt at
accomodation within the capitalist social and economic
order. The intention was to maintain labor relations on
the existing basis of a "two-class" society and at the
same time to improve wage rates among the workers.[12]
It is only with the encyclical *Mater et Magistra* (1961)
that the basic concepts taken over from capitalism—
ownership, capital and wage-agreement—are called in
question and relativized for the first time.

Now I do not wish to do less than justice to the very

12 Paul Jostock, *Der deutsche Katholizismus und die Uber-
wingdung des Kapitalismus* (Regensburg, 1932) p. 138.

great deal of good that has come as a result of Catholic social doctrine; but honesty compels us to recognize that social thought and action in the Church got going too late and too slowly. Unhappily, they have been governed by a spirit of cautious compromise and have left little scope, generally speaking, for a more radical Christian humanism.

We should not be allowed *now*, therefore, to forget that Marxism and also Communism in its later Marxist-Leninist form were (and still are) a terrible indictment of a "churchified," remote, middle-class, *laissez-faire* Christianity. When we turn our thoughts to the question of a dialogue with Communism, we must be fully aware of our compromising record; and when in the conversation it becomes our turn to speak, we shall then do so with all the more diffidence and consciousness of guilt.

"Applied Religion" and the Established Order

Atheistic Communism is an imputation of guilt laid at the door of a desiccated, saltless Christianity, riddled with ecclesiasticism. The fact is that in many parts of Europe Christianity during the eighteenth and nineteenth centuries had undergone a fatal curtailment and constriction, so far as its living expression was concerned. Religion had become a "private affair." Permeated with a drawing-room atmosphere, the practice of the faith was nearly always relegated to a man's closet or confined within the walls of some sacred edifice. Christian witness played no active and effective role in public life. The aristocracy, imbued with free-thinking notions, and the so-called higher classes made a point of keeping religion and the life of society in separate compartments, and saw to it that most of the clergy remained sufficiently in leading-strings to serve their own turn.

The Christianity of our grandparents and great-grandparents was infused with a mystical *Weltflucht* (a "fleeing from the world"), a strong *Jenseitigkeitserlebung* (cultivation of other-worldliness), that refused to contemplate in any way the injunction to build here and now a world in which *all* people might find it good to live. The Catholic community was like a fortress within which the faithful clung hard—and in some trepidation —to the apron-strings of Mother Church. The clergy in Russia and in most of what are now the satellite countries (especially Czechoslovakia and Hungary) for the greater part took their stand on the side of the feudal overlords and big landowners (if they did not themselves belong to that class anyway)—and thus on the side of the very class that occasioned the misery of so many thousands.

By way of illustration, here is an outline of the situation as it was in Hungary. Prior to the Second World War, not only were 67 per cent of its population Catholic, but the Catholic Church was also the principal landowner in the country. The bishops (with the Cardinal Primate at their head) were at that time still in possession of the vast territories which St. Stephen, first king of the Hungarians, and his successors had given to the prelates of their period: a gift in kind which should have enabled the Church to discharge her religious and cultural avocation without undue embarrassment or difficulty. What had seemed natural enough in the past, however, in the twentieth century had become a source of scandal and vexation among the faithful, who gradually began to ask themselves why the Catholic Church did not give up—in part, at any rate—her right to possess so much land. There were two and a half million peasants living in the bitterest poverty, because there was no land available for them. It was expected of the Church that of her own initiative she would carry through an agrarian reform, that she would surrender her position as a feudal power, the better to fulfill her spiritual mission. But *no member* of the ecclesiastical hierarchy did anything to deliver the Church from the clutches of this ancient feudal structure. Only the Cistercians—and then not until 1943—distributed five thousand hectares among the poverty-stricken peasants on their estates. When at last the Russians came, agrarian reform was put through, by main force, within a matter of days.[13]

In Russia and in various other countries social and economic wrongs were inflicted for centuries not only by the aristocracy but by the clergy too. These mal-practices, built into the structure of feudalism, were not actually written into the legal codes of the countries concerned; but years of exploitation, the fact that whole sections of the population were without legal rights or status, and sheer human wretchedness at length aroused the people's sense of justice in the face of these social and economic wrongs. When the Communist revolution came and the relationships preserved by the old legal system were abrogated, the new sense of what was right and just took a course that was, to begin with, quite uncontrolled. The profiteers of the old order were massacred in their thousands; and others received long terms of imprisonment. That many innocent persons fell victim to this orgy of hatred and that the actual punishment administered was often arbitrary and atrocious must invariably appall us; yet such things belong to the nature of a revolution, when feelings of hate,

[13] Tibor Kovacs, *Het drama Hongarije* (Utrecht-Amsterdam, 1957), pp. 67, 68.

pent up for centuries, are released with the force of an explosion.

During and after the Communist revolution all who had been in any way concerned with the old regime were the objects of hatred and an urge to destroy. Because the Christian Churches almost everywhere had compromised with that regime or had been a part of it, the urge to hate and to kill was turned upon them also . . . and, albeit to a lesser extent, is turned upon Christians still.

In the light of history the problem of the conflict between Christianity and Communism appears in its true perspective. It would seem that the Catholic Church also has a murky record; and it is a *sine qua non* that we should be aware of that, before we start thinking and talking about the potentialities of the dialogue. We Christians may identify Communism with the devil; but what if this particular devil has been conjured up by the *errors and shortcomings of Christianity itself?*

III. THE FEASIBILITY OF THE DIALOGUE

In the article by Professor B. Delfgaauw to which I have already referred[14] we find summarized a number of insuperable objections to a dialogue with Communism. The professor declares that any rapprochement is out of the question: (1) because Communism is too dogmatic, (2) because within the Communist world the expression of opinion is subject to censorship, (3) because Communism aims at worldwide domination, and (4) because force counts for more than freedom.

Professor Delfgaauw very properly relativizes these objections. It occurs to me, however, that unless her

14 See note 5.

self-knowledge is extremely defective the Catholic Church cannot easily maintain objections of this sort. A frank scrutiny of her history must surely reveal that she has herself suffered under more or less of the evils enumerated (and perhaps does so still). We shall leave these objections on one side, therefore, and turn our thoughts to the possibilities offered by a dialogue with Communism.

Some people immediately think of such a dialogue in terms of a "round table conference" or a discussion group. However, when we speak here of a "dialogue," we mean a "colloquy" in a wider sense. A dialogue is primarily a "game" or round of listening and speaking, in which two parties are prepared to open themselves to a *logos*—the truth-revealing word—and in that way arrive at a joint understanding and consequently to an understanding of each other. It is assumed that each party will approach the other on a footing of equality and mutual trust. A dialogue in which one party sets itself *a priori* above the other or insists on delimiting the themes to be pursued is naturally doomed to failure.

The points which now follow are intended to indicate the ways in which this dialogue would be feasible.

Readiness to Listen

The Catholic Church has already had a good deal to say about and against Communism; but it has not done nearly the same amount of listening. In my view, what such "listening" involves in the first instance is a ready sense of the conflict between Christianity and Communism as it presents itself to us in history viewed as a whole. We have had a rough shot at achieving this in an earlier part of the chapter; and in so doing we made the discovery that Communism passes a very real judgment on our Christian society. It is in the first place a judgment regarding a specific social and economic system with which the Christianity of the Churches had identified itself or has at least compromised. Next, it is a judgment passed on a middle-class, world-denying Christianity that neglected its duty towards humanity on this earth; and finally, it is a judgment given against the Christians' conception of their God—for they had cut God down to size, so as to make him the servant of a kind of Christian party interest.

All of this should lead us, perhaps, to declare our suspicion that Communism is not so much an assault on the Message of the Gospel, as on *what we have made of that message*.

Again, our "listening" will make us alive to the positive values in Communism. We shall have to try and discover what that sense of values is which inspires the voice of Communism today. I say "discover" here, because in the past we have all too easily either denied that Communism is sensible of any values or insisted that there could be "nothing in it" of positive worth, anyhow, so far as Christianity is concerned. What Catholicism has to proclaim exerts little hold over the contemporary world, because Catholicism presupposes too great a degree of perfection in its own camp and so has no eye to that world's sensibilities and to the moral values that go with them. The Catholic Church must not only preach to its own constituency but proclaim the message of Christ to the world. She cannot address herself to Communism unless she knows what the values of that system are and acknowledges them.[15]

[15] See W. Luijpen, *Fenomenologie en Atheisme* (Utrecht-Antwerp, 1963), pp. 67, 68.

A start is being made with all this, as can now be seen from the "Copernican revolution" in Vatican diplomacy and from the generally new attitude to Communism. An obvious token of this was the sympathetic reception accorded to Mr. Adzhubei, editor-in-chief (at that time) of *Izvestia* and son-in-law to Mr. Khrushchev, by Pope John XXIII. Church authorities and diplomats conduct negotiations with Communist government officials. These new contacts at a diplomatic level and the change of tactics that they reveal are no doubt the initial outcome of the extensive information supplied to the Vatican by the sixty bishops from behind the Iron Curtain who have been attending the Council. It is regrettable, perhaps, that these negotiations have so far been pursued with too exclusive an eye toward an amnesty for imprisoned priests and bishops and to restoring a certain hierarchical-canonical *status quo ante*. But in themselves the contacts made are still of value in that they offer the possibility of discussion at a deeper level.

An Historical-Cum-Existential Approach

Communism is not an ossified system, but is continuously on the move—a fact which has become more evident over the last ten years. In a recent article[16] Professor W. Banning has rightly cautioned us against the current *dogmatic* and fixed position with regard to (Russian) Communism; and he pleads for a historical approach, based on the living and shifting reality. For Communism is going through a process of profound change in many respects; and this we must know and

---

[16] "Na tien jaar," *Wending*, 18 (1963), pp. 570–578.

comprehend before we can reach a judgment. There is an internal process afoot that arises out of the immanent logic of an advancing industrialization and the social, intellectual and cultural development of whole sections of the population. Of course, we can say that the totalitarianism and the dictatorship are still there. But a new generation of industrial managers, intellectuals and artists have learned how to find ways of resolving the tensions with the regime, as and when these occur, in a sound and sensible fashion.

Not so very long ago Mr. Khrushchev was making a point of the fact that Marxism is not a fixed and settled dogma but a method which in every period of history has to be applied to changing circumstances. "It is not enough," he said, "to reach for the book and look up what Lenin said. *We must think for ourselves*, study life assiduously and analyze the prevailing constellations."[17]

It is heartening to be able to record that Pope John XXIII was also most emphatic in urging a historical-existential approach to Communism. In the encyclical *Pacem in Terris* the Pope argued for making *a distinction between the false philosophical theory and the historical movement that has arisen out of it* and can be considerably affected by the changing circumstances of life. With this the Pope combined a clear suggestion pointing in the direction of a dialogue: "It may be, therefore, that *positive encounters* at the practical level, which until now have looked to be inopportune or fruitless, now offer real advantages or bid fair to do so in the future." This new approach is related to the actual distribution of power in the nuclear era, which could very well be exploited in favor of a dialogue. That is why the next section is entitled:

[17] Quoted in *Time*, vol. 83, no. 17 (1964), p. 21.

Reaching an Understanding— an Indispensable Need[18]

Even allowing that the Communist is fundamentally intolerant, still tolerance is wrung from him by the actual course of history, which as a matter of sheer fact has led to the "balance of power" situation. At bottom the Communist may not see the West as a serious partner for a discussion; but dialogue is forced upon him by the dilemma of peace or annihilation. Those who are opposed to dialogue are right enough when they point to the doctrine of Marx and Lenin as the ground of the present religious persecution and oppression; but then they fail to reckon sufficiently with the changes that are taking place in the world and in Communism today, the importance of which it is hard to overestimate.

The question of a dialogue must be examined not only in the light of a past phase of Communism but also from the standpoint of the future; and here we refer to the prospect being opened up by the course events are taking now. The situation today offers these possibilities: (1) atomic war—which implies, however, total annihilation; (2) unilateral disarmament—which would upset the balance of power, the very thing that constitutes the basis of the enforced tolerance; (3) maintenance of the status quo—but to go on living under the threat of atomic war is risky in the extreme. There remains only one further possibility: to accept the unavoidable and reach an understanding. This would involve going all out, in the future, to turn the so far negative point of

[18] The phraseology and the ideas are taken from a very constructive article by Professor L. van Bladel, *Streven*, 16, vol. II, no. 8 (1963), pp. 765–772.

departure which we share into a positive kind of cooperation. "Self interest and the instinct for self-preservation are powerful motives that have given evidence of their effectiveness," says Professor R. C. Kwant. "Never in history have such cogent motives been at work in favour of mutual understanding and unification."[19]

Positive cooperation—as has been said already—has become a real possibility also by virtue of the fact that the received Soviet system of dogma is being confronted by the course of history with such novel problems that the traditional ideology and its equally traditional interpretation no longer provide the answer; and this has given scope for some relatively independent thinking within the Communist camp.[20] Here is an aspect which the Christian must seize upon in his efforts to further the dialogue.

Correcting the Distorted Image

The Communists—not altogether without cause—have fashioned a caricature of Christianity. Christian candor constrains us to correct the distortions and the caricature of Communism current in the Western world; for the view that we get of Communism is a warped one. We live under the proscriptive influence of a counter-propaganda that is inspired by the American press and backed by a considerable part of the West European press and is carried on against the victims of "hidden persuaders" who impose upon us, through the mass media, a particular image of Communism.

In the United States Communism has always been a

[19] R. C. Kwant, "Het christelijke geweten en de bewapening-swedloop" (The Christian Conscience and the Armaments Race) in *Anti-revolutionaire Staatkunde*, 33 (1936), p. 140.

[20] See, for example, the articles by H. Fleischer and D. D. Comey in *Studies in Soviet Thought*, vol. II, no. 4 (1962).

"political issue"; and it is certain that the political bosses there have an interest in systematically keeping the fear of Communism on the go. This fear (which carries over onto the European scene) was at one point so intense that serious politicians were contemplating the possibility of a "preventive atomic war."

It is a commonplace of psychology that fear almost always distorts reality. American conflict-psychologists made an interesting study of the East-West conflict and reached some surprising conclusions.[21] The proclivity, in cases where there is never—or hardly ever—any personal contact, to attribute to people all sorts of bad or even monstrous characteristics, coupled with the tendency to mold reality into a logical unity and so to think in terms of simple opposites, has given rise on both sides of the East-West conflict to a stereotype of "the others" which is at a considerable remove from reality. Naturally, therefore, tourist encounters occasion a good deal of amazement; but they do not usually result in a definitive correction of the faulty stereotype. On its own ground, conflict-sociology comes to similar conclusions.[22]

The researches of these two new sciences only make one wonder just how much psychological and sociological subjectivity persists quite unnecessarily in the East-West conflict.

A Comprehensive Christian Social Program

It is a disquieting fact that Communism is successfully taking root in countries that are traditionally Catholic (or at any rate Christian). A rigid ecclesias-

[21] A write-up of the research appears in *The Journal of Social Issues* 17, no, 3 1961).

[22] *Cf.* Doubt, De Moore, Thurlings and De Vooys, *Het Conflict als maatschappelijk verschijnsel* (Conflict as a Social Phenomenon) (Utrecht-Antwerp, 1962).

ticism or the identification of Catholicism with a particular established milieu or class is often the reason that
an effective Christian social program is lacking. If Communism alleges that religion alienates man from his true
being as man by extinguishing in him every effectual
desire to achieve a socially and economically well
ordered world (the "opium"), we should not give the
Communists any opportunity to substantiate this idea
with facts.

An active, socially concerned Christianity, drawing its
inspiration from religion, but well organized, too, from
a human standpoint, must show the meaning of love for
one's neighbor on a world scale. The Catholic Church
ought to be giving a lead anywhere in the world where
social injustice is occurring; and she must do this without hidden motives of proselytism. In a number of countries or areas of the world there is need for sociological
studies designed to discover ways and means of detach-
ing the Church from antiquated colonial or feudal systems with which in the course of centuries and in some
territories (such as South America) she has come to be
identified.

Special attention must be paid to the developing
countries; and this should take the form more of a
concern for the human being and less of a desire to
introduce an ecclesiastical system beautifully structured
from a canonical standpoint. A program of social action
on a global scale and deriving from an authentically
Christian inspiration (the depth dimension) is part of
the essential task of a true Catholicism.

A New Study of Communism

There are already a fair number of systematic studies
on the subject of Communism. In view of the new

developments and of the new attitude, which is becoming more and more widespread, towards Communism, however, there is a pressing need for a fresh study of Communism as a phenomenon—and most especially where the Christian Churches are concerned.

As to the possibility of a dialogue—in the sense that we have in mind—this has never before been envisaged; and the absence of this element from the method of approach has produced a "blind spot" in every investigator, however thorough and scholarly he may have been. Thus a Protestant professor could declare, only a few years ago, that the real confrontation of Christianity and Communism has perhaps scarcely begun.

Scholars of the Reformed Churches in Germany are aiming, therefore, at a renewed study of Marxism (*Marxismus-Studien. Schriften der evangelischen Studiengemeinschaft,* Tübingen). The driving force behind these studies is the conviction that Marxism in its European form may be a seminal factor in the work of communicating the Gospel. Professor Banning discusses this in an article entiled: "Can Marxism Still be Relevant?" and answers as follows: "There is a process at work in which Christians are making the astonishing discovery that the basic starting point of the young Marx may be fruitful. If so, it is possible to support the thesis that the real confrontation of Christianity and Marxism is only just beginning. That this process is going on in Germany, France and the Netherlands is more important than individual statements to the effect that 'it can't be, it ought not to be' and so forth."[23]

On the Catholic side also, Marxism is beginning to be studied in a new way. We have mentioned already the work of Professor Delfgaauw in this connection. In a book that appeared recently yet another writer has

[23] W. Banning, *Om Mens en medemenselijkheid* (For Man and His Shared Humanity) (Amsterdam, 1960), p. 101.

pointed to the value of the Christian Marxist confrontation:

Christianity has to learn specifically from Marxism that the present time makes special demands upon its peculiar ethic. One of the central points in that ethic is 'love for thy neighbour." Love is to be defined here as accepting, willing, supporting and furthering the subjectivity, self-hood, freedom of the other. But the subject that "the other" is a subject in existence, a subject that is implicated in the world and that has to work itself up to its authentic being, in the world and upon it. Now the world in which the subject is implicated is not merely the world of nature but also the totality of economic, social and political structures that human history has thrown up. Because man is a subject-in-the-world, it makes no sense whatever for the Christian to claim to be loving his neighbour, unless his love finds its realisation in opening the world to the neighbour and in making it accessible to him. But how is this to be done, save through economic, social and political activity? In so far as such economic, social and political structures as may exist render the world accessible to man, the Christian is in duty bound—at the imperative demand of Christian love—to reshape those structures.[24]

The one thing that these studies overlook is that contemporary Communism does not draw its basic inspiration solely from Marx. An investigation into the *fait primitif* on the basis of which modern Communism thinks and acts is an undertaking that would be much to the point and would fill in the gap.

So far as this goes, I have been working for the establishment of an institute or center for experts who would study contemporary Communism with a view to confrontation and a possible dialogue. In odd places here and there some extremely important and useful work is

[24] W. Luijpen, *op. cit.*, pp. 200, 201.

being done in this sphere; but it all urgently requires coordination, and for all the Christian Churches to work together at the international level (this too bears on the plan of a real Catholicism conceived as a task to be fulfilled). From an institute of this sort the initiatives for an active dialogue ought surely to come.

IV. THE ACTUAL DIALOGUE

If I am asked of what the actual dialogue consists, then I am bound to say that no one can form a concrete idea of it at this stage. I have tried to suggest what the new attitude is that should prevail on our side. A lot of traditional taboos and assumptions still have to be eliminated. Even so, up to a point one can already surmise what the stages of this dialogue are likely to be.

The first thing to aim at is an improvement in relations between East and West. Taking an optimistic view one might suppose that such an improvement is already —if only in a vague way—apparent. Where economic relations are concerned, progress is already on record. The economic situation in the world is such that by an intrinsic logic it is almost certain to lead to an increase in trade relations.

This development will demand of the Soviet Union and of the West some degree of adjustment of their economic structure. Eventually, the economic development will reach a point where any further advance is not really feasible without some corresponding political *entente* to ratify and support the links already established. It is then that East-West relations will enter the phase of political dialogue. The next step will be the cultural and scientific dialogue (although to a limited extent this exists already). As soon as this stage has been attained, the ideological dialogue will become possible.

Of course, this summary outline is not meant to suggest a chronological order of events. In practice, these various phases of the dialogue will interlock or overlap with one another. Nevertheless I believe that this is the likely course of development and that the ideological discussion will come only at the end of it. This should not be allowed, however, to discourage us from making our preparations for that phase here and now.

There are many aspects of the dialogue with Communism that we have still not considered—and yet others that we have deliberately left to one side (such as Chinese Communism and its conflict with the Soviet Union). We might do well to remember that "the dialogue" has become more than ever a vital necessity for us, because the issue at stake is whether our civilization is to continue in existence or not. Thus it is by no means a question of a few simpletons riding their favorite hobby-horse in a state of ecumenical fuddle or intoxication. Rather ought we to say perhaps that the dialogue is an imperative Christian duty, in that the Christian is certainly called to make his contribution to the unification of mankind and to peace on earth.

II

Priest and Communist

ALAN ECCLESTONE

> It seemed, indeed, that modern Communism might well be
> that half of Christianity which had been dropped by the Church
> in favour of an accommodation with Rome, coming back to
> assert itself against the part that had been retained.
>
> JOHN MACMURRAY, *Search for*
> *Reality in Religion*

I JOINED THE Communist Party of Great Britain in 1948
and, along with my wife who joined a few days later,
began to attend week by week the meetings of the
local branch of the "Party" in the east end of Sheffield.
I have continued to do so ever since, taking what part
I could in the work of a Party member: selling pam-
phlets and the *Daily Worker* on the streets, taking part
in public demonstrations, speaking at public meetings,
standing as a candidate in municipal elections, playing
a part in the Peace movement locally and at international congresses. All this adds up to the "chores" of an
ordinary Party member and meant sharing in the circumstances of such work, i.e., I did not get many votes
as a candidate in municipal elections nor sell many
newspapers nor convince any large number of people
that they must join the Communist Party. On the contrary, it meant incurring a good deal of suspicion and
hostility and spending a good deal of time and energy

ALAN ECCLESTONE is a priest of the Church of England.
He has been rector of an industrial parish in Sheffield for
the past twenty years. In 1948 he became a member of the
British Communist Party. This is his personal apologia. It
has not previously been published.

in repetitive and seemingly fruitless work. This was all to the good in the sense that it enabled me to look at the political situation from the standpoint of the obscure person in the street who is concerned about the social problems of his time and finds himself grappling with great difficulties which discourage and exhaust him. The Communist Party, being few in numbers, makes big demands upon its members, and one can learn much even from seeing the devoted self-effacing work which many give to it.

When I joined the Communist Party I was, nonetheless, slightly eccentric because I was a Christian, a priest of the Church of England, and the vicar of a parish in the industrial-dormitory area of the steel-producing city of Sheffield. I was then fifty-three years old. The assumption in British society, then and now, is that no Christian in his senses could take this step because the Communist Party is "atheistic" and is believed by many to be devoted, among other things, to the extirpation of religion. The special position of the Church of England with its traditional role of buttressing the established social order made my position more ludicrous and my decision heinous. I was, like the aristocratic combatants in Shakespeare's *Richard II*—except that I was ignoble—"a traitor to God and King." The utmost charity could do, as shown in a comment made by the then Archbishop of York, was to convict me of being "illogical."

Needless to say, I received some abusive scurrilous letters to this effect, and other people no doubt said as much about it, though not to me. On the other hand, I was often surprised by messages of encouragement from quite unknown people, making it clear that in British society there are numbers of people who want to connect Christianity with radical political action, and numbers whose inspiration for radical politics is rooted in a residual Christianity.

The Cold War period brought its own peculiar difficulties so that it was never easy to begin to explain what one stood for or hoped to say. The Korean War, the Berlin Wall, the Polish and Hungarian uprisings, the Stalinist trials, all made discussion difficult because they could not be ignored or related to the over-all situation in straightforward intelligible terms. The partisan tends to fall back on stock answers, to give nothing away, to score what points he can. The demands of the day no doubt played their own part in damaging my judgment on a great many matters. In a highly charged emotional situation, the partisan is often at the mercy of his own personal weaknesses. In the defense of a minority position, the garrison mentality tends to become second nature. All too easily one is persuaded to defend the indefensible. Believing as I do that the decision to join and stay in the Communist Party was a right one, I hasten to say that I do not claim to have acted or spoken or thought wisely on innumerable occasions in the working out of the consequences of this decision. Honesty of purpose does not absolve one from follies or errors. I do claim, however, as an outcome of having belonged to the Party for almost twenty years, to be able to speak out of experience and from the standpoint of one more critical of the Party than I might otherwise have been, and one more convinced than ever of the necessity of its work.

"How can a Christian belong to the Communist Party?" The first answer must be that he can do so because the Communist Party of Great Britain does not debar him from doing so. It is open to "those who are prepared to work for the achievement of socialism" and its aims and constitution propose no religious test. Its

Party program—The British Road to Socialism—declares that "freedom of religious worship needs to be guaranteed and all religions, creeds and beliefs respected." In saying this, I do not lose sight of, nor do I seek to minimize, the great difficulties that have been faced by Christians in other countries where the Church-State conflict has been open and bitter, and where persecution on grounds of belief and practice has been prolonged. I would say that many Christians have suffered such persecution as a result of accumulations of evil often perpetrated or condoned by the Churches in the past, but persecution is not to be justified on any grounds. But I have always recalled the article "Between Yesterdayday and Tomorrow" by D. Josef Hromádka which appeared as a *Christian Newsletter* supplement 12 May, 1948 in which he pointed out that the February change in Czechoslovakia had to be accepted as a step in the unavoidable and justifiable process of the social transformation of its life. "Communism is partly heir of the age-long craving for social justice and equality, partly the child of the errors, blindness and greediness of the decadent bourgeois society." Dr. Hromádka made no secret of the difficulties to be faced by Christians but he insisted, as he had a right to do because he returned to Czechoslovakia to share in them, that the "Christian witness has got to be carried out where there is no security."

Having been able to join the Communist Party as a Christian and a clergyman, I can say that nothing in the work of the Party has appeared to me to conflict with the standards of morality which I believe a Christian should endeavor to live by. I can say that my fellow Party members have invariably given me courteous treatment, encouragement, trust and scope. They have not necessarily "understood" why I chose to be a

clergyman, any more than many Christians have understood why I decided to join the Party. Nor did I think
it to be my job, supposing I could have done so, to set
about convincing Communists that they should be
Christians, or Christians, *qua* Christians, that they
should become Communists. The whole matter of
attempting to convert people is not quite so clear as
it was once assumed to be. There are other things to be
done first. I had joined the Party to work for the
achievement of Socialism in Great Britain. That did not
mean that I disavowed the Christian faith or interpreted
my ministry wholly in terms of making socialists. It did
mean a recognition of different spheres of action, and
in particular of the political-social world of socialist
activity with its own proper relative autonomy, comparable to those other fields in which a Christian rightly
engages in action and joins with non-Christians in the
pursuit of common purposes.

"But is not Marxism avowedly atheistic?" How is it
possible for a clergyman to work honestly inside a
Party whose philosophy is said to be clean contrary to
Christian understanding of the nature of things? Very
properly the Communist Party encourages its members
to study Marxism as a guide to action. Without its help
it is inconceivable that human society will ever advance
to socialism. "Without it," writes Gordon Leff in *The
Tyranny of Concepts*, "there can be little hope of gaining a worthwhile understanding of society or of being in
possession of a viable method of approach." Paul Tillich
in *The Protestant Era* declared that "nobody can understand the character of the present world revolution who
has not been prepared for it by the Marxian analysis of
bourgeois society, its contradictions and its decisive
trends." Marxist methodology has its essential position
in socialism. That does not mean that the *obiter dicta*

of Marx constitute a sacred dogmatic text, and Marx
would have repudiated fiercely the attempt to employ
them in this fashion. Marxists and Christians may well
believe that they have some insights into the nature of
Reality: both are none the less committed to a never-
ending critique of these insights lest they become idola-
trous servants of their cherished notions and obstinate
enemies of the pursuit of Truth. Christians need all
the help they can get from any discipline of thought
which illuminates life: Communists, as Sean O'Casey
has written, "should always be going about learning."
The fact that a great many Christians and some Communists do not want to live like this should not prevent
us from seeing that Christianity and Marxism alike suffer
as soon as they cease to be self-critical in this way.
God does not need to be protected from those who
relentlessly question the nature of things. Socialism does
not need to be shielded from any possible exposure of
fallacious reasoning and false evidence.

The question of atheism has, in any case, during the
past twenty years undergone a remarkable re-presenta-
tion. My own approach to it was largely shaped by the
teaching of John Macmurray, who in the 1930's was
teaching the necessity of posing the question, not in
terms of "does God exist," but rather as an inquiry into
the nature of the Reality with which men in action—
their real life—had to do. It was "astonishing," to use
his own words, written many years later, "to find how
correct the conviction was that the study of Communism was a necessary prelude to the understanding
of Christianity." I have quoted these words on many
occasions to groups of Christians to see if they ever
showed signs of surprise at being told that the study of
Communism was a necessary prelude to the understanding of Christianity. That they did not do so con-

vinced me that Macmurray is right in his contention that we have substituted an idealist religion for Christianity, and that its devotees feel constrained to defend this idealism against the "materialism" of Marx.

Even so, and notwithstanding the fact that Macmurray's teaching has been treated largely as a rather eccentric fashion of thought, the question of atheism has taken on a new form since Christian theologians have begun to write in terms of Christian atheism and the death of God. I have found myself saying to Communists that the strictures on religion pronounced by Marx are as nothing compared with those that appear daily from Christian theologians. The battle is no longer one between Marxists and Christians contending for the honor of God or God's dismissal, but between groups composed on both sides of Marxists and Christians who are searching for an adequate foundation of human life today.

One consequence of this remarkable change has altered very profoundly the situation in which the Communist-Christian now finds himself. The past few years have witnessed the beginnings of more prolonged discussions and more fruitful dialogues between Marxist and Christian thinkers. My own approach to this came through years of endeavoring to work out for myself a position honestly relating Christian beliefs and Marxist insights when called upon to explain myself to Christians or Communists. As the Cold War abated, invitations to do this became very frequent. Communist Party branches, Church discussion groups, sixth forms at schools, university study groups, have all in the past six years inundated me with invitations to speak, listened very seriously, and helped me very considerably by question and discussion to clarify, rethink and restate my judgments about it. As the dialogue between Marxists and Christians has developed internationally, and as journals like *Marxism Today* and *World Marxist Review* have given more and more attention to the question, I have been greatly helped to see how my own thinking on the problems was related to that of others. The strange thing about it, as a contributor to *Slant* has pointed out, was that it did not begin earlier, since the roots were obviously there in the 1930's and showed signs of active life immediately after the war when French priest workers and Marxists were vigorously involved in their common tasks. There was so much, for example, in Henri-Charles Desroches' book *Signification du Marxisme* (1948) which could have been followed up, and it is good to realize that such a book received its "imprimatur." In English, Tiran Nesoyan's book *The Christian Approach to Communism* (1942) was quite outstanding and deserves to be republished. I mention these from among many simply to make the point that what is happening today is not a strange aberration but a pressing deeper of the indications to understanding which were given in the hard years earlier.

Now, from all directions, come the insistent demands for a fearless attempt to reason together. When I read in the Teilhard *Review*, for example, that Roger Garaudy, the eminent French Marxist, declares that "the future of man cannot be constructed in opposition to communists nor without them," and go on to read his books *De l'Anathème au Dialogue* and *Marxisme du 20ème Siècle*, I recognized the full-growing features of what I have experienced in this city of Sheffield and in my own dialogue with workers and students in this country. We have come through to a situation more hopeful in terms of understanding than we might have dared to hope for fifteen or twenty years ago. Of course, people in Great Britain have had this matter

before them on less exacting crucial terms than people
on the continent of Europe, and they had a residual
legacy of radical interpretation of the Christian faith
which had never died out. John Ball and Gerard
Winstanley and their kind live in our present efforts.

But why join the Communist Party? The first thing to
be said is, of course, that Christians, and this must
include clergymen, must not stand outside the political
life of the people, but must take as full a share as possible in political action. Belonging to a Party is simply
one stage in so doing, showing publicly where you stand
and giving you opportunity to learn from and contribute
to the shaping of the outlook and life of the community.
This is a matter of real responsibility and calls for more
serious commitment than is commonly given to it by
Christians.

Secondly, I joined the Communist Party in 1948
because I believed that the British Labour Party had
by that time made it clear that its concern for socialism
at home and abroad was quite dead. Internationally, it
was patently anti-Communist; at home it had ceased to
be able to will the transformation of society towards
socialism. The socialist impetus—such as it had been
—which gave rise to the Social Democratic Federation,
the Independent Labour Party and smaller groups, and
which helped to put the Attlee Government into power,
had spent itself and was not being renewed. Labour
leaders like Herbert Morrison made it very clear that
such renewal was not even being contemplated. The
Communist Party alone was wholly committed to the
cause of socialism. That it was small, that it had made
many mistakes in the past, that it was suspect and
obnoxious to many people, that its members were
treated as potential if not actual treason-workers, made
joining it a difficult decision. The fact remained that

socialism was the purpose of the Communist Party, and
if open declaration of one's concern for socialism was
important, as I believed it to be, then joining the Communist Party was the right step to take.

I come now to the matter of socialism which I make
the great point at issue. The concept of socialism
needs restatement and amplification and something like
re-creation to meet the imaginative and scientific needs
of this generation. It needs exposition in world terms.
For the moment I should prefer to express its meaning
in this way. As a human being and as a Christian one is
against certain things and for certain things. Socialism
is a movement of political action against a social order
which discriminates against some human beings in order
to maintain and extend the wealth and power of others.
This is so repugnant to a Christian intention in life
that such a social order must be rejected. It would be
objectionable if those discriminated against were simply
a handful of people: as it is, they constitute millions of
poor working people throughout the world. They are
discriminated against by being excluded from the means
of better livelihood, better health, better education,
better social intercourse.

These are human beings and, in Christian terms, my
brothers, and if I am convinced that they are discriminated against, I cannot, as a Christian, ignore this or
pretend that it does not matter or leave it to others to
attempt to do something about it; I must endeavor to
bring this discriminatory order of society to an end and
to replace it by one which is free from this evil. Those
discriminated against are, in Christians terms, "the least
of these my brethren," whose condition Jesus Christ is
said to have made the criterion of the judgment of the
nations. They are the people whom the Old Testament

prophets invariably drew attention to when they endeavored to recall Israel to the true service of God: "See
that thou deal thy bread to the hungry and let the
oppressed go free." They are, as far as this country is
concerned, the people among whom I have spent my
working life: people who endured years of mass unemployment, people who live in dreary bad houses, whose
children go to dreary bad schools, whose health is
damaged by their bad conditions of living. In my lifetime their condition has vastly improved, but their place
in society as "discriminated-against people" has not
substantially altered. The circumstances and conditions
and deprivations built up to discriminate against them
are still there as powerful as ever. Socialism as a witness
and movement against this discrimination is something
to which I believe as a Christian I must give what help
I can. Jesus Christ identified Himself with such discriminated-against persons.

I am fully aware of the fact that many so-called socialists and so-called socialist states have permitted discrimination against people to go on. They stand condemned
by socialism itself and it is part of our job to expose fraud.
This gives us no liberty to prefer our present discriminatory order or to denigrate efforts to do better. Christians do not expect men to be other than men who need
help and forgiveness and encouragement in their efforts
to do better. That socialists have behaved badly at times
is no more a reason for leaving the Communist Party
than religious persecution and witch-hunting and anti-
Semitism are reasons for leaving the Christian Church.
The fact that some people will turn the Promised Land
into a dreary repetition of the society from which they
were released is no reason why the Long March, the
Exodus, should not begin. But you have to be inside the

movement to have the credentials for criticizing it adequately.

Socialism is the utilization of all human resources to enable all human life to be fulfilled. Socialism is the recognition in practice that nothing human must ever be handled in a contemptuous way. "Every pot in Jerusalem shall be holy to the Lord." This too I see as an essential part of my Christian commitment, a concern for the growing up to their full stature, by a process of mutual nourishment and common concern, of the whole family of God's people. All this has taken on a new significance in human affairs since men have begun to see themselves called upon to shape their own destiny, to be creative in the most profound sense, to make their own history with an ever-increasing awareness of what this means. Forty years ago men laughed at the Soviet Union's First Five Year Plan. We are all planners now, but the intentions of our planning are under judgment. Something which agitated men like Saint-Simon and Marx has grown to maturity. Marx's theses on Feuerbach have clothed themselves in our flesh and blood, and Christians should be the first to see what kind of words do this and dwell among us for good or ill.

Socialism then is the deliberate construction of a home for the human family—the full "economics" of human livelihood—involving every kind of human activity and drawing upon every kind of scientific and imaginative resource to improve the home conditions and home relationships. Christians, I believe, are committed to such ordering of human relationships as may permit and encourage such a constructive purpose to engage the activities and resources of the human family. Communism is an integral part of this purpose. Communism, as John Macmurray has taught, is the highest term of

religious activity and experience, and Communism calls
for community, and community must be founded upon
Communism.

How then does this work out in terms of belonging
to the Communist Party? It is significant that wherever,
throughout the world, discriminated-against people are
restless, subversive, angry, militant and hopeful, they
are branded as Communists. This is both foolishly wide
of, and perspicaciously near the truth. Communists are
the evidence of the world campaign growing to end
discrimination against people and to build a social order
which is for them all. The Communist Party in one's
own country may be great or small, immature or experienced. Joining it is the gesture one makes to affirm one's
belief in the triumph of that movement of the whole
human family to take its affairs into its own hands and
to order its life in the ways which the Spirit requires.

III

Towards an Alliance of Communists and Catholics

(New Features of the Spanish Scene)

SANTIAGO ALVARES

THE OPPOSITION MOVEMENT now gathering momentum in Spain surpasses anything seen during the years of the Franco regime or for that matter in the past fifty years. The starting point and impelling force of this opposition is the new movement of the working class, which has its source in the workers' committees and is permeated with the spirit of unity.

Sections of the population far removed from the proletariat have joined the movement. The protest actions of university students at their "freedom assemblies," and especially their public demonstrations, which are supported by many faculty members, go far beyond the bounds of the students actions of previous years.

The opposition also enjoys the sympathy and support of the clergy and even of some of the dignitaries of the Church.

Basically this ferment has its source in the objective situation in Spain.

While recognizing the role played by other political forces and groups it can be said that one of the prin-

SANTIAGO ALVAREZ writes as a spokesman of the Spanish Communist Party. His article was first printed in the *World Marxist Review*, June 1965.

cipal subjective reasons for the scope of the opposition movement is the unity of action between Catholics and Communists.

The Catholics are our main allies today in the struggle against Franco. This is a fact. It is perhaps the most characteristic and encouraging feature of the Spanish scene today.

The ideas expressed in this article about this new development and our experience are, of course, to be regarded as talking points that still need to be concretized and amplified.

I.

This development in the Spanish Catholic movement did not come about suddenly and spontaneously. It originated in the intensification of the struggle of the working class and especially as a result of the joint actions in which Communists and Catholics participated beginning with the end of the '50's.[1] The support accorded the working-class struggle by the Workers' Brotherhoods of Catholic Action during the strike movement of 1962 aggravated relations between the Church and the government. This process of rapprochement between Catholics and Communists has quickened in recent months.

Members of the Catholic Association and Catholic Working Youth join our members in strikes, public demonstrations and other forms of the working-class struggle. Many of them are members of the joint committees leading the new working-class movement.

[1] S. Carrillo, "The Underground Party and its Contact with the Masses," in *Problems of Peace and Socialism* (Prague, 1961), no. 4.

Whereas in the past Catholic participation in joint actions with Communists was more or less sporadic, it is now broader and more conscious. Not only have masses of Catholic workers broken away from the control of the Church, and their striving for unity and their militancy played an extremely important part in the entire process, there is also what could be described as a new orientation on the part of some Catholics, the "line" of the National Union of the Apostolic Laity (although this "line" has not been fully elaborated and is not consistently pursued).

To cite some facts: At one of the trials of Asturian miners the parish priest of the mining village of Mieres, on behalf of the clergy of his province and with the authorization of the bishop of Oviedo, testified at the Tribunal of Public Order in Madrid in defense of the miners. Priests have also participated in a number of workers' demonstrations. In many cases leaflets or appeals to strike are printed with their help; the workers' committees often meet on premises placed at their disposal by priests who keep watch to warn the workers of the approach of the police; meetings banned by the authorities are often held on the premises of the parish.

These and other facts show that priests are continuing to act side by side with Communists in this new stage of the struggle being waged by the working class and the entire people.

And the feature of this stage is an alliance of Communists and Catholic *workers*. Based on the struggle for common aims and loyal cooperation, this alliance is the cornerstone of the unity of the new working-class movement.

Catholic students, too, are beginning to take a more direct and active part in the struggle. In the recent student demonstrations members of the Democratic University Federation were joined by members of the Union of Democratic Youth and Catholic Student Youth, and by students in the Catholic universities in Comillas and Deusto, and of the "Opus Dei" student movement in Navarra.

The stand taken in defense of democracy by the abbot of Montserrat monastery, Father Escarre, and his group at the end of 1963 (and also the actions by three hundred Basque priests in 1960) was an important step by clergy towards the formation of a more open and decisive opposition to the Franco regime. Father Escarre (now in exile) and his group, who pressed for an amnesty for political prisoners, freedom of conscience and democratic liberties, and for the restoration of nationality rights in the Spanish state, voiced the views of considerable democratic and nationalist Catholic circles. When the hierarchy sought to ostracize Father Escarre some four hundred priests in Catalonia rallied to his defense.

When the Tribunal of Public Order, which convicted Sandoval and other Communists, instituted proceedings against another Catalonian priest, Father Dalmau, there were renewed demonstrations, in one of which one hundred priests marched outside the courthouse.

This is the first time that Catholic clergy have engaged in such "plebian" forms of action as meetings and demonstrations—characteristic primarily of the working people—in order to express their protest against the fascist methods of government. The aforementioned examples and also the demonstration by Basque clergy in Guernica, in defense of a fellow priest who in a sermon denounced the police for torturing prisoners, are a sign of the times.

Prominent Catholic personalities, too, are voicing their

views on internal issues, including the issue of freedom and democracy. In a recent lecture Professor Aranguren, Catholic philosopher, made an impassioned plea for democratic liberties.[2]

Various Catholic journals, among them *Serra d'Or* and *Cuadernos para el Dialogo*, favor the idea of a dialogue with Communists, uphold trade union freedom and the right to strike, and stress the need for structural reforms and, primarily, for a profound agrarian reform.

Comrade Santiago Carrillo was referring to the concrete experience of our Party when he wrote ". . . in Spain in particular, Catholic organizations are participating, at times very actively, in the fight for social demands and democratic liberties," that "they frequently join forces with the Communists in the struggle for the vital interests of the masses."[3]

The events of recent months have confirmed and amplified this experience.

Some weeks ago, Professor Manuel Gimenez Fernandez[4] discussing the papal appeal to Catholics to participate in political life (*Pacem in Terris*), pointed to the need for deep going structural reforms in Spain. Fernandez believes that this can be accomplished in cooperation with other groups or political parties even if their philosophy is the opposite of Catholicism (for instance, Communists), "provided there is agreement on concrete issues pertaining to the government of the country."

[2] Lecture delivered at the Friends of UNESCO Club, on the U.N. "Declaration on the Rights of Man," and on the encyclical *Pacem in Terris.*

[3]*Problems of Peace and Socialism* no. 11, 1964, p. 18.

[4] Professor Manuel Gimenez Fernandez occupies the Chair of Canonic Law at the University of Seville. At the time of the Republic and the Government of the Rights (1933–34) he was Minister of Agriculture and adviser to the Catholic agricultural trade unions. He is one of the inspirers and leaders of the Christian Democratic Union.

The formation in January of the Christian Democratic Union corresponds, to some extent, with Fernandez' proposal. The Union's program and its "Declaration of Principles" have many points in common with our democratic program (agrarian reform with the land being handed over to those who till it; nationalization of the banks and big monopolies and respect for the rights of the nationalities). But there is the danger that this program might became just another document if it is not reinforced by mass action, if it does not reflect that which is now usually referred to as social tension. True enough, some of the points in the program are the product of mass action and social tension.

Even more important perhaps than the program and the Declaration was the discussion around these documents when they were being worked out. During the discussion the anti-Communists had to retreat; they even had to agree to some formulations being modified, which could have been interpreted to the disadvantage of the Communist Party.

Recently a document of very great importance for the nation appeared, signed by 1,161 representatives of the working class and intelligentsia, among them Catholic leaders, priests, Communists and people of other democratic trends. The points contained in this document coincide with the platform of our Party (freedom of association and especially trade union freedom; the right to strike, freedom of information and expression; freedom for all political prisoners and the annulment of responsibility deriving from the civil war).

One of the signs of the new situation in Spain is the *retreat of anti-Communism,* the failure of the attempts by the dictatorship and agents of imperialism to impose anti-Communism on the opposition, especially in Catholic circles. Significant in this respect is Professor

Ruiz-Gimenez's actions and his rupture with the regime
following the debate in the Cortes on the Law on Associations, which should be seen in their relation to the
new trends in the Vatican with respect to Spain and
the steps taken recently by the Spanish Church itself.
We have in mind the objections raised by the National
Union of the Apostolic Laity and *Ecclesia,* central organ
of Catholic Action, to the aforementioned Law on Associations; the editorial in the same journal on the significance of strikes and student demonstrations which, it
wrote, "reflect aspirations that have become urgent"; etc.

*Thus the positive attitude adopted by the Catholic
working-class movement and by substantial sections of
the Catholic laity toward the necessity of ending the
fascist form of government and clearing the way for
democracy is merging with the new trends in the Church
itself, and with the trend of the apostolic laity.*

*It would be a mistake, however, to think that this is
a one-way process of smooth development,* that it is
not meeting with the resistance of some groups pursuing
their own ends in the political struggle, that it is not
encountering obstacles in the trade unions placed in the
way by the hierarchy, that it does not have to contend
with the pressure exerted on the Church by the regime
and by circles of the monopolistic oligarchy. Be that as
it may, one of the features of the present situation is
that *the Catholic Church, envisaging the collapse of the
Franco regime, is, consequently, gradually disengaging
itself so as not to be engulfed with it when the crisis
comes.* But whatever its ulterior motives, the fact is that
the Church's attitude benefits the democratic movement.

What is even more significant perhaps is that we are
witnessing a deep-going process, one in which efforts
are now being made to renovate the Church in Spain
and to effect a radical change.

Let us hear what some Catholic leaders have to say about the factors impelling them to advocate change.

"The Church," Miguel Benzo, General Secretary of Catholic Action, has declared, "knows of three types of pastorals: the 'Pastoral of Authority,' the 'Pastoral of Segregation' and the 'Pastoral of Persuasion.' . . . The 'Pastoral of Persuasion' is appropriate when *Christian unanimity* is absent, when lack of faith asserts itself not as an external danger but as something within ourselves. . . ." In Spain, Benzo continues, "Catholic action up to 1939 was guided by the 'Pastoral of Segregation,' after 1939, by the 'Pastoral of Authority' and since 1959 it has been guided by the 'Pastoral of Persuasion.' . . ."

After stressing that profound "changes in the structure of the Church, in its way of thinking and in its action" are absolutely necessary, Miguel concludes that the present situation in Spain and throughout the world makes it imperative for Catholic Action to "adapt its activity to the era of rapid change."

This "era of rapid change" is the era of the transition from capitalism to socialism, of the abolition of the antagonistic social system based on exploitation of man by man, of the era of scientific-technological revolution, whose significance cannot be overestimated.

For a number of historical and social reasons these contradictions, universal in their implications, are of a specific nature in Spain owing to internal factors of very great importance.

Constantinian views and the deep-seated integralism predominating universally in the Church hierarchy are rooted in Spanish reality with its archaic structure and its semi-feudal survivals. However, the existence of a strong and militant working class whose political consciousness is steadily growing, the growth of the revolutionary movement that is renovating the nation and more and more isolating the exclusive social group of the monopolistic oligarchy, and also the growing ideological influence of Marxism-Leninism—all show that definite changes are taking place in the Catholic movement and in the Church itself, more so in Spain than in any other Western country. It is not accidental that at the Ecumenical Council Monsignor Guerra Campos, Councillor of Catholic Action, Secretary of the Spanish Episcopacy and President of the National Union of the Apostolic Laity, strongly supported the idea of a dialogue with the Marxists.

However, we should not forget what happened during the civil war and afterwards, the fact that the Church bears its share of responsibility for this war and that it has to atone for this grave historical sin which hangs like a sinister shadow over its pastoral calling. The Church's support of the fascist revolt; its indifference over the years to the thousands of shootings and to the reprisals generally; its silence about the tortures; its support of the social policy of the regime and its attempts to reconcile the classes in the interests of monopolistic capital—all this prepared the way for a profound process in the country which some Catholic commentators have described as "dechristianization."

As more far-sighted Catholics admit, the "humble classes" began to lose faith in the Church. The Church's spiritual influence has waned. "The youth, particularly the university youth," according to the Bishop of Astorga, "is moving away from the Church." "Surely it is clear," says Father Dalmau, "that in our country the Church has still not convinced a multitude of people."

If the Church really wants to regain some of its lost spiritual influence it will have to be self-critical and, more important still, it will have to thoroughly revise its old attitude, that is, steer a new course. This seems to be the underlying meaning of Monsignor Guerra Campos' speech at the Ecumenical Council.

The period of intoxication with the "victory" of 1939 has ended; the grievous wounds inflicted on the people by the civil war have healed; there is a resurgence of the vital forces of democracy and progress; the class struggle has entered upon a new phase—these developments could not but affect the Catholic movement and that section of it most sensitive to the new situation.

Compared with the end of the 1950's when the Catholic Action's switch-over to a "Pastoral of Persuasion" had for its background the battles of 1956 fought by the working class and students—a now post-civil war generation not swayed by fascist ideology—the "speed" at which top-ranking Catholic clergy and laymen are now changing their attitude is a response to the speed at which the working-class and mass struggle is developing. This means that the course this struggle takes will be of decisive importance both now and in the future. And this struggle, operating as the principal factor, is reinforced by other factors.

These include, first of all, what the Catholics themselves have described as the "new frontiers of the Vatican," which began with Pope John's encyclical *Pacem in Terris*. This encyclical, which opened a new period in the life of the Church, has not only made for better relations between Communists and Catholics, despite the efforts of the conservative forces to detract from its influence; it also set into motion forces within the Church who want renovation.

At this point the question arises: To what extent is renovation possible?

The main thing is that in our rapidly changing

world the general law of the class struggle (in its broadest and universal meaning) affects both the Catholic movement and the Church itself as an institution. Inside the Church a sharpening struggle is taking place between those who do not want the Church to remain a class, political and ideological instrument of capitalism and imperialism, on the one hand, and on the other the archreactionary elements who adhere to "integralist," "traditionalist" and "conservative" views, as a leading Spanish Catholic describes them. The reactionaries want to prevent the Church from taking the path indicated by John XXIII, and even threaten a split if they can't have their way.

How will the struggle develop? Will the adherents of "modernization," who are inspired by Pope John's precepts, triumph? Will the conservatives be able to impose their views, even temporarily? Or will there be a split?

At the present stage of social development and scientific-technological advance, the physical impossibility of destroying socialism (which for decades was the object of the Church) without destroying humanity is a fact of immense significance. Having realized this, John XXIII wanted the Church to keep in step with the times. If socialism is a reality, then this reality must be accepted, taken into account, by entering into contact with it and having dialogue with it.

This reality and all that it implies for the general development of the class struggle (including the ideological sphere) will continue to influence favorably the course charted by John XXIII. The Church's movement in this direction is apparently irreversible.

But this in itself does not guarantee the triumph of John XXIII's ideas without struggle, does not guarantee the evolution of the Church in this direction, does not remove the possibility of a split. Despite the changes that have taken place in the world, the experience gained by the Church at the dawn of capitalism when the Reform movement arose cannot be overlooked.

If the forces fighting for the renovation of the Church are to be stimulated, if they are to develop and exert a decisive influence on Church life, we Marxists must take into account the aforementioned circumstances and the influence which, with the development of the class struggle, our own attitude can exert on these forces.

Our ability to see the new and to facilitate, on a principled basis, the unity of Catholics and Communists in working for common national, democratic and revolutionary aims is extremely important.

It is clear to Communists and to millions of Spaniards that the theses advanced by our Party in 1954 on its attitude to Catholic worship, and particularly its policy of national accord, elaborated in 1956, made a profound impression on broad circles of Spanish society and particularly on Catholics. We thus facilitated for them unity of action with us, despite the threats of excommunication made by the Holy Office and despite the traditionally reactionary attitude of the church hierarchy.

In our view this experience confirms Lenin's idea, which he expressed some fifty years ago, that it is far more important for workers to have *real alliance* here, on earth, in the name of winning common earthly aims, than differences about the existence of another world in heaven.

We Spanish Communists are sparing no efforts to create such an alliance, for we are convinced not only that it is necessary to fight together with Catholics for these aims right now, but also that it is possible to continue this alliance in the future.

People who take a narrow pragmatic approach might ask what the purpose of establishing such an alliance is if the Church is losing its spiritual influence over the masses. The answer is simple. Despite the obvious weakening of the Church's spiritual influence in recent years, it is still strong in Spain, particularly in the countryside and among the petty-bourgeoisie and women.

The two most important ideological trends in Spain today are the revolutionary Marxist ideology and the Catholic ideology. Hence *a truly popular, democratic and revolutionary struggle implies the participation in it of millions of Catholics.* Even if a new religious conscience exists outside the Church, our aim to draw it into the struggle morally, or at least to neutralize it, is one in which all the people are vitally interested. The experience of the civil war is instructive in this respect. But we repeat, we do not approach this alliance from a purely pragmatic standpoint. We do not consider it as something accidental and limited to the present stage of the struggle against the fascist form of government, but as something substantial and permanent, something which should continue—as we envisage in our long-range program—throughout the period of democratic development as well as in the socialist future of Spain.

II.

Engels wrote that Christianity originated as a movement of the oppressed, that it appeared at first as the religion of the slaves and freemen, of the poor and the downtrodden. Both Christianity and socialism, he noted, preached coming salvation from slavery and misery, but whereas Christianity sought salvation in another world, in heaven, socialism sought it in this world in a reconstruction of society. Lenin, too, stressed the "democratic revolutionary spirit" of primitive Christianity.

These views hold true today too. In the past twenty-five years Spanish Catholic workers and peasants, who are exploited in the same way as non-Catholics, often had to wage an underground struggle, to seek refuge in the "catacombs." Many Catholics are still persecuted by the regime which proclaims itself to be a Catholic state.

Catholics now see the decisive contribution made by Communists in defense of the working class and the people, the lofty moral spirit, integrity and revolutionary passion they have displayed in the fight for a better social system; Catholics now understand many aspects of our ideology. They also see that Communists respect their religious beliefs.

The objective conditions which have led many working people to lose faith in religion have created a new frame of mind among Catholics. They frequently now turn to the past, to early Christianity. But unlike two thousand years ago when Christianity taught that salvation would only come in the other world, after death, growing numbers of believers are now fighting, without renouncing this salvation, for a paradise on earth.

The struggle is also teaching revolutionary Marxists a great deal. In contrast to previous years, the religious beliefs of workers are no longer considered an obstacle to their participation in the struggle.

Just as there is a growing understanding that socialism, for which the Marxists are working, is a pressing necessity, and that the dialectical materialist philosophy is affirming itself as the only philosophy that can offer a vision of the future, so there is a growing convic-

tion that personalities whose philosophy is not materialist can take part (and they are taking part) in the
revolutionary struggle for democracy and socialism.
This, needless to say, opens up new horizons.

Those sections of Spanish Catholicism demanding
that greater attention be paid to social problems are
growing. The desire to advance towards a society in
which there will be no exploitation of man by man
exists not only among the Catholic workers, but is
shared also by Catholicism in other walks of life. The
changes in the Catholic movement are not only prompting the church to "modernize" itself; they are also
prompting Catholics to speak about socialism. What
in the past was comprehensible only to some outstanding minds and later to progressives is now becoming
a more or less conscious phenomenon.

This is not accidental. Socialism is definitely leaving
its imprint on Spanish reality. The anti-Communist
crusade cost our country millions of lives. For years
the forces of socialism were hounded and persecuted,
only to revive and grow stronger. What is to be done
under the circumstances? The words spoken by Professor Ruiz-Gimenez in defense of the Communists at
their trial are truly symbolic: "If Communism is an
historical fact, it means that God chooses that it
should be so."

Father Dalmau, a Catalonian priest, believes, rightly
or wrongly, that a "large part of the Left wing of Italian
Christian Democracy holds firm socialist convictions"
and asserts that this is a heavy blow to those who think
that socialism is irreconcilable with religion and religion irreconcilable with socialsm.

Marxists have never said that socialism is incompatible with the existence of religion among broad
sections of the population. Everyday life in the Social-

ist countries is the proof of this. But what interests us particularly is Father Dalmau's statement that this irreconcilability does not exist in Spain either. That is why he has identified himself with those who believe that "socialism as a technical instrument brings the world more justice than all previous socio-political structures." "Man's attitude to labour, the condemnation of capitalism, abolition of classes, the building of socialism—on all these points we must soberly and honestly compare ideas," writes the priest Jose Maria Gonzales-Ruiz in *Juventud Obrera*, organ of the Catholic working youth, discussing the necessity for a dialogue with Marxists. These facts show how insistently the ideas of socialism are knocking at the doors of the Catholic working-class movement and the Church.

Some Catholic thinkers in our country are more and more sharply taking issue with the existing system of property and raising the question of the need for structural changes.

Miguel Benzo, for example, says: "How can we speak of the duty of self-perfection when access to the treasures of culture is closed to proletarians and even to the most well-to-do peasants? This is precisely where it becomes the duty of all Christians to contribute to the rapid evolution of social structures since it is these structures that influence the destinies of people on earth and in the hereafter."

Professor Ruiz-Gimenez expressed a similar opinion. "Political power," he says, "is entitled to expropriate property or companies which, because of excessive concentration of economic power, are hampering the fair distribution of the national income and even the independence of the government."

Ruiz-Gimenez goes on: "I have in mind 'socialization' as it was interpreted by His Holiness John XXIII, i.e., as a process of the development of relations between people, as affirmation of the forms of social life which will make it possible for all people and all nations to enjoy the achievements of civilization and technology. But I also have in mind, 'socialization,' where this is necessary, in the narrower sense, in the sense of the transfer to the State, the trade unions and co-operatives or the smaller associations, of the right of ownership, or management, of the sources of the production of wealth which ensure a strong social and political power, but this power should be in the hands only of true representatives of the national or international community."[5]

In his *Critical Attitude to Social Problems,* the Reverend Jose Maria Diez Alegria, professor of the Gregorian University in Rome, quoting from St. Paul's Second Epistle to the Thessalonians that "he who does not work shall not eat," likewise criticizes the existing system of property. Defending only private property in articles of consumption and means of production that are not of decisive importance, he states that "our system of private property, taken as a whole, is contrary to natural law."[6]

At the Ecumenical Council Bishop Guerra Campos expressed the wish that the Church should be "a reality, standing above the various socio-economic structures. A reality and not only [of] the past; a transforming force looking to the future."

The meaning of the words "various structures" is clear. But the phrase "a transforming force" can be interpreted to mean that the Church should not link its destiny with capitalism. Can this future be other

[5] Open letter to Jose Maria Peman, "Cuadernos para el dialogo," no. 1, 1963, p. 5.
[6] Pedro Altares, "Cuadernos para el dialogo," nos. 5–6, 1964.

than socialism, the objective inevitability of which is
becoming more and more evident?

It is true that none of the authors clearly define their
views on socialism. While recognizing the need for
structural reform and social changes they see the solution in neo-capitalism or reforms. Be that as it may,
it should be noted at this stage of the transition from
capitalism to socialism that the basic socialist alternative
stemming from the dialectics of development is increasingly taken for granted also by non-Communists.

The socialist alternative will gain ground all the
faster and all the more "naturally," the more revolutionary Marxists develop mass action and involve the
Catholics in this action, by giving constructive answers
to the questions posed by them and by the Church.

Spanish Communists have been giving thought to
these answers. They concern the secular character of
the state; guaranteeing freedom of conscience and performance of religious rites; aid to Catholicism by the
state; the possibility of the revolutionary transformation
of society without resort to violence; the Party's support
of a multi-party system, including Catholic parties, in
the period of building socialism.

Some events of the past decade have had particular
repercussions in Spain. The socialist character of the
Cuban revolution has greatly attracted the youth of
the middle classes. The youth is impressed also by the
fact that the Algerian people's religious beliefs, although
very different from Catholicism, have not suffered in
any way as a result of Algeria adopting a socialist form
of government.

Speaking of this reminds me of the surprise of a
Communist intellectual when on a visit to Cuba he
saw in a house the image of Christ beside pictures

of Marx and Castro. He was quite taken aback. He failed to understand the significance of this fact, namely that the concept of socialism and its practical implementation are increasingly appealing to people's minds.

As Lenin foresaw, the concept of the specific features associated with building a new society is being amplified and enriched. Here, too, the problems can be discussed and solved in ideological and political debate between Communists, Catholics and other democratic groups.

And in a socialist Spain, too, there will be no coercion, no administrative measures against religious beliefs, against Catholicism. This means that, without weakening the ideological struggle and renouncing our materialist world outlook, we foresee coexistence of Church and socialism for an indefinite period, until there will be created, as Marx said, "a certain material groundwork or set of conditions of existence, which in their turn are the spontaneous product of a long and painful process of development."[7]

Catholics and the Church itself may accept our statements with varying degrees of confidence, but for all that the changing reality should be borne in mind.

Today, as distinct from the 1930's, the last decade of the monarchy, the situation in the country is no longer determined by the petty-bourgeois anti-clerical who, while attacking the priest, left intact the economic power of the landlord and the oligarchy. It is no longer the reformist Social-Democratic Party, swayed by anti-clericalism, nor the anarcho-syndicalist trend of unprincipled radicalism, which decides the basic issues of the working class. *Today the Communist Party—the embodiment of the Marxist-Leninist ideology, the champion*

---

[7] *Das Kapital*, vol. I, p. 80.

*of the interests of the working class and democracy—
is the guarantee that the revolution will not be diverted
from its path into anti-clerical channels.* We will prevent this from happening by virtue of our principled
philosophical outlook, and all the more so if Catholics,
understanding the full significance of the times through
which the world and Spain are passing, will fight with
us to elevate man to "a higher level of self-knowledge"
(Jose Maria Gonzalez-Ruiz).

III.

When in the new correlation of social forces growing
numbers of Catholics are upholding peace in the spirit
of *Pacem in Terris*, when a radical improvement in
conditions is demanded, when the right of women to
participate in public life is recognized, when abolition
of colonialism is hailed and the general belief confirmed that all are equal, irrespective of sex, class or
race, when at the Ecumenical Council freedom of
conscience is upheld, when proposals are made for the
purpose of putting an end to the moral and material
bondage in which the Church kept millions of people
or which it helped to maintain by its power—when
all this is happening, there are unlimited opportunities
for unity and cooperation between Catholics and Communists. They are, first of all, the opportunity for joint
action at a definite stage (for the restoration of democratic liberties), or over a period of time (for the
development of democracy), the opportunity to wage
a joint struggle against the moral decline engendered
by neo-capitalism, which is more and more turning
man into a robot; against the violation of human values
by the latest forms of exploitation; for structural reforms

that will ensure a socialist future; in defense of freedom generally, and in particular from want, oppression, and the alienation associated therewith, including, to quote Father Ruiz, freedom from "religious alienation."

When Spanish dignitaries of the Church declared at the highest level (for example, Bishop Guerra Campos at the Ecumenical Council) in favor of a dialogue with the Communists on questions of both ideology and the future, Communists responded at once. *We believe that a dialogue is not only possible but urgently necessary.* We accept this dialogue because, among other reasons, our concept of an alliance between Catholics and Communists is broadening out, due to the factors mentioned earlier, especially the influence of the expanding spheres of socialism. We accept a dialogue with Christians also because we "hope to find in it elements of mutual enrichment," to quote Bishop Gonzalez-Ruiz.

This approach makes it incumbent on us to study some problems more closely. The social practice of our time and the principles of Marxism-Leninism demand of us that we treat questions of religion and of the Church more profoundly than has been the case up to now.

Bishop Gonzalez-Ruiz, whom we have quoted so often in this article, speaking of Marxism (thus giving added proof of the interest displayed in Spain in our ideology), said that one should "not pass unattested judgment on an ideology which influences the lives of so many people and so many nations, and which gives hope to so many of the oppressed and the exploited."

For us it is important to establish what points of contact the Church proposes as a basis on which millions of believers would help us to realize this hope, proceeding from the immediate material demands of the common social struggle.

Religious misery, Marx wrote, was at one and the same time expression of real misery and a *protest* against this real misery, religion was the sigh of the oppressed creature, the kindliness of a heartless world, the spirit of unspiritual conditions; it was the *opium* of the people.

In the hundred and twenty years that have passed since Marx expressed this view of religion, it is the final phrase that has been most often quoted. Generally speaking, this is correct and necessary, considering that the ruling classes have always used religion as an opiate. But this is not the only aspect Marx had in mind. If we confine ourselves to this aspect we will not find the solution to the concrete and important theoretical and practical social problems which face us today in our relations with believers, and which will crop up in the future as well.

As materialists we deny the "transcendental," the idea of God and the existence of something outside matter. But we should not ignore the fact that millions believe in this "something," that religion exists and that with all its complexities it is a real and tangible superstructural phenomenon.

In the rapidly changing world when opportunities are opening up for millions of Christians to help bring about these changes together with Communists, if we accept religion as a form of protest against the "real misery" of which Marx spoke, this will stimulate this protest and bring it to its logical conclusion—a struggle to abolish the capitalist system of exploitation and oppression, the social base that engendered this protest. Christians want to find the answer to their protest against "real misery" today, not in the hereafter, "in the millennium to come," the solution offered by religion. Hence their growing opposition.

Ignorance and fear of the forces of Nature, helplessness in the face of his surroundings, impelled man to create his own gods. Later, with the division of society into antagonistic classes religion became a vital part of the superstructure serving the interests of the exploiting classes.

The different historical and social ways of development of the different groups of peoples or civilizations determined the emergence of different creeds, the creation of definite canons and religious norms. In most parts of the world and at all times religion has hampered social development. However, at certain stages of history, when religion was used by rising classes it gave shape to the real, positive content of the struggle and thus played a positive role. Engels recalled this in his *The Peasant War in Germany*. Lenin too mentioned this in a letter to Maxim Gorky: "There was a time in history when, despite the varying origins and actual meaning of the idea of God, the struggle waged by democrats and the proletariat took the form of a struggle of *one religious* idea against another." "But," Lenin added, "that time has long since passed."

That is quite true. But in the ideas of good, equality and fraternity, preached by the Christian religion—and reflected in the honest and sincere consciousness of believers—there are elements which could be a positive contribution to the liberation struggle. These elements stem not from religion as such; they have been borrowed by religion from the nonreligious, objective forms of relations between people as members of society. These elements could be a stimulus and not an obstacle to the struggle. That is our view. Instructive in this respect is the example of Algeria which is carrying out revolutionary changes (not to speak of the processes taking place in our own country). Religion can be an inspiring banner in those instances where the religious movement supports social reforms and socialism. This has been corroborated by some leading Catholics in Spain who have expressed themselves in favor of united action with the Marxists, of "religion not being considered and exploited as an obstacle to human progress."

These developments call for serious reflection. We should give thought also to the changed forms in which religion manifests itself as a reflection, although a "fantastic" one, of the rapidly changing world.

Engels in his *Anti-Dühring* showed the evolution of Christianity through the ages. This evolution continues, reflecting the new reality.

In the encyclical *Pacem in Terris* and at the Ecumenical Council, the very essence of the religious idea is being examined, revised and renovated. In many of the speeches and the draft documents distributed at the Council less is being said about religion's relation to the transcendental, to God, and more about its relation to concrete ideas and moral values. Marxist philosophers should take note of this.

Nor should we overlook the different encyclicals determining the Church's attitude to socialism.

The encyclical *Rerum Novarum*, for instance, which appeared in 1891, before there was a socialist country, speaks of socialism in general terms as a "false solution which would worsen the conditions of workers." The encyclical *Quadragesimo Anno*, published in 1931, when the Soviet Union already existed, draws a distinction between "socialism" (reformist) and "communism," which it says "preaches and tries to carry out by all means, including the most violent, a bitter class struggle and gradually to destroy private ownership"; in contrast to this "communism" the encyclical extols reformist socialism. The encyclical of Pius XI, *Divina Redemtoris*, which appeared in 1937, the time of the Popular Front in France and the civil war in Spain, spoke about "atheist communism" and condemned it. Pius XII, referring to the same theme, singled out "materialist and atheist communism" so as not to confuse it with "socialism" (reformist). The encyclical of John XXIII, *Mater et Magistra*, published after the meeting of representatives of eighty-one Communist and Workers' Parties in Moscow in December 1960, refrains from emphatically condemning communism; it might be said to mark the beginning of a transitional phase. And the encyclical *Pacem in Terris*, far from condemning communism, opens new opportunities for Catholics cooperating with socialism as a social system, with Communism as "an historical, humanist movement."

"The religious reflex of the real world," Marx said, "can in any case finally vanish, when the practical relations of everyday life offer to man none but perfectly intelligible and reasonable relations with regard to his fellow men and to Nature."[8] This means that even under socialism, when class contradictions and exploitation cease to exist, the disappearance of religion will be a gradual and prolonged process. Referring to Marx's idea that religion will die a natural death as the result of progress in a society which can only be a Communist society, Jose Gomez Caffarena, a Jesuit *padre* of the Faculty of Philosophy and Literature in Alcala de Henares, says: "We Christians can fully accept this challenge."

But Marx's thesis cannot be accepted without accepting, at the same time, the idea of cooperation between

8 *Das Kapital*, vol. I, p. 19.

Catholics and Communists in creating the society referred to by Marx. This is what Caffarena evidently has in mind.

Bishop Guerra Campos also appears to have been thinking along these lines when, at the Ecumenical Council, he proposed beginning a dialogue between Catholics and Marxists: "If in the future society, no matter how perfect it will be, people will still aspire to the transcendental, then we must recognize that this aspiration is inherent in man's nature and consequently admit that the subjective has an objective basis."

We on the contrary believe that at a certain stage in the development of Communist society, when the relations between people and Nature will be "perfectly intelligent and reasonable," as Marx said, the yearning for the transcendental, for the other world, will disappear. Thus, logic tells us that the way to test the two positions—the Marxist and the Catholic—is to begin right now joint actions to reconstruct society and to advance, through successive stages, to the creation of a society where both ideologies will be put to the test; so why not make the experiment?

IV

Spain 1967: A Catholic Commentary

ELIZABETH POWER

IN THE PAST year or two, the liberalization of conditions and attitudes in Spain, especially among certain
sections of the Spanish Church, has been frequently
noted in the press. There has also been much speculation about the succession to the reins of power held
by the aging General.

But increasingly we have heard of workers' protests,
strikes, street battles with police, widespread arrests
of priests involved in the workers' struggle, and also
repressive action against the right of assembly, with
increased control of the press and all other mass media.

Thus it appears that all is not well in Spain, that
there is growing social unrest and political opposition.
There are also signs that the Church is divided against
itself, the establishment against the people.

It is on these aspects of the Spanish scene that I
shall concentrate in this paper. For the Christian-

ELIZABETH POWER is a young Roman Catholic housewife
who has made a study of non-violent methods of revolution in Spain, in various parts of Africa, and, together with
her husband, as a member of Martin Luther King's staff
in 1966. This chapter has not previously been published.

Marxist collaboration that exists today in Spain can only be understood in the framework of a truly popular resistance movement, most of whose actions and alliances arise not from theoretical or ideological considerations but from the practical needs of the Spanish poor who do not have even minimum human rights at present.

This is the nature of a revolutionary situation. People with a common goal of freedom and dignity, people united by oppression and hardship will by-pass the luxury of "Christian-Marxist dialogue," but will work side by side, militant atheistic Communist and committed revolutionary Christian, for the freeing of their people.

This is the situation in Spain.

In order to understand the united workers' movement, we must trace some of the background of the Spanish economy, of the conditions of the working class, and of the Catholic Church.

There are three industrial pockets in Spain: Barcelona (and surrounding region); Bilbao (and surrounding region) and Asturias. The latter is the mining region, supplying the fuel for the other two regions which are areas of heavy industry, and the only areas producing industrial exports at all. The rest of Spain by and large is agricultural, although Madrid is a fast-growing industrial area, assembling foreign cars, foreign televisions, foreign sewing machines, etc. If it were not for the American military bases, the booming tourist industry, and the presence of two million emigrant Spanish workers in Western Europe, the Spanish economy would collapse.

Spain is suffering from a recession after the rapid development of the last five years. This is producing increased unemployment and underemployment at home. At the same time a recession in Germany and Switzerland is causing Spanish workers (as well as other foreign workers, of course) to be sent home, swelling the economic problems in Spain. Several foreign factories in Madrid have closed in the past year, and Marconi, one of the largest industrial employers, is cutting back drastically on its working force. This means that while the supply of labor is increasing, job prospects are shrinking. The tourist industry (which has brought such economic advantages to Spain) adds to the problem, i.e., it is sending prices constantly higher for the home consumer, and the tourist wealth is not redistributed among the masses.

Thus the situation seems to be getting worse for the worker. Because of the resulting unrest, state control appears to be tighter now than ever before—house searches are made in the night without warning; batons and hoses are readily used on crowds, even crowds gathered for religious celebrations (so traditional and so common in Spain); and any worker who adopts a position of leadership in the factory is watched, put to work where he cannot communicate with other workers, sometimes dismissed and even arrested.

A recent case will illustrate the situation. A Catholic leader in the movement was involved early this summer in an illegal assembly. With others, both Communists and Christians, he was arrested shortly afterwards. On his release he found that his factory had dismissed him, after twenty-five years of service with an outstanding record of reliability, skill and competence. (He was a skilled, technical worker.) He has five children. Inevitably he will receive no unemployment benefit, nor any other form of pension. Nor is he likely to be employed elsewhere. His fellow workers began a fund which by August had raised over 60,000 pesetas for his family (roughly equivalent to six months' wages).

This case is important, not only in showing the individual plight of leaders, but also in showing the new mood of the ordinary workers, their readiness to sacrifice, and their feeling of identity with the leaders in the movement, whether they are Christians or Communists, or "non-aligned."

It seems that as the struggle intensifies the determination and solidarity of the workers also grows and so repressive actions by the regime are having the reverse effect and creating more opposition, rather than reducing it.

Now to trace the engagement of the Church in this struggle. One must not minimize the strength of traditional Catholic policies and attitudes and interests today. The Church as a whole implicitly supports the regime, is vigorously anti-Communist, and has large vested interests in the status quo. One should add that since the civil war in Spain the word socialism is equated with Communism. It is also important to note that Catholic schools and universities educate the middle and upper classes (with a few notable exceptions), that the fascist party, the "Falange," is fanatically pro-Catholic, and that Franco, himself a devout churchgoer, is given widespread credit for "having brought twenty-five years of peace to Spain." Rarely if ever is mention made of his twenty-five years of harsh dictatorship by the Church leaders.

The Church is in a difficult position. It is a huge and wealthy institution, part of the Spanish Establishment, and it cannot disengage itself overnight. But there are signs that it wishes it could. Several bishops have made statements, couched in delicately chosen words, which lend some support to social liberalization. But it is fair to say that at no point does the institutional Church identify itself with the workers' movement. Its approaches, if any, are cautious, defensive and self-protective. In other words it risks little or nothing. Therefore it has no relation to the movement.

But fortunately the Church is not only an institution. The Church in the primitive Christian sense of the word is a movement as well. Thus among the young clergy, particularly in the industrial provinces of Bilbao, Barcelona and Asturias, they are looking for a new relevance in the Christian message. They have tried to translate brotherhood and love—the essence of Christianity—into real terms among their people. Inevitably they have identified with the poor and the suffering, and inevitably they have been infected by the militancy, bitterness and rebellion of the poor. So they have joined the *Movement*. They see no difference between their commitment to justice and equality through Christian love and the workers' commitment to justice and equality through the need to survive. In some cases the young priests have left their parish jobs, replaced their cassocks with overalls, and become workers. So there is complete identity of interest.

The young priests are the cause of many headaches to their bishops, who, as I have already explained, do not want to fall out with the regime. Some have been silenced; many are transferred to hillside peasant parishes where they can do less harm; one young priest I knew was removed from a fishing-port parish outside Bilbao to a retired Monsignor's residence, where he became private chaplain to the eighty-four-year-old invalid.

But just as repression by the army and police helps to unite the workers, so authoritarianism and caution by the Church help to forge the links between the young clergy and the workers. The Catalonian priests, demonstrating on the streets their solidarity with the workers, were clubbed and beaten and arrested by the police, and many of the workers have a picture in their homes of this event. (It was later admitted by certain officials that the police had allowed themselves to be provoked and had behaved with insufficient restraint in public.)

The other sector of the Church where the interests of the workers' movement have been adopted is among certain lay Catholic organizations. Because of the rigid class divisions in Spain, with enormous disparities of wealth and opportunity, the Church has sponsored groups which are specifically working-class whose members and leaders are all workers, and whose major task has inevitably become the solution of working-class problems. These groups some years ago had as their objective "the Christianizing of the working-class environment"—winning workers to the Church. However, as Catholic workers became increasingly disillusioned with the institutional Church, and aware of their own plight, they realized two things: first, that their true identity and commitment lay not with the hierarchical Church but with their fellow workers; and second, that their Christian commitment involved not so much their working for the return of lapsed Catholic workers to the sacraments, but the presence of committed Christians in the struggle for a just and brotherly society. Their task became the building of a *Christian society*—not a society in which all members were Christians, but a society based on the concepts of love, justice, equality and freedom. This ambition the Christian workers held in common with other workers' organizations, including the Communist Party.

This fusion of interests has, in the last year or so,

led to the emergence of a workers' front called the "Comisiones Obreras."

During Spain's long history of inner turmoil, there have been many occasions when Catholics and Communists have found themselves side by side. The Basque provinces (in which Bilbao is situated) are traditionally the most Catholic provinces in Spain; they also have a long history of separatism and of industrial militancy. In the civil war many Basque Catholics and Communists fought together against the Franquist armies and the Nazi-German air-raids.

And in the recurring mining disputes in Asturias, the Catholic and Communist workers share the same grievances and take joint action. There are many other such examples.

But until recently there was no organizational collaboration. Contact was haphazard and common action sporadic. There was no common front.

It is the gathering strength of the workers' movement that has brought Communists and Christians together in a new form. And it is the increasing urgency of the situation and a growing desire for revolutionary change in the economic and political structures that has led to the forging of a common structure, under the name of "Workers' Commissions."

The "Workers' Commissions" were first formed about eighteen months ago, and they represent the major forces in the workers' movement, i.e., Catholics and Communists. Below is a passage translated from the closing statement of the National Assembly of the "Workers' Commissions" held in June 1967. The meeting was illegal, the document was duplicated and circulated secretly. Many arrests were made as a result, but the crucial fact is that the meeting took place. The meeting was only known previously to the highly trusted representatives of the "Workers' Commissions" in different regions of Spain. Eight provinces were represented. Since the meeting was arranged and held in the highest secrecy, I can only give the following quotation as an indication of what the present alliance of different religious and political groups means to the workers involved:

The Workers' Commissions do not comprise an organization, but a coordinated force, a movement which attempts to involve all workers who hold in common the rejection of the present Trade Union structure, and who are prepared to fight for their rights and for class justice, and in particular at this moment for the right to free Trade Unions. . . .

The Workers' Commissions have a unifying character. They are not a federation of groups of elements in the struggle. They are united in a common participation in the movement of working-class people, without making distinctions of political ideology, philosophical notions, or religious beliefs. . . .

The Workers' Commissions are independent in their actions of all political, religious or trade union groups. The action of the Workers' Commissions will be guided exclusively by the will of the workers who participate in their movement and in general by the feelings and aspirations of all the Spanish workers. . . .

The Workers' Commissions will be guided in all action by a *democratic* spirit. This democracy will be based in the workers themselves, especially by means of workers' assemblies. . . .

There are two points which are extremely important in relation to the above statements. One is that today in Spain there is a genuine popular revolt. The workers feel a stronger class identity than they feel a political or religious identity (which does not mean that they have lost either political or religious affiliation). It is this that has enabled them to forge a militant union which presents a real threat to the present regime.

The second important point is that the workers have found ways of organizing themselves, of holding illegal assemblies, of distributing anti-government literature, and of keeping enough leaders out of jail to prevent the Movement from coming to a halt.

The Communist Party, which is banned, operates effectively and consistently, with ever-increasing membership (more and more of whom are returned young workers from France and Germany). The Catholic Groups have now made their position clear vis-à-vis the established Church. Their prime concern is the revolution in conditions for the ordinary Spaniard. They too are rapidly gaining support among the workers, and many of their leaders are in the most trusted positions in the "Workers' Commissions" and in clandestine trade union groups.

In spite of the dangers, the arrests, the worsening economic situation, there was in the summer of 1967 an air of confidence and optimism among the workers in the movement. The major cause is undoubtedly the success of the "Workers' Commissions," the unity they have fostered among workers and the strength and resilience they have shown in a common front, which they have previously failed to summon through their separate organizations.

The alliance of Communists and Catholics in Spain at grass roots level is unique in the history of Western Europe. All the signs described above indicate that it is meaningful and effective.

The implications for the Church, for the Communist Party and for a possible socialist society in Spain are extremely encouraging.

V

Opium or Leaven?

An American in Prague

CHARLES M. SAVAGE

"WE ARE WORKING night and day to overcome the damaging diseases of the body, we must also cure the soul of society of its greatest infection: Communism!" Applause filled the high school auditorium as a leading anti-Communist finished his speech.

In the late 1950's it was not difficult to believe him when he compared Communism to cancer. Later I asked him how one was to combat this malignancy. Everything seemed so clear and simple. There was a good side and a bad side. The object was to expose and halt the bad.

Shortly after entering college I again encountered this "Christian" crusader who sought to save the world from "atheistic" Communism. The oversimplification of his position and his dogmatism frightened me. Communism in his eyes was a force with no humanity. It was to be opposed by high defensive walls. How

CHARLES M. SAVAGE, a Presbyterian seminary student from the United States, went to study theology at the Comenius Faculty in Prague. In sharing the life of Christians in Czechoslovakia he learned to understand something of the nature of Christian commitment in a socialist country. This chapter is part of his personal testament. It has not previously been published.

could one possibly reason with a Communist? Were not all Communists little Stalins trying to out-do one another in their brutality and tyranny?

My study of history in college showed that this simplified view did not correspond to reality. It would be like accepting white light simply as white light. However, in science class we had learned that white light was composed of many colors blended together and disseminated according to a wave or particle theory. Was Communism to be seen simply as white light? No. I knew that one had to analyze its components in order to understand its historical development and its driving force. Only in this way could we really begin to deal with it. This was a much less vulnerable approach than either falling under its spell or hiding behind a protective wall. Moreover, humanity was somehow mixed up with it. Could we not approach the Marxists as human beings?

Several years later, while studying in Boston, I received a scholarship from the World Council of Churches and the United Presbyterian Church in the United States to continue my theological studies at the Comenius Theological Faculty in Prague, Czechoslovakia. I had become interested in the writings of Professor Joseph Hromádka, a leading Czech theologian and until recently Dean of the Comenius Faculty. He made sense when he explained that the dividing line of good and evil did not necessarily correspond to the configuration of the "Capitalist Christian" West and the "Communist Atheistic" East. Instead, he drew the line between those deeply and honestly concerned with human development and the egocentric opportunists who were more concerned about their own empires. He spoke often of the fact that Marxists and Christians were at the "threshold" of a dialogue. He pointed out that

Jesus was not concerned about defending a particular ideology; instead, he shared deeply of man's suffering and humiliation in order to free man to be truly creative. Hromádka, therefore, fought for the idea that a Christian could witness even in a "Communist" country. It was my desire to discover the truth of Hromádka's position which ultimately led me to Prague.

I arrived in Prague in September 1965. A thick fog made the dark night even more mysterious. Here I was a Christian in a "Communist" country. I felt a bit uneasy. Even though I wanted to be open and objective, the many prejudices I had picked up in the West shrouded me like the fog. Only after two months did I begin to emerge from the ghetto of the "Iron Curtain" mentality. Sure, I still heard stories of injustices which would have given the "anti-Communists" some credibility. But I also knew that there were great injustices in my own country. It was more important to achieve a balanced and not "sensational" picture of Czechoslovakian life.

It is impossible to cram an account of a year's experiences into a short essay. Instead, the following are several "snapshots" of individual experiences. Taken together they convinced me that it is possible to talk fruitfully with persons living in "Communist" Czechoslovakia, and second, that many Marxists are ready to modify their positions in response to changes on the "other side." It should be remembered that the philosophical and historical traditions of Czechoslovakia and the Soviet Union differ immensely and therefore it is dangerous to make generalizations which are too sweeping. Moreover, I found a real distinction between the intellectuals with whom I could speak openly and the bureaucrats who were adequately described by Franz Kafka as being remote yet powerful.

The Theological Faculty had about forty-five students

and about twelve professors. We lived in an excellent location in the middle of Prague. The students there told me of a regular seminar at the Charles University between Marxists and Christians.

How was such a seminar possible? Was it composed of opportunists, Marxists who were trying to use Christians to spread their political programs and Christians who wanted to chalk up "Brownie points" in order to gain better positions? On what basis could Marxists and Christians talk together? All I had heard earlier was that the Marxists considered religion the "opium of the people." It took several months and many conversations before I found answers to these questions.

After attending several of these seminars in a crowded classroom at the university I asked a young Marxist participant to lunch. He noticed I was having a difficult time understanding his train of conversation and so he asked me why. I told him that he did not fit into the image of a Marxist I had brought from the West. He did not quote Marx at every turn. As we discussed this I realized that he took Marxism more as a method rather than as a dogma. He said Marx had begun by analyzing a concrete historical situation. Therefore, he felt he should have this same freedom to begin afresh. He would return to Marx at those points where Marx still offered insights, but he did not feel "strait-jacketed" by Marxism. After all, he pointed out, Marx was critical of philosophers who just described the world; the point was to change it. He was a Marxist not because he was bound by Marx's dogmas, but because he saw the need to create a more just world and he felt Marx provided the needed insights for making the changes.

Later I spoke with Dr. Milan Machovec, Professor of Marxist Ethics at the Philosophical Faculty of the

Charles University. It was through his initiative that this seminar had begun. He explained its history.

In the mid-1950's there was an order from the government to increase the atheist propaganda. He felt much of the propaganda was naively and stupidly conceived. Therefore, while speaking against religion he also criticized the simplified atheist propaganda. He was in great demand as a speaker, for it seemed that everyone wanted to do something against religion at that time.

Occasionally a few Christians would attend his lectures. At a lecture in 1958 a young Christian pastor asked Professor Machovec a question concerning Protestant theology. Machovec said he had to admit that he did not really know much about Protestant theology. This encounter led him to begin studying theology more seriously. In the following weeks and months the questioning pastor and another Christian theologian met now and again with Professor Machovec to discuss more deeply problems of Christian theology and atheism. Between 1958 and 1961 Machovec wrote a book on Protestant and another on Roman Catholic theology. Although he freely admitted the weaknesses and omissions of these books, he felt they were an advance over the "stupid" atheistic propaganda.

His books awoke an intense interest among other Marxists and Christians. Soon he found himself in discussions with different persons almost every evening of the week. He could not hold so many individual conversations and at the same time get his other work done, so he proposed the establishment of a seminar to which persons interested in these problems could come.

He was able to begin a seminar in the fall of 1964 at the Philosophical Faculty of the Charles University in Prague. It was attended by about five Marxist philosophers, a like number of Christian theologians, and about ten university students. Professor Machovec said he had not asked permission of the Party or University to hold this seminar. He felt it was better to risk it on his own. If he had asked the Party and they granted permission, then others would say it was revisionist, while if it refused them some could say it was too dogmatic. Machovec's feeling for the situation has proved correct, for the seminar is still meeting each Monday afternoon at 4:30 with sometimes as many as one hundred in attendance and still without official sanction.

The seminar has discussed the writings of the Young Marx, the Ecumenical Movement, Modern Catholic Theology, Islam, Masaryk, Prayer, and Biblical Criticism, among many other topics. A Christian or Marxist would give a major presentation, then someone from the other side would respond, and afterwards there was always an open discussion. In addition to Czech speakers other internationally known men including Erich Fromm, Gustav Wetter, Herbert Braun and Charles West have spoken at the seminar.

The discussions at this seminar were open and free. Although I understood the history of the seminar I knew I had also to understand the theological and philosophical rationale for the seminar. A friend explained that the recent discovery of the "Young Marx," his "Economic and Philosophical Manuscripts" of Paris, written in 1844, had made it possible for the Marxists to think more humanistically. On the other hand, as modern Christian theology emphasized man's responsibility in this world, it found itself dealing with many of the same social problems with which the Marxists were dealing. Therefore, it became clear that the object of a dialogue was not to convert one another but to be open in order to share common insights in facing the problems of the modern world. A Marxist participant wrote that the first condition of a dialogue is "the courage to open oneself to the other . . . to unveil not only one's strengths but one's weaknesses, not only one's certitudes but one's doubts, confusions and gropings." Although idealistically stated, this does characterize one goal of the Machovec seminar.

I asked Professor Machovec to summarize the effect of several years of the Czech dialogue. He mentioned several points. First, it is not attempting to convert one side to the other, but to look at the problems of the world through each other's traditions. Second, those involved would admit that Christianity can no longer be sandwiched into the "opium" phrase. Third, it has proved that even a weak dialogue is better than strong monologues. Finally, it has become clear to the participants that both sides need each other and that they can legitimately work together. I noticed that at these seminars the Marxists did not defend Stalinism or all that the Party had done. Likewise, the Christian participants did not feel the necessity of defending any one economic system as "God-given," nor were they willing to hide mistakes of the Church. Instead, each side seemed to emerge with a clearer and sharper vision of its own possibilities.

My contacts were not limited to Professor Machovec or this seminar. Through my interest in the work of UNESCO I met a professor of the Technical University in Prague who also did research in computer systems organization. When we first met we took a long walk through the beautiful parks in Prague, then sat in a café and drank coffee for another hour, all the while talking about the relation between science and religion. Could science and religion ever be reconciled? he asked. He displayed many naive prejudices of a scientist against religion. He was still "hung up" on the Church's treatment of Copernicus. I tried to explain gently enough that modern Christian theology rejects the practice of using God as a working hypothesis to explain that which man can explain in no other way. Modern theology wants to rid itself of the "stop-gap-helper-god" concept. Modern theology no longer says that man is dependent on God for everything; instead it stresses man's responsibility in this world.

As I continued to meet with this professor of the Technical University I noticed a change in his attitude. He was interested in reading Bonhoeffer and Harvey Cox's *The Secular City*. We discussed the reports of the World Council of Churches' "Church and Society" Conference held in July 1966. He was bothered by the loose and vague theological language in these reports. I had to admit that Christianity was to blame for much of the scientist's suspicion because it often expressed itself in archaic language.

Another philosopher scientist and I discussed the relationship between the French Catholic Theologian Teilhard de Chardin's "Omega point" and the problem of negative entropy. He wondered if this was the Christian equivalent to the Marxist goal of a more perfect society. I introduced him to a professor of the Comenius Theological Faculty with whom he has explored this matter in greater depth. His interest in the future parallels that of many contemporary theologians who find heaven no longer "above" us but "before" us; no longer separated from this world in a vertical relationship, but intrinsically bound into the future development of human history.

One afternoon I visited the home of a pastor in a town near Prague. He was in his study talking with the local government secretary who was responsible for supervising church affairs. The pastor's wife brought in some coffee and we all sat and talked. I learned that the government secretary had been a member of the Communist Party for many years. He had grown up in a family of nine and had been a house painter before being given responsibility for the churches in this area. He proved friendly and willing to answer my questions. I asked him about relations between the Church and State.

He explained that just after the Communist revolution in Czechoslovakia in 1948 the Church sided with the capitalist interests. This is quite understandable when one considers the vast landholdings of the Roman Catholic Church. He said 60 per cent of the land was under their control. Naturally this led to a clash of interests. However, he explained that the state began to liberalize its position towards the churches when it noticed that some pastors were interested in the problems of the workers. He cited England as an example of where this was happening. This trend toward liberalization continued, he explained, as the Communists saw that the Christians were sincerely interested in working for peace. The work of the Christian Peace Conference, which originated in Czechoslovakia, dramatized this concern. The secretary said he had followed with interest the American Church's involvement in helping the civil rights movement. I was intrigued by the sensitivity of this local Party official to the developments in the Church in other parts of the world as well as in his own country. The pastor told me later that not all the Party secretaries were as sensitive and open as he, and that other pastors did have trouble from time to time. He warned that it would be unfair to present a clear and simple picture of the situation. There have been and will be setbacks for the Christians. But it is also important to understand the humanity and sensitivity of some of the Communists.

Another pastor complained that the state censor refused to let him include anything about the Christian attitude towards work in a Sunday School manual he was writing. It is not only the Christians who are given a bad time by the bureaucracy. A Marxist philosopher told me he had been refused permission to attend an important philosophical conference in West Germany because, as he later discovered, a junior bureaucrat felt he had been to the West enough times. Another Marxist explained that even though they might have overcome Stalinism philosophically, they had not overcome it bureaucratically.

I found this true myself as I returned to Prague after a summer vacation, intending to study for a second year. After an uncertain period of two months, it became clear that for some unexplained reason the government was refusing to renew my visa and therefore I would have to leave Czechoslovakia.

Nevertheless it was possible several months later for me to return to Czechoslovakia as a tourist to attend a conference between about two hundred Christians and Marxists from the East and the West. It was sponsored jointly by the West German Paulus-Gesellschaft (Society of St. Paul) and the Czechoslovak Institute of Sociology, part of the Academy of Sciences. During the last three days of April 1967 they discussed "Creativity and Freedom in a Human Society." This was the third annual conference held for Marxists and Christians by the Paulus-Gesellschaft, but the first in Eastern Europe. The French Marxist Professor Roger Garaudy summed up the present position of the dialogue by saying that it has passed beyond what Hromádka had called "the threshold." He documented this further development with three references: first, this conference itself; second, the publication of the Roman Catholic encyclical *Populorum Progressio;* and third, the urging of the leader of the Spanish Communist Party, Dolores Ibarruri *(La Passionaria)* at the Karlovy Vary Conference of Communist leaders held in April 1967 for them to become more open to the positive social forces of Christianity. (She was speaking out of her practical experience in the Spanish situation in which Christians and Marxists find themselves working constructively together to rebuild Spanish society on a more just and democratic basis.) Garaudy hoped this dialogue would become a model for a greater pluralistic "Dialogue of the Citizens of the Whole World." He might have been reminded that this is not the only model, for the Pugwash Conferences have been gathering persons from east and west, north and south for many years to speak as scientists to the practical problems of justice and peace.

These are only a few of the "portraits" I took while in Czechoslovakia. Those who attended the Montreal World's Fair know something of Czech creative genius. Were they to visit Prague they might meet this creativity in many diverse sectors. They might be intrigued by a series of articles which has appeared in the leading intellectual newspaper written by a Professor of Marxist Philosophy, Vitezslav Gardavsky, under the title "God is Not Quite Dead Yet." They would be amazed at the deep thinking which has been going on at the Philosophical Institute concerning the social implications of the scientific and technological revolutions. The Christian Peace Conference under the able leadership of Professor Hromádka has held its third major assembly (March 1968) in Prague bringing together Christians from all parts of the world to think seriously about the concrete problems of this world. Professor Hromádka has repeated many times the warning that the ideological differences between the East and West are less important than the economic differences between the rich nations of the North and the poorer nations of the South.

As I look back over my year in Prague I realize it was one of growth from a distrustful "cold war" mentality to one of deep concern for the concrete economic, social and political problems of this world. I found my own Christian faith had been deepened and made clearer through these encounters. I no longer see the world as a great tug-of-war between Communism and Capitalism. Instead I feel the need for us to use the best insights of Capitalism, Marxism and Christianity in meeting the real problems of hunger, poverty, social injustices and economic and political colonialism. Finally, I have come home with the conviction that Marxism can be a positive social force, and Christianity need no longer be considered an "opium" but the "leaven" for creative social change.

VI
Tasks for the Dialogue

A radio discussion between Milan Machovec and Helmut Gollwitzer with Hans-Joachim Girock in the chair.

GIROCK: I think that, as the starting point for our
deliberations, we should take the question: Are Christianity and Marxist atheism "tomorrow's partners"?
Partnership is certainly more than coexistence. And
both of you, Professor Machovec and Professor Gollwitzer, are among those in the two camps who consider this partnership to be a necessity for the future,
irrespective of the question of how this can be
achieved in practice. This point of view does not pass
unquestioned on either side. Professor Machovec,
what makes you, as an atheist, devote so much
energy to spreading your conviction of the necessity
to come closer together?

MACHOVEC: I am convinced that this is one of the most
important questions for mankind as a whole. In

MILAN MACHOVEC is Professor of Philosophy in the University of Prague and a member of the Czechoslovak Academy of Sciences. Formerly a Roman Catholic, he is one of
the Marxist pioneers of dialogue.
HELMUT GOLLWITZER is Professor of Protestant Theology
in the Free University of (West) Berlin. A Lutheran, much
influenced by Karl Barth, he took a prominent part in
the German Churches' struggle against Hitler. He is the
best-known writer on political ethics in the German Church,
taking a radical position.
H. J. GIROCK is a director of religious broadcasting. This
discussion was first broadcast in 1967 by Südwestdeutscher
Rundfunk.

Czechoslovakia, too, men experience certain unfortunate and tragic situations in their lives and I think that the question of a confrontation with those who think differently is one of the most important aspects of the search for authenticity, for happiness, or, as we have said, for the meaning of man's life. In the West I have often noticed that when Marxists, especially those from the East, talk about the importance of meeting or dialogue, people do not believe that they really mean it. They presuppose that it is just part of their tactics, but I should like to say that this is not true. We sometimes make similar mistakes in that we see our opponents, us for you in the West and you for us in the East, in a rather rigid mold. But I must say that we in Czechoslovakia, for example, have twenty years' experience that includes a number of problems; for example, in the atheist education of our young people. And so we cannot simply say we are atheists, or that we are right and the others are wrong; we know that there are weak points in our *Weltanschauung* as well and when—as I find very often in Western literature—the Marxist is portrayed as a person who has a kind of power complex, I must say that I am scarcely aware of any such people in Czechoslovakia.

Therefore this is not just the concern of a few artists or theoreticians. In Czechoslovakia over the last five or six years there has been the spontaneous development of something like a desire to meet those who hold different views for dialogue, in order to come together instead of merely living side by side. We also do not merely want to discuss, because in my opinion dialogue does not only mean rational discussion; in the realms of morality and emotion it means a meeting with those who think differently, with one's "neighbor" as Christians say.

Secondly, dialogue seems to me an essential means to any form of human maturity. I believe that a man, be he Buddhist, Marxist or Christian, in some sense can only be mature and live maturely when he is living in dialogue. In my opinion in Czechoslovakia we are discovering that work and specialization, possessions and evening entertainment, are not all that is required for human maturity. If a modern man lives surrounded by all sorts of things but despises human encounter, he is living at a level lower than his humanity offers, and I think that in this sense the dialogue with views other than our own can also serve for us Marxists as a means of overcoming our individual limitations. Therefore for me it is not merely a political question. We also have to be realistic about the fact that we are not the only people on this planet.

But for me it is not primarily a question of respecting others because we are not alone; it is an existential question of atheism and Marxism as such.

Thirdly, I want to say that this meeting, this dialogue, is really the only method which corresponds to so-called peaceful coexistence. This is the only method which can do justice to humanism. And I should like to add, especially in the dialogue between Marxism and Christianity, we have not only realistically to accept that mass Christianity is the most widespread non-Marxist movement and ideology in the world, but also to take seriously that the—as I would describe it—Christian elite, or certain groups of the Christian intelligentsia within the ranks of the theologians, in my opinion, if I am not mistaken, have experienced crises similar to our own and that these theologians are prepared to talk with us. When I visited the theologian Karl Barth in Basle, he asked me what we, as atheists, valued in his work. I thought about this and then said: perhaps the most important thing is that he, on the theoretical plane, had done so much to renew the forms of Christianity's own internal criticism of the Christian tradition. And I believe that Pope John XXIII in a quite different way has done something very similar for the Catholic Church. This is why the confrontation with the theoreticians of Christianity is also of interest to us.

And as far as Christianity is concerned, of course, twenty years after the revolution we are discovering that it is not enough to base life on purely political and economic factors, that we have to take more interest in moral questions, in existential questions, in the so-called ultimate questions of human life. And there we have to take seriously that Christianity has a very old and far-reaching tradition of seeking answers to these questions.

And, finally, it seems to me that we are facing a perfectly legitimate question when we are concerned with finding our own roots. This is something very widespread among thinkers in Czechoslovakia at the present time. There is a desire not simply to live Marxism from day to day but to discover the deep— perhaps the deepest—roots of history. And if we find in the Jewish prophets, for example, something like openness to the future, and in Jesus an openness in his claims related to the moment, this naturally does not mean that, because it interests us, we therefore become Christians. But at present this has reawakened in us an interest in the Christian tradition and we can in some way gain from this dialogue; I could say we can become more ourselves.

GIROCK: In what you have said, Professor Machovec, there may be much that you, Professor Gollwitzer, would also say from the Christian point of view, that you perhaps can subscribe to. Could you say more about your impetus as a Christian?

GOLLWITZER: What Professor Machovec has just said indicates the motives—he has said it so convincingly that from my point of view I can accept it to a large extent—indicates the motives which move me and many Christians and Christian theologians. On the one hand we see Communism today in the midst of a great internal hopeful development and we have living experiences, for which I would cite Milan Machovec himself as an example of a Communist devoted to this honest search, of a readiness to discuss; it would be most unchristian to reply with a "no" and with a closed mind.

Secondly, as Professor Machovec has pointed out, we are going forward together into the future. The phenomenon of religion, the phenomena of Christianity and Marxism, are not going to die out, at least not in the foreseeable future, in the future that we can foresee, however much each may have prophesied the death of the other. They will have to live together in the world of tomorrow and each will have to share with the other in that world's development.

Thirdly, this means for Christianity that we must do all in our power to ensure that Christianity is not used, as it has so often been in the past, as a means to warm up the "cold war," leading eventually to "hot war." The disputes or dialogue between Marxism and Christianity cannot be tackled with weapons or on the political level alone.

And finally, we have gradually learned, even some of us Christians when we look at Communism, to see each other as positive factors—not as something which has to be overcome and removed as fast as possible, but as something positive and constructive in the world of the present and of tomorrow. I should like quickly to explain this: Marxism's guiding principle—and this is its real motive power—is a vision of a human society in which all the inhumanity of society in the past is clearly and critically examined—even a self-critical examination of the inhumanities which remain today in its own socialist society. This criticism, this vision of the future, is inspired, in my opinion, by Christianity. We are responsible for it. A life which men can live together, in which the strong do not exploit and subjugate the weak, nor the privileged the underprivileged, but in which the strong help the weak, in which all live together as brothers—that is the vision of the New Testament. It is ridiculous to postpone this vision for the never-never or to restrict it to the next life. It was the driving force which led the first Christians to work out their communal life in the Church. It must be the driving force which enables us to change the world today. A Christianity which, as has often been the case, shows itself to be uninterested in changing the world for the better, would in my opinion be a Christianity which has not yet understood the relevance of the New Testament for today and for tomorrow. And this brings Christians and Marxists together today.

GIROCK: Could one sum up what you have both said so far as meaning that you both recognize and admit that the one side cannot in the long run exist without the other . . .

GOLLWITZER: Yes, yes.

GIROCK: . . . and that you are both determined to seek the way into the future together?

GOLLWITZER: . . . and that each has something to say to the other which, in fact, when they are alone they will not say to themselves but only hear if the other one, the partner, says it. This is why they so badly need one another.

MACHOVEC: I could not subscribe to that word for word but I find that it contains many valuable points. I, too, could say that, in my opinion, now in this age of confrontation—not only the meeting of modern Christianity with modern Marxism, as it were, but also the meeting with a thousand years of seeking like, for example, the question of the meaning of the teaching of Augustine or Thomas Aquinas, of Pascal and Luther—this is also very important now for the Marxist, but of course I do not want to prophesy for the distant future. As you know, it is part of the so-called ABC of Marxism that religion is basically superfluous and that we can reach a time when religion will no longer exist. I do not want to prophesy when this will happen; such attempts seem ridiculous to me. As far as prophets are concerned I believe that both of our movements have had some unfortunate experience of them . . .

GOLLWITZER: Yes, yes.

MACHOVEC: . . . and yet I should not like merely to leave it on one side. Although we were convinced fifteen or twenty years ago that it would be relatively easy to do away with religion and that all that was necessary was to develop new economic structures, now after twenty years we know that this task which Karl Marx set us of overcoming religion, if we are to carry it out, is really an enormously difficult task and, as I understand it, it means for us that the possibility which Karl Marx outlined can only become a reality if, I might say, the genuine, the human, the deep, the seeking, all that is in the Jewish and Christian tradition and has so deeply marked Western history—if we do not simply negate this but rather try and see to what extent we can adopt it and further it, on a new theoretical basis, of course.

GOLLWITZER: Of course this brings us to our differences.

GIROCK: Yes; I did not want us to go on to the differences yet, but rather to ask the question as to whether we have not seen so much good will expressed on both sides that we have to take care not to be carried away by a euphoria of good will. It is easier to demand that we should have things in common than actually to share them. Do not the problems initially arise because the concept of man is very differently defined by the two sides? In the Marxism which is predominant today, if I have rightly understood it, the logical consequences of historical development are in a sense seen as absolute guarantees for the future. Man finds his self-fulfillment by submitting to these consequences for the well-being of all. Would you, Professor Machovec, be able to accept that, not as your personal view but as the predominant view within Marxism at the present time?

MACHOVEC: I must admit that one can relatively often find this or similar views in our country among the "men on the street," but in my opinion it is neither Karl Marx's view nor one which will help us to go further. So-called historical determinism, when it is interpreted as a sure guarantee of the future, for example "our victory is assured," or as meaning that we can lay down a complete blueprint for the man of the future, seems to me to be something repulsive and I have never found anything of this sort in Karl Marx; and it is clear to us that we cannot define our concept of man so clearly. For example, we cannot develop a concept of man without considering the disciplines of anthropology, nor can we in any sense absolutely predict what the man of tomorrow will be like. In this sense it seems to me that the conception of determinism as a guarantee for the future can play a part among atheists similar to, if you will allow me, that of so-called divine providence—Professor Gollwitzer might say: to mistaken interpretations of divine providence—which I believe was also typical in mass Christianity; I mean the interpretation which believes that in the end God corrects the world's failings, cares for his children and so on. That is determinism understood as a tranquillizer, it is opportunism, something which satisfies human laziness and passivity, and this is one of the things we have to fight against in Czechoslovakia at the present time. Only action, only individual involvement will usher in the tomorrow, and otherwise we shall end up in a cul-de-sac.

GOLLWITZER: Professor Machovec, a question on that: the conviction that the laws of history will lead us on to the classless society of the future has not encouraged laziness in classical Marxism. It was a comfort to the fighter which gave him the certainty that his fight was in line with history itself and did not contradict this line. Our conviction today, even within the realm of Marxism, that historical processes inevitably bring about the establishment of socialist and Communist society, has been very much shaken. We observe today with great concern that society can also fall prey to barbarism and the extermination of humanity. The same is true of the reliance on God's presence, his care for his humanity, which we see in the Gospel— it is possible for this to have the effect of opium, encouraging laziness, as has often enough been the case.

But this is not inevitable. Among people in the history of Christendom who have believed in a very strict predestination, like Cromwell, for example, and the Puritans, it certainly did not produce laziness. And so I should say, if we take up this antithesis for the moment, that a Christian's conviction springs from the promise that God is always in command of his world and guiding it to his goal. We see this promise in the coming of Jesus Christ which is directly connected with the future: atoning death, resurrection, forgiveness, this all points to future life, surely. And so my question to you is—and there will then be other questions—where does the Marxists conviction that his fight for a humane future will not be in vain come from?

MACHOVEC: Professor Gollwitzer, before I answer I should like to thank you for interpreting classical Marxism so well. Because it is certainly true that in classical Marxism the doctrine, as it were, of historical determinism was no pill for laziness at all. But I must say that for more than twenty years I have been living in a socialist society where people do not always embrace Marxism for purely scientific reasons— quite opportunist motives . . .

GOLLWITZER: Of course.

MACHOVEC: . . . one can say it is human, yes, but above all we must combat this pseudo-Marxism as well. You have made similar distinctions in the history of Christianity.

Yes, I could subscribe to that too. My Marxism does not mean that I have to assume *a priori*, as it were, that everyone who believed in God was, to the same degree just because of his belief in God, an opium-taker. For example, in the history of our country men like Hus and Comenius had a firm belief in God but they were, so to speak, awakeners of a new search for greater depths in man. Or in the present, who could say, for example, that Gandhi propagated an opium ideology; that would be a very naive view. But then the question arises again as to how this idea, the idea of God, is effective basically in history and in general. And of course I should say that in millions of cases it has resulted in human passivity. But now, where Marxism is not just in opposition that has become the ruling ideology in many countries, we cannot just oppose this misinterpretation of the Christian faith; we have also to oppose the misinterpretation of and tendencies to misuse our own theory.

GOLLWITZER: Yes, but then I have two questions to ask: Firstly, wherever an idea is associated with the ruling power it faces the temptation of opportunism. We can see this in the history of Christianity as well as in the history of the Communist states. This calls for internal self-criticism. Why do you conclude from the history of Christianity, which was linked with the ruling power from the time of Constantine, that Christianity, in general at least, apart from a few notable exceptions, must of necessity be reactionary? Secondly, can one discuss all religions in the same breath at all? There may be some religions whose very essence encourages fatalism and induces apathy. This can certainly not be said of Christianity. So I should like to talk here only about Christianity. One can interpret Christianity both as an exaltation of the status quo, that is reactionary, and as a mobilization of forces for change, that is revolutionary. Why, unlike early socialism, does Marxism not simply criticize empirical Christianity? Why does it go on to reject religion as a whole? You yourself have just said of religion that it may not be abolished in the foreseeable future, but that you believe one day it will be. Why is that your ideal at all, this disappearance of religion?

MACHOVEC: My main argument against Christianity does not of course apply to all the modern theologians' interpretations of Christian theory but rather to what you have called the empirical view of Christianity in history. In my youth this was what you can call an existential question: Why were there so many crimes committed on classically Christian soil? Why, in countries with a Christian tradition, was something like Auschwitz possible, for example, or why were people in general indifferent to existential questions altogether?

Yes, Professor Gollwitzer, when we meet a deeply committed Christian we are sometimes impressed. But, in practice, how many such Christians do we meet? We find more that is—as I sometimes call it—Sunday religiosity on the fringe of the average life in a consumer society. It seems to me that the influence of Christianity on the population in the last two or three centuries has grown so weak that the conviction that the future can be based on this theory represents too great a risk. I believe that, alongside its other causes, Marxism also arose because Christianity was no longer able to play its ethical part in the nineteenth century. Naturally, as far as religion is concerned, Karl Marx's criticism was applied to the Church as it was in the nineteenth century, the Church which we could say had become bourgeois, if you will allow—

GOLLWITZER: Of course—

MACHOVEC:—or one can say that Karl Marx's atheism was a denial of the form of theism which was widespread in the eighteenth and nineteenth centuries; one must admit that. But it appears to me that Western man has had so many unpleasant experiences of this weakened tradition that mankind is fully justified in building a new life on a completely new theoretical basis. This does not mean that I can now explain my conviction to you without any reservations.

On certain points I can admit quite openly that I do not know. I do not know, for example, how to deal with the problem of death in a Marxist way. I know that, in a way, on this all too human point the Christian tradition has achieved more than atheism, including Marxist atheism, during its history. But, although I admit this weakness of mine, this is not a reason for becoming a Christian.

GOLLWITZER: No, Professor Machovec, when you said that, because of the shortcomings of Christianity, Marxism now raises the flag of humanity, I would go still further and say that the Marxism which you represent—and you are not one white raven among a lot of black ravens; I know that your sort of Marxism has a large number of supporters—that Marxism is nothing less than the continuation of the work of Jesus Christ in a new form, without its knowing about Jesus Christ at all. But it is a consequence of our failure as Christians that now you carry on this work in an atheistic way. This does not make us Christians superfluous. But in your Marxist humanism I recognize a Christian movement rather than Christianity being superseded. That is the first thing I wanted to say.

Secondly, when a Christian, a real Christian, faces all the crimes of two thousand years of Church history —I cannot go into all of that now, but you know that we do recognize them clearly—they do not in fact make us cast Christianity aside but, rather, force us all the more to take Christianity seriously in another way and find a new way to try and be Christians.

But the weakening of the Christian influence to which you referred is not the weakening of a true Christian influence, because this was never present in the Church of the masses; it is rather the weakening of an old, pseudo-Christian tradition among the masses. In this way Christianity again becomes the concern of smaller groups, "shrinks itself better" as Augustine rightly expressed it, surely, and can only then seriously be the subject of discussion. I do not believe in the Christian Middle Ages or in a bygone Christian culture. They were not Christian. And now, thirdly, when you said what a great problem the question of death is for you, for example, then the—or rather I shall put it in the way I usually like to say it: the Gospel does not render the battle for a better human society superfluous, nor, on the other hand, will the best of human societies make the Gospel superfluous, because there are human problems which society, even the best society, cannot solve. And this is why the question which has led to the development of religion in all times will always be vital. And this is why the answer which Christianity gives to the question of guilt, of the meaning of life, of death and also of the relationship between the individual and communities in situations of conflict, which arise in the best of societies: inequality, which will also exist in the best of societies, people who suffer from biological defects, sickness, and so on—these questions will always make Christianity's answer relevant. And so I must ask my question again: Why do you in fact want religion to disappear?

MACHOVEC: But here we have to make a distinction: religion is not the same thing as Christianity. And I should like to ask in return: Why should these questions you have mentioned—the question of conscience, of the meaning of life and of guilt—why should they be called Christian? Of course I admit . . .

GOLLWITZER: No! Those are general human questions.

MACHOVEC: Yes!

GOLLWITZER: There are various answers to them . . .

MACHOVEC: In Buddhism, for example . . .

GOLLWITZER: Precisely! Precisely, but society as such, however good its structure may be, can never, in my opinion, answer these questions which are vital questions for individuals.

MACHOVEC: Well then, Professor Gollwitzer, if you admit that these general human questions, which are so important to men, that these questions also exist in a non-Christian tradition . . .

GOLLWITZER: Certainly!

MACHOVEC: . . . for example, in Hinduism, Buddhism and so on, then I do not understand why you call yourself a Christian, because it seems to me that Gandhi, for example, was not a Christian but he nevertheless very much admired the figure of Jesus Christ; it seems to me not only that the atheist, too, the Marxist atheist, can, as it were, admire this figure, but that he even has many grounds for taking this figure very seriously and admiring it. But then I can never understand why I have to see something so absolutely unique in this figure. It is a great figure in which the great human questions are epitomized in a specific way. But in a similar way these questions are epitomized in Buddha, Confucius and, one can also say, in Marx.

GOLLWITZER: Professor Machovec, because our time is short we cannot now go into the question as to why, for me, the answer of the New Testament to these general human questions is so compelling, whereas it is not for others. But when Marxism refers to the death of religion, this expression means that in the successful society of the future these questions will die out because this future society will have answered them. I would rather say that even the best and most successful society of the future may make these questions more acute but will not answer them. And therefore religion will not die out. And therefore Christianity's answer will still be relevant.

MACHOVEC: I see this question in a rather different way. We have both admitted that these questions are neither Buddhist, nor Confucian, neither specifically Christian nor Jewish. Why do we now have to say that these are religious questions? In my opinion, they are deep human problems, one could say anthropological questions. Not only Marx, but many philosophers who did not think religiously at all, have still taken the question of the conscience or of the meaning of human life seriously. I could say that these questions must not die out because then, of course, first humaneness and then humanity would be destroyed. If the Marxist statement about the death of religion is understood in this way then I would say that, of course, in this sense religion cannot die out, but I do not know why I should call it religion. But I must say—and this is the second and more important part of my answer—Marxism, at heart, in the works of Marx and now too, is not merely a socio-political and socio-economic theory and doctrine, but a philosophical doctrine. Marxism is concerned with man as he is. Marxism is not only concerned with changing social problems, social conditions; it is seeking a new form for man's existence and moral life, and therefore Marxism has also to be concerned with problems of *Weltanschauung*, morality and so on, and has therefore also to ask, not only what part Christianity has played in society, but also to what extent Christianity as a theory is or is not true. I remember a discussion I had with a theologian who said that in Marxism nothing as significant as a conception of resurrection could ever arise. And I replied: Yes, I admit that the concept of resurrection has been very important in history. But Marxism as a *Weltanschauung* also has to ask to what extent this was illusion, to what extent ontologically, as it were, this idea in reality does or does not correspond to something. And this is also a reason why Marxism is concerned with Christianity.

GIROCK: Forgive me for interrupting you here a bit abruptly. That was rather a lightning tour of mutual criticisms and perhaps, for the time being, we can leave it at your view, Professor Gollwitzer, that the ultimate questions referred to in this discussion can be more convincingly answered by Christianity than by Marxism.

GOLLWITZER: At least we are agreed that, looking at the mental state of future society, if this future society should succeed, we cannot prophesy about it except perhaps to say that these questions will still be vital then.

MACHOVEC: Yes indeed!

GOLLWITZER: And therefore your reply would give me hope for my theory that Marxism, in its essence, does not spell a "no" to religion, but that it is only concerned that religion should not continue to play an obstructive, opium-like part in the struggle for future society, a struggle which has now become a vital fight for life for man today.

MACHOVEC: Yes, if we make the distinctions we have referred to, I can subscribe to that wholeheartedly. I

would go even further. When I come across the fact
in modern society that we men only live from day to
day, are only concerned with consumer questions,
and when I find a desire in certain people—and not
only a desire, but action—to combat this stupid, or,
as we say, vulgar materialism, this vulgar epicu-
rianism, then of course I do not first ask whether you
are a Buddhist or a Marxist or a Christian; I ask to
what extent this involvement is useful. Because in my
opinion it is not only Christian mistakes which are
a danger in our time.

GIROCK: May I interrupt this train of thought a bit
brutally. Our discussion should also deal with the
question of how opportunities for discussion between
atheists and Christians can be developed. Both of you
start from the premise that each of you, on the basis
of his own view, is seeking a reliable hope. Professor
Machovec, once in a lecture you referred to three
conditions for the search for reliable hope. The first
was "the recognition of false paths and of self-decep-
tions." What were the two others?

MACHOVEC: If I remember rightly, that was in Essen at
the conference of the Evangelical Academy. I probably spoke there of the importance of the so-called
cosmic awareness. By that I mean something like
what Teilhard de Chardin has worked out; that is,
the question of the significance of man's entry into the
cosmos, and perhaps one can also say that, precisely
because this awareness of our common cosmic tasks is
deepening, it could help us to resolve quite practical
humanistic questions better on this planet. In this
respect everything which furthers this cosmic awareness seems to me very important and hopeful. But
there is a second aspect to this: for example, why we
are interested in discussion with Christianity; perhaps

this is connected with the fact that, in these meetings, we find something in common not just on the fringe but at an original basic level, something I would call universalism or universal humanism; I mean the fight against any national or racial exclusivity or the like.

And thirdly, I referred to a tendency to modesty which, in my opinion, is a hopeful sign in Christianity, in existential philosophy and in philosophy as a whole, but which has also been developing in recent years in Marxism as well. This means that every intelligent being has a certain feeling of impotence in our modern, super-organized world. We cannot change the world in a moment, but perhaps no one is so impotent that he has no possibility of joining the battle against fanaticism in his own ranks. That then was the third point: the hope of combating fanaticism in one's own ranks.

GIROCK: But now, at the end of this discussion, I should like to express an uneasiness which haunts me a bit. In a sense this conversation has been conducted with a harmony of good will; and I have the feeling that this harmony of good will does not entirely correspond to everyday reality. In fact, today, when we look at socialist societies, we see that Christianity may be tolerated there but it is considered to be a relic of the past, both in everyday theory and practice; a thing of the past which is rather a hindrance than a help on the way to a better future. And on the other hand I think that, on our side, in our Western democracies, Professor Gollwitzer, it is not different basically, but at least up to a point. In theory we give the atheist exactly the same freedom as the Christian. But in his confrontation with society he will at once encounter difficulties, and when it becomes clear that his atheism springs from Marxist roots, then his thoughts and ideas will come up against real barriers. And so my question is: How can this "harmony of good will," which I have sensed in your discussion, be translated into the reality of everyday life? Professor Machovec, do you see some means whereby the degree of tolerance for Christians within a socialist society could be increased?

MACHOVEC: If you come to Prague, and now many guests from the West are coming to Prague, then you will see that this question is not closed, that it is not even fossilized, but that it is being tackled. I can say that we do not want a silent Church. Of course, we cannot be indifferent to what Christians say. Perhaps you will agree that tolerance in the sense of indifference would not be enough. In this sense I can respect another's views; but I also respect him insofar as he tries to convert me. That I am not absolutely satisfied with the relationship between Christians and atheists in Czechoslovakia is surely quite natural, otherwise I should do something different. The fact that I am involved in this field means that there are many problems which we have not yet solved.

GIROCK: But perhaps you, Professor Gollwitzer, would like to say one or two things from our side on the subject of how we can increase the measure of tolerance here.

GOLLWITZER: Yes, we must say that we are, firstly, struggling on both sides with a heavy burden of the past. Christians have been shocked by the initial "no" which Marxism flung uncompromisingly at religion, by the acceptance of atheism and the prophecy of the death of the Christian faith and of all religious attitudes. Secondly, we have been shocked by the brutality of the revolutionary fighting, the Communist acceptance of force as a legitimate means in the revolutionary struggle. And of course they forget that force played a significant part in Christian Western society as well, that Christians have also accepted war and so on and so forth. They forget all of this when they express horror at the Communists' brutality. But this is all ballast. On the other hand, you referred to the fact that Marx faced the bourgeois Church of the nineteenth century, and our mutual friend Hromádka once said that the attitude of the official churches in the West confirms the Marxist criticism of religion. So that is the ballast of which we have to free ourselves so as not to use it to judge the nature of our partners. We must give our partner a chance to come to terms with the weight of his own history. This is necessary for a future meeting.

Secondly, on the question of tolerance, we are naturally not satisfied that, as a result of this tradition, the policy of countries in the East towards the Church does, thank God, tolerate the churches and allow a certain measure of freedom for the practice of religion; in most Communist countries we do not consider this adequate yet. We hope that there will be an improvement. But only those can demand and hope for this who are prepared to exercise such tolerance on their side that is among us in the West. To put this quite clearly, those who support the banning of the Communist Party in West Germany cannot demand that Christians in the East should have more freedom. The one is very closely related to the other.

GIROCK: I am afraid that there we must break off, rather than close, this discussion. Like all discussions of this sort, it was not intended to supply a bundle of answers and instructions for usage which we could then happily take back home. It was rather an attempt to raise the problems and questions and at most take a small step forward. If we have succeeded in this discussion and in this series of broadcasts in removing a few of our mutual prejudices and relaxing some of our rigidity, then I think that all those who took part in this series and in this discussion have achieved their aim. I should again like to thank you, Professor Gollwitzer, and you Professor Machovec, very warmly, and I thank you especially for speaking so frankly and often so directly, as well as for presenting your arguments so clearly.

VII

Creative Freedom

ROGER GARAUDY

Prefaced by an Interview of the Author
by Tannequy De Quenetain

"WE CONCEDE THAT THERE IS A
POSITIVE SIDE TO RELIGION"

Question: What makes you think that a fruitful
dialogue is possible today between Marxists and
Christians?

Answer: Evolution on both sides. Let us look first
at the evolution of Christians. This is characterized by a double dissociation—first, faith is being
dissociated from traditionally conservative attitudes;
secondly, faith is being dissociated from an ideology
which acted as a brake on rational and scientific
thought.

Q.   But is it true to the facts of history to say that
the Church has always been a conservative force?

ROGER GARAUDY is Professor of Philosophy in the University of Poitiers and a member of the Politburo of the
French Communist Party. He is author of *From Anathema
to Dialogue* and numerous essays on Christianity and
Marxism. His essay "Creative Freedom" first appeared
in the journal *Dialogue*, Vienna, 1968.

A.   Not always, but it has been in the great
majority of cases since the time of its triumph over
paganism. From Constantine to Salazar, the Church
has supported the established order, and this means
that it has defended the cause of the privileged.
St. Augustine justified slavery, in which he saw
a consequence of sin; in the same way, Thomas
Aquinas justified serfdom, and Bossuet the Negro
trade. And I would remind you that in the nineteenth century, the basilica of Sacre-Coeur was
built as expiation for the Commune.

However, if the Church as an insitution has
been on the side of the established order, Christian faith has led some of the great popular revolts
against political and social injustices. This was
the case with John Huss' movement in the fifteenth
century, and with the Peasants' War in Germany
in the sixteenth century. At the present time, there
is talk in the Catholic Church of rehabilitating
John Huss. That is no mere chance. An outstanding turning point was reached with John XXIII's
Pacem in Terris, and the work of many theologians
to liberate the Church from the "Constantinian"
tradition which has made her, as many Christian
theologians recognize today, the church of the
employer rather than of the employed.

Q.   You also said that faith was being dissociated
from an "ideology" which hindered rational and
scientific thought. What ideology do you mean?

A.   I mean the fact that Christianity as traditionally presented was bound up with an obsolete
view of the world, the view of Ptolemy and Aristotle. There has been a spectacular evolution on
just this point. At the recent Council, Msgr. Elchin-
ger, co-adjutor Bishop of Strasbourg, requested the

official rehabilitation of Galileo; and in a speech at Pisa, Paul VI said that Galileo was a great Christian. Among the great architects of this evolution I must mention the Protestant theologian Rudolf Bultmann and the Jesuit scholar Teilhard de Chardin. The theology of Bultmann is an attempt to release the Christian message from the mythology in which it has been enveloped until now. Bultmann distinguishes very clearly between what he calls the "Kerygma"—that is God's call expressed in the proclamation of the Gospel—and the myth which is the form in which the irruption of the transcendant into human life is expressed. This form depends on the view of the world current in each epoch.

While Bultmann is attempting to "de-mythologize" the Bible and the Gospels, Teilhard de Chardin has released the Christian message from the fixed view of the universe, and replaced it with a form of evolutionism which gives a cosmic dimension to Darwin's transformism.

Q. Has it been the reading of the works of Teilhard (for which you profess a great admiration) which has led you to rethink the relationship between Marxism and religion? And if so, for what reasons?

A. What I like first of all about Teilhard is his optimistic view of the evolution of the world and of man, a view incompatible with social conservatism, which is closely linked to a pessimistic view of the world. Teilhard was certainly not a Marxist, and indeed he said a number of silly things about a philosophy about which he knew very little; but in his work one finds a high doctrine of human work, and of our historic future, which approaches

that of Marx. I would add that Teilhard's evolutionism is also in many respects close to Engels'
Dialectic of Nature. Moreover, Teilhard tried to
make theology evacuate the realm of science. One
of the great classical temptations of Christian apologetic consists of locating God and the supernatural
in the provisional gaps in our human knowledge.
The trouble with this method is that theology
is continually giving ground as our knowledge
advances. Teilhard deliberately refuses to make
of God what Father Dubarle calls "the little recom-
pense for our intellectual inadequacies." He vehe-
mently opposes an apologetic based on miracles,
pointing out that very probably many Christians
remain believers not because of, but in spite of,
miracles. This beginning of a re-evaluation of
Christian thought (and it is certainly not the work
of Teilhard alone) makes dialogue possible because
the theologians with whom we talk are now speaking a language which is modern and accessible to us.

Q.   Is there a parallel in Marxist thought to this
evolution in Christian thought? Has Marxism also
undergone a mutation?

A.   The problem is rather different. Marxist
thought needed not so much to change as to wake
up. One could say that in the second half of the
twentieth century, Marxism has emerged from a
theological slumber of twenty-five years. It fell
asleep around 1935–36, with the publication of a
work of Stalin which summed up materialism in
three principles, dialectic in four laws and historical materialism in five stages. This work fixed
Marxism in structures which claimed to be definitive, although Engels had shown that materialism
should take on new forms with every great dis-

covery in the evolution of science. After Engels
we have had in Marxist thought the stage on which
Lenin left his mark, but since Lenin the development of science has been much more rapid than
it was in the period from Engels to Lenin.

Q.   Then what form has Marxism taken, and what
forms should it have taken, since Lenin?

A.   Without pretending to solve the problem, I
should like to raise several points. First of all,
Marxist materialism cannot leave out of account
the critical work of Kant, in particular the idea
that whatever we say about things, it is *we* who
are saying it. We set out to meet things with what
in cybernetics are called "models." A "model" is
a reconstruction of reality according to human
plans, and science progresses from corrected
hypothesis to corrigible hypothesis in a never-
ending dialectic. This is how we move from
Ptolemy's model to Newton's and then to Einstein's.
Every model is part myth, because myth is also a
reconstruction of the real according to a human
plan; but the scientific model, unlike the myth, is
subject to experimental verification. Between the
model and the real there is established a dialectic,
of which the cybernetic theories of retroaction
and auto-regulation give us the mathematical
image. And to think that some people have regarded
cybernetics as a bourgeois science!

Now to the second point: For Marx and Lenin,
the fundamental problem was the construction of
a new social order. For this reason, the problems
of subjectivity were well down in the list of priori-
ties, although they were not entirely ignored. But
these problems are now primary, and they can
be formulated as follows: Will new *human* rela-

tionships automatically develop hand-in-hand with the construction of new *social* relationships? Experience says no. Human relationships are not mechanically determined by social relationships. Even in the class system there were sublime forms of love which transcended the feudal or bourgeois scheme of relationship between human beings: for example, the mystic love of St. Theresa of Avila, courtly love, the passionate love of Tristan or of Phaedra.

On the other hand, one can see in a socialist society the persistence of feudal or bourgeois forms in the relationship between the sexes. In short, the advancement of socialism has not led to the rise of new forms of love. Even in the most beautiful works of art, such as the novels of Sholokhov or a film like *The Ballad of a Soldier,* there is nothing as far as the presentation of love is concerned which surprises or disconcerts men who have been formed in our class system.

Q.   Then what is the point of changing social relationships if ultimate relationships are not also improved?

A.   The changes in social relations are, if I may say so, a kind of negative contribution. They are salutory because they suppress certain things. Socialist society suppresses the commercial side of love; the marriage for money, the whole question of dowry and inheritance. It suppresses prostitution, the statistical curve of which follows that of unemployment in capitalist societies. In Cuba there were 110,000 prostitutes before the Castro Revolution; now there are 10,000. In the Soviet Union prostitution has almost entirely disappeared, and what remains represents a psychological rather than a social problem. The conditions are present for the changeover to new historic forms, but man is not merely the product of the conditions in which he lives.

Q.   You have touched on the problem of love. But is there not here, when we start to talk about love, a fundamental difference between Marxism and Christianity, which is to the advantage of the latter? You can see among Marxists a striving for justice, brotherhood in combat, class solidarity; but absolute and unconditional love—is not this the prerogative, the trump card, of the Christian message?

A.   It is true that there is something sublime in Christianity, and Marxism would be impoverished if it were not to take into consideration, and not to seek to enrich itself, by all that is best in the Christian heritage. However, it must be said that in practice, this appeal to love has too often served as an alibi in order to condemn the just revolt of the oppressed. And when, under the pretext of love, you condemn the revolt of the slave, you become the accomplice of the man who is keeping him in chains.

Q.   Just over two years ago, you publicly criticized the report of Ilytchev, Secretary of the Central Committee of the Party in the U.S.S.R., which advocated the intensification of the anti-religious struggle. For what reasons did you condemn this report?

A.   Because this report is the resurgence of the idealist atheism of the eighteenth century in France, and of the scientific atheism of the nineteenth century. The atheism of the Encyclopedists considered that religion was a fable, entirely invented

by "tyrants and priests." The atheism of the nineteenth century is based on scientism; science, it is
said, can answer all the questions with which man
is faced. Now this is false, at least at the present
stage of scientific knowledge. Science does not give
answers to the questions raised by our deepest
preoccupations: the meaning of life, for example—
the confrontation with death. And religion touches
directly on these questions. That is why you cannot
simply dispose of the problem of religion by saying
with Bichat, for example, "I have not found
God at the end of my scalpel," or with Titov,
"I have not found God in space."

Marxist atheism approaches this problem from
a different standpoint: liberty. If God exists, is
my liberty decreased? Is God alienating where
my liberty is concerned? And Marxist atheism
answers: "Yes, God is alienating insofar as he is
regarded as a Moral Law existing before the creation of Man, as a heteronomy, opposed to the
autonomy of man."

Q.   To what extent do you agree with Marx's dic-
tum that religion is the "opium of the people"? Is
that all that religion is for you?

A.   Historically, religion has played, and still does
play, the role of opium. But it is not only that.
The Marxist theory of religion is not limited to
this formula. Religion, like all ideology, is a way
of tearing oneself away from the past: it is a scheme
whereby one anticipates the real, either in order
to justify it, or in order to transform it. The myth
is a "model" which enables man to act. It is a
pre-scientific, irrational model, which marks the
beginning of the great speculative adventure in
the history of mankind. It gives man access to the

world of causes beyond the world of sensible effects.

Q. But today it is to science that man turns when asking about the causes of phenomena. What role role then can myth play?

A. Beyond science there are all the questions to which science has no answers. They are in the realm of myth and of philosophy. But myth belongs to the irrational order, while philosophy is rational. To my mind, myth expresses reason while it is being made, while the philosophical concept expresses reason when it has been made. Moreover, myth witnesses, in a pre-rational way, to the possibilities for man that are open in any given situation. Nothing expresses this infinite possibility better than the Resurrection of Christ. By his Resurrection, Christ breaks through man's absolute limitation, which is death. I should like to add that the Jewish faith, continued in the Christian faith—when it is dissociated from Greco-Roman ideology—is particularly suited for releasing man from a given situation in order to launch him into action by its high doctrine of the possibility of historical development. For the prophets of Israel, as for the early Christians, God is "He who comes." He is present as a challenge, as a permanent future. To believe is to make oneself open to the future—to respond to God by tearing oneself away from the past. You find this idea nowadays in the works of Teilhard de Chardin, for whom God is not only above, but also ahead. You find it also in the works of Father Rahner, for whom God is "the absolute future," actively and demandingly present in every man.

In contemporary Christianity, there is a current which is already very strong, running in the direction of making a clear distinction between faith and religion. Religion is a way of thinking, whereas faith is a way of acting. Paul Ricoeur goes as far as to say "religion is an alienation of faith."

Q.   What does Marxism stand to gain, in your opinion, from a dialogue with Christians?

A.   Christianity raises questions which, even if they are wrapped up in mystery, require answers. There are areas which Christianity has explored, where the fruit of its experience could be enriching for Marxist thought. Take, for example, the problem of death. I am invited to a colloquium with the Dominicans on this question, and I arrive with empty hands. As a Marxist philosopher I shall probably learn a great deal about this question from Christian experience. In short, I think that all the answers which religion gives are out of date, and I think that some of its questions have been wrapped up in mystification, but I believe that the human experience which underlines these questions cannot be ignored by any doctrine, including Marxism. Perhaps the role of religion is to go on raising questions indefinitely, and the perversion of religion is to provide answers. By the questions which it raises, Christianity prevents the Marxists from going to sleep. I find that very beneficial.

Q.   And Marxism, for its part, prevents many Christians from going to sleep?

A.   I certainly hope so. That is what makes dialogue possible, for it witnesses to the fact that each can bring something to the other. The Christian faith is being cleansed of its Platonism, thanks to Marxist criticism, and Marxist atheism is being enriched by the need to answer the objections of faith.

Q.   And what other benefits do you think that Christians can gain from the study of Marxism?

A.   That is not for me to say. That is a question for the Christians.

Q.   After all that you have just said, I should like to ask a last question. After Marxists have seized power in any country, may the Church retain the right to exercise its apostolate in the whole of society, making use of normal means of propaganda?

A.   I will answer quite frankly: Yes. The arrival of socialism should not lead to atheism becoming the state religion. Engels already reproached the Blanquist emigrés in London, after the Commune, for raising atheism to the level of a state religion. And Lenin was always opposed to having atheism written into the statutes of the Party, saying that this was an anarchist proposal. Certainly in a Communist society, the Party can, and should, struggle against religious ideology in the name of Marxist philosophy, and armed only with theoretical criticism. But what applies to the Party does not apply to the State. You must distinguish clearly between their respective roles.

Creative Freedom

IN THE WESTERN tradition the concept of freedom has two sources: Greco-Roman and Judaic-Christian; that of creation has only one: Judaic-Christian.

Greek humanism discovered and elaborated one aspect and one essential element of freedom: that of necessity and the cognition of necessity. Divine necessity, then rational necessity. From Prometheus to Antigone, myth and tragedy express the confrontation of the hero with Fate. Necessity has neither been created by the gods, who are but demiurges subjected to fate, nor, by men, subjected to fate and to the gods. The hero can pit himself against this sovereign law, but he cannot destroy it. He will be vanquished by it. From Heraclitus to the Stoics, the order of the cosmos and the city *(polis)* will become an interior part of reason, but for man, discovering himself to be a particle or fragment of this order, freedom in its highest form is the cognizance of necessity. Free man identifies himself with this inflexible law. When, in this non-created universe, Epicurus wants to establish the autonomy of man, he has to postulate an arbitrary rupture of determinism from nature and reason.

In the Hellenic conception of the world and of man, the idea of creation is absent. The world, Heraclitus wrote, has not been created by any god nor any man; it is an eternally living flame that lights and extinguishes itself according to determined laws.

In the Judaic-Christian conception, on the contrary, creation is primary, and man's freedom is no longer defined as the awareness of necessity but as participation in the creative act.

The gospels of the New Testament announce this "good news." Man is able at any moment to begin a new future, to free himself from the laws of the world, of nature and of society. The resurrection of Christ is the paradigm of this new liberty. Death, the very final frontier determining our inexorable finitude, death itself has been vanquished.

This actual experience of the possibility of tearing oneself away from the "given" world and of inaugurating a new future is that of a double transcendence: the radical transcendence of God in relation to man establishes the transcendence of man in relation to nature, to society and to his own history.

For if man is more than the inevitable product of the laws of nature, or of the structures of society, the prolongation or outcome of his past, he can only exercise this right of intervening on the inevitability of the world if he participates in the actual act of its continual creation.

This presupposes two conditions:

First, that the world does not suffice unto itself: there is a process of creation.

This creation cannot be thought of *in* time, for it is precisely creation that institutes time. In the Greek conception time and history do not exist. They are only the mobile images of the immobile eternity of a world that has not been created. If this world is a totality that suffices unto itself, which is the definition of a non-created world, nothing really new can occur in it, that is to say, nothing that would not be a mere reorganization of that which already exists, since it derives from no outside, transcendent source. This is the logic of that radical immanence explored by Spinoza or Hegel.

Real time and history can only exist if something new is able to emerge; and something new can only emerge if the totality of being does not suffice in itself, if it leads us on to something entirely different.

This ontological dependence was at first expressed naively; in the Bible, in the form of creation in time, whilst, however, as Descartes perceived, this creation either occurs continuously or it never occurs at all, it is everywhere or nowhere. Creation, far from being a unique miracle, is the most constant actual experience: it is the continuous emergence of something new. St.

Paul expressed this actual experience when he said, "In God we live and move and have our being."

But would we not then be overcoming this autonomy in relation to the order of the world, only to fall under another yoke, to stand before God in the relationship of the heteronomy of the slave before his master?

It is here that the second condition operates: not only is the world not sufficient unto itself, and, in order to take account of the emergence of the new, calls for something quite novel, but it is not the necessary emanation of the entirely new, the entirely different. Otherwise we would be faced again with the previous problem. We can as little remove God from the world (then He would only be the totality of the world closed to itself and immanent, like the God of Spinoza or Hegel's Absolute Spirit) as we can withdraw the world from God (or this God would set us the same problem of self-sufficiency that the world set, and we would revert to the endless regressions of the Indian philosophy of emanation: the world is borne by an elephant, the elephant by a tortoise, and so ad infinitum).

The originality of the Christian experience of creation is the cognition of the ineluctable schism in the weft of concepts. Neither being nor thoughts in process of being born suffice in themselves or are able to account for themselves.

Hence the scandal and the folly, for the Hellenic wisdom of the sages, of asserting that the final law of being is not reason but love.

For if the final law of being is, as the Greeks thought, reason, then we are a fragment or an element, necessary and rational, of the closed totality of the universe or of a God who is but a name for this totality.

Breakaway and freedom are only possible by an act of creation, and one that is not inevitable. This is

what Christianity expressed in saying that creation was
a gratuitous gift, an act of love. For, unlike the relationship between master and slave (where the slave
has no value in himself save that of serving his master),
or the relationship between cause and effect, the relationship of love is the only one that implies the unity
of oneself and the other person, each being for himself and for the other person, both an end and a
transcendence of himself.

Thus, as Harvey Cox shows, the following become
possible:

— The removal of sacralism from nature, free of the
spirits and god of animism, as from the unchanging
essence of dogmatic reason;

— the removal of fatalism from history, free of pre-
tensions to an order of divine right or a finally rational
order;

— a removal of alienation from religion, no longer
giving God the appearance of an idol and demanding
that in him he recognized the entirely other, which is,
by the very principle, neither non-being nor a concept.

The radical novelty of this relationship of man and
the world has been blurred every time the fundamental
experience of Christian creation and freedom has been
translated into the language of Greek philosophy, which
is radically foreign to it.

This has occurred at least twice: with St. Augustine
at the decline of slavery, and with St. Thomas Aquinas
at the decline of the feudal world.

The extraordinary experience of inwardness and subjectivity with St. Augustine, paralyzed by the dualism
of Plato and Plotinus, leads to the loss of the cosmic
dimension with St. Paul and, by this rejection of the
world, to the orientation of man towards another world.
For centuries Christianity thus became in effect what

Nietzsche with justified contempt termed "Platonism for the people," renouncing the continual creation of the world and giving only an illusory freedom, that of "liberating" oneself from the world by escaping from it. Making Christianity a confraternity of fugitives has always proved a windfall for the established powers.

It was another historical turning point when, for the second time and once again for centuries, Christian experience was translated into the categories of Greek thought: St. Thomas Aquinas in terms of Aristotle.

Contrary to St. Augustine, St. Thomas endeavored to overcome the dualism inherited from Plato: Grace is neither opposed nor juxtaposed to nature, it is its perfecting. Faith is not heterogeneous to reason, it is the opening of reason. Freedom is not exiled outside the determinisms of nature or of the structures of society. God, as Father Chénu said, is "a creative presence at the very root of my being and an ontological source of my freedom."

But this effort to reconquer the world, to recognize its dignity and true value is, in its turn, paralyzed by the schema borrowed from Plotinus and the Greek Fathers, according to which the universe and man, who is part of it, are conceived as an emanation from God and a return to God. This schema determines the structure of the "summa theologica" of St. Thomas Aquinas. This emanation reintroduces a conception of freedom no longer based on the creative act of a new reality, but on the sacral hierarchy of the world. And it is this that was to permit, for centuries to come, a transforming of Thomism into the instrument of immobilism and of the existing order.

It appears that in the middle of the twentieth cen-

tury a mutation began to take place in Christians' attitudes to the world that enabled Christianity to rid itself
of the vestiges of Platonic dualism and of the philosophy of emanation.

The first breakaway was effected by Karl Barth,
when he affirmed transcendence in its most intransigent form.

Every concession to anthropomorphism, every conception tending to establish a continuity between man
and God, set God up as a rival to man. All that is given
to the one is taken away from the other. Humanism
is profane, and the religious man is he who, in order
to choose God, turns his back on the world. As Father
Girardi writes: "God only ceases to be man's rival
if he possesses no common measure with him. Man
only becomes true man when God is truly God."

In the major currents of contemporary theology there
are three essential characteristics. In the first place,
these are not pre-critical theologies; they are aware that
all that is said about God is said by man. The second
trait derives from the first: they are centered on man,
as the Council itself. In his study *Theology and Anthropology* Father Rahner writes, for example: "The question of man . . . must be considered as the very essence of dogmatic theology." Finally, they endeavor to
distinguish religions as ideology always linked to institutional or cultural structures and faith as actual experience of transcendence. Some of them, like Paul Ricoeur,
go as far on occasion as to consider religion as an
alienation of faith.

This new attitude by the Church to man, which has
continued to gain ground since the Vatican Council,
permits a profound meeting with Marxists on the level
of humanism; that is to say, the affirmation of the

autonomy of man that is so powerfully recognized in the constitution *Gaudium et Spes* and in the encyclical *Populorum Progressio*.

Marxism's particular position on this problem of humanism, of the autonomy of man and the identification of freedom with creative activity, is to join the two links of the chain, to integrate, in going beyond them, the two antithetic traditions: Greco-Roman and Judaic-Christian.

Marx—whose "historic initiative" Lenin often said he appreciated the most—binds together in one fundamental formula creation, freedom and necessity. Men, Marx wrote, make their own history, but not arbitrarily. They do so in conditions that are always shaped by the past.

To reduce Marxism to the single Greek tradition expressed in the Hegelian formula that Engels takes up—freedom is necessity become conscious—would be to impoverish it in a singular fashion. The recognition of necessity is indeed an indispensable element of freedom. But human history is not merely a particular case of the dialectics of nature. The difference, as Marx points out in *Das Kapital*, is that men have made the one but not the other. Marx emphasizes the specific differences of levels and stresses the emergence, with man, of a new qualitative form of coming into being. With labor in its specifically human form, that is to say, labor that is preceded by the awareness of its aim, a history arises that is the creation of man: man by his work transforms nature and in transforming it transforms himself, creates new needs, new horizons and new meanings.

In the course of this history, in which man objectifies himself in the products or institutions, the social division of labor, the private ownership of the means of

production, the rise of conflicting classes all lead to
an alienation: when the product of labor has become
a commodity, when it belongs to the owner of the
means of production, the laborer is deprived not only
of the product of his own labor, but of the means
and ends of this labor, which are decided over his
head by the owner of the means of production. His
labor and his very life become alien to him, because
work no longer has its proper human character for
him, that is, determining his own end, which then
becomes the law of his labor.

Labor is no longer objectivation of oneself but alienation of oneself. And alienation is the opposite of creation in that the object then dominates the subject;
relations between men, says Marx, take on the appearance of relations between things. Human history
thus begins to resemble the history of nature. As Engels
reminds us, in the jungle of capital everyone com-
petes with everyone else, individual projects cancel one
another, and the result, the historical event, is something no one consciously desires.

According to Marx, in man's history necessity takes
on two basic forms: that of an external necessity which
expresses man's alienation and, more particularly, the
fetishism of commodities, by which men's relations to
one another take on the appearance of relations between
things; and secondly, that of an inner necessity, which
comes about through man and is expressed in the
struggle against alienation: the "subjective" element
of awareness, as Lenin stressed, plays a major role in
the class struggle.

In the alienated world, where for the most part
external necessity rules, man tends to be only a link
in the chain of things and events. Human history, as
Marx wrote, tends to resemble natural history.

This type of necessity dominates, for example, the development of capitalism, a system in which man becomes the *object* of history, since the alienation due to the private ownership of the means of production degrades him to the status of things.

When, on the contrary, Marx speaks of the *necessary* advent of socialism, it is a much more profound necessity. It is no longer a matter of the *external* necessity of the development of a system where man, treated as a mere thing, is not present, but of an *inner* necessity in which man is part and parcel of the problem itself.

The victory of socialism will not come about by itself, by a kind of necessity of things, as if the working class were urged by the sole force of the inertia of the mechanisms of capital. This mechanistic determinism has always led to reformism, to the idea of a progressive and automatic integration of socialism in capitalism.

The dialectical necessity of the revolutionary negation is the very opposite of mechanical necessity. The one takes place without me, the other requires my participation. The one teaches passivity and resignation, while the other is the master of energy and historic initiative.

Truly external necessity depicts a range of possibilities. It radically excludes certain possible factors: a return of capitalism to the feudal system is, for instance, excluded, or even a return of monopoly capitalism to liberal capitalism. But it imposes no choice. To say that, at the present stage of capitalism, the advent of socialism is necessary does not mean that it will come about by itself whatever we do. It means that the contradictions of capitalism are of such a nature that they can only be resolved by the elimination of the private ownership of the means of production and the passage to socialism. But if we are not aware of this necessity, or if, being aware of it and assuming this task, we commit a multitude of errors of strategy and tactics, the contradiction could remain unresolved, and lead to a deterioration of history marked by convulsions and catastrophes as the inevitable result of this unresolved contradiction: crises, wars, etc.

Class consciousness is therefore the necessary condition for the conquest of freedom.

For Marx, as for Hegel, freedom is the overcoming of alienation. But while with Hegel and Feuerbach this operates only in the individual consciousness, for Marx it demands a real transformation of the world and not merely the idea that we would make of it.

For Marx, alienation is not merely the schism of the individual, but social reality, the reality of classes and their antagonisms.

Thus for Marx the problem of freedom is not simply an individual problem but a historical and social problem, a class problem. It is closely linked to the revolutionary tasks of the proletariat.

The external necessity of alienation engenders many types of illusions: for instance, that of the freedom in what we call a bourgeois "democracy." In a society based on the private ownership of the means of production, freedom is the privilege of those who own the means of production. In the classic epoch of Athens, "democracy" is a political system in which 20,000 citizens rule over 400,000 slaves who are deprived of all rights. In the preamble to its first constitution, the bourgeois French Revolution of 1789 proclaimed: "All men are born free and equal in law," and it straightaway rejected as "passive citizens"—because they are non-owners—three quarters of the nation, following the principle proclaimed by the great bourgeois ideologists of the Encyclopaedia: only he who possesses is a citizen.

Yet the winning of universal suffrage through revolutions has not changed things fundamentally. Freedom remains a class privilege

Dependence begins in the factory, where those who do not possess the means of production have only the freedom of obedience.

It continues on the political level, where the main means of expression are owned by the owning class (newspapers and mass media); opinion is shaped by them. "Ruling ideas," said Marx, "are the ideas of the ruling class." And that is only one aspect of the means of pressure. In the center of Paris, at the Citroën works among others, to reveal oneself as a Communist is to lose one's job.

As regards culture, the fundamental inequality is even more flagrant. Only a tiny minority of working-class children have access to higher education. Thousands of children who perhaps possess the genius of a Mozart or an Einstein will never develop their true creative capacities because their parents' position has not allowed them access to higher education.

True freedom is not a formal freedom. It is the opportunity given to everyone to develop his capacities and his gifts to the full.

A true democracy is one that makes a man of every man; that is to say, a source of initiative, of responsibility, of creation on all levels of social life—that of economics, politics and culture.

But in every system based on the private ownership of the means of production, this capacity for initiative and creation remains for the most part a class privilege. It is pure deception to say there is freedom for all as long as the material means are left in the hands of a few and millions of men are deprived of their initiative and, if they protest, of their bread. There is no more deceptive theory than that of the free fox in the free chicken run.

This is the great deception of the so-called free world. Each ruling class calls freedom the maintenance of its class privileges. Marx humorously told the story of how, in 1850, an American arriving in England was prevented from whipping his slave and cried out: "Can one call it a free country where one is prevented from punishing one's own Negro?" Today, the big landowners who are expropriated by agrarian reforms that give the land to those that work it, and the exiled capitalists whose enterprises have been nationalized, voluntarily subsidize the sending out by the radios of "Free Europe" all the necessary calumnies to justify their former privileges, which they call "freedoms." But the fact remains that, from China to the Soviet Union and Cuba, it took socialism to liquidate in a few years the illiteracy that had been maintained for centuries by class systems. Socialism does not give everyone the genius of an Einstein, but it allows every child who possesses genius in him to use it to the full.

Whatever the dramatic events and insufficiencies, historic experience shows that only socialism can, in our age, rapidly overcome the disparities in the standard of living and of culture and give to the greatest number of people the means to live and the opportunity to create.

The most typical example in our epoch is that of the colonial or dependent countries, where the colonialists of the so-called free countries have destroyed freedom and the capacity for initiative and creation for millions.

Let us take the case of a country that has been dependent for a long time, Cuba. In the course of ten years of the dictatorship of Batista, a vassal of the United States, the proportion of illiterates did not decrease by 1 per cent. Three years after the advent of socialism, illiteracy has disappeared, while it continues to remain in all the other countries of Latin America, which are dependent on the United States.

With all the present storms raging over China, it is enough to compare the speed with which it is overcoming underdevelopment, hunger and illiteracy by socialism with the stagnation in all fields of practical freedom which men are condemned to in India, whose leaders have chosen the road of capitalism.

A century ago, Marx showed that the disparities and contradictions are not diminished by the spontaneous play of the laws of capitalism. He foresaw that there would be a growing discrepancy between the historically determined needs of workers and their chances of satisfying them. Today we are able to note with pleasure that the latest encyclical of Paul VI not only takes account of these disparities, but emphasizes that they are growing worse. It notes that in a system based on profits, competition and private ownership of the means of production considered as an absolute right, the spontaneous play of free enterprise, of "liberalism," risks the rich growing even richer, the powerful stronger, while confirming the misery of the poor and adding to the servitude of the oppressed.

These growing contradictions that reveal the situation in the underdeveloped countries, however, take on other forms in the big industrialized capitalist countries.

Here the big new fact is that, starting with the middle of the twentieth century and as a result of the second scientific and technological revolution characterized by automation and the growing importance of electronic computers, a trend that has been constant since the start of capitalism has begun to be reversed:

the proportion of unskilled workers has stopped increasing; it is now the number of qualified workers that is growing. Two concomitant phenomena can be seen. First, there is the change in the very conception of professional qualification. In a completely automated factory, the characteristics of qualification in work become the same as those of culture: an aptitude for grasping processes in a global manner; the capacity for renewal and change, for flexible training and deployment; the ability to pose questions, the machine relieving man of the job of calculation, of forecasting problems and solving them. Second, the gearing down of the centers of decision-making turns out to be more profitable than of concentrating them in the hands of a number of technocrats.

Thus the very development of techniques demands working with ever more initiative and creative activity. A new subjectivity is in the process of being born and growing, due to the objective development of the productive forces; but it then becomes more and more contradictory to demand that a worker devote the maximum of initiative and creative energy in his technical tasks and at the same time to demand from him unconditional obedience to the private owner, whether individual or collective, of the means of production.

The problem of freedom and creative activity has thus been posed in a concrete way by recent developments.

From now on, the following are outdated in our epoch: from the economic point of view, the era of managers and technocrats in the service of invisible owners of the means of production; from the political point of view, the era of dictators and personal authority, where one individual thinks and decides for all;

and in culture, the era of the supposed elite and class barriers to the access of all to culture and creative activity.

Only socialism, that is to say, a system in which the private ownership of the major means of production, of transport, credit and exchange has been abolished, permits each worker to attain practical freedom, to deploy initiative and creative ability.

Only in this way will the unlimited creative power of all men be liberated.

A curious question is sometimes posed about the future of a world in which the liberation of so many forces would in practice reduce to nil the work necessary to satisfy need. It is a strange question, first, because the world of hunger reminds us of the most urgent problems; but above all, it fails to take into account the fact that this continued creation of man by man calls forth new and unlimited requirements. It is not a question merely of increasing needs *quantitatively* in a consumer society in which the capitalist society functions in such a way as to condition the consumer to buy the products which are profitable to the seller without any relation at all to their human significance. It is a question of a *qualitative* growth of needs; that is to say, a growing predominance of the needs of *culture* over those of *nature*, and above all, this fundamental need that is specifically human, that of creation.

What will man do with the leisure gained from his techniques of production?

Leisure will no longer be merely recreation and distraction. It will be work in its highest form, creation; unlimited creative work in the field of scientific research, of literature and the arts, and in the infinite knowledge of man that is love.

Why should men only be able to create under the

incentive of want, while, for example, Christianity has conceived a God whose creation is not an inevitable necessity but a free gift of love? Is it not a fact that some of the finest works of science and art have been accomplished without any consideration of interest or need, but from the irrepressible need to create? And could not the rare case today become the joyous rule of tomorrow?

Marxism, the indivisible synthesis of dream and struggle, conceives this world peopled with untroubled gods inaugurating a specifically human epoch of history that will no longer be governed by need or the strife of the jungle but by the new dialectics of a creativity of infinite opportunity.

Perhaps this is the highest level on which our dialogue can proceed. Whether Christian or Marxist, we identify freedom with creation. Our humanism shares in common the desire to make a man of every man, to make him a creative being.

The final problem that remains outstanding for us is to know which of our two conceptions of the world most fully recognizes man's responsibility for his own history and provides him with the most effective method of creating his own future.

This is no sterile confrontation, for each can only grow in stature by asking of himself the questions that his partner poses to him. What would your faith be if it did not bear within it that latent athesim that prevents the service of a false God?

What would be our atheism if it did not learn from your faith, not the transcendence of a God of whom we have no actual experience, but the transcendence of man whose full development demands that he never limit himself to what the past has made of him?

Perhaps our atheism and your faith are only two

approximations of this actual and continuous experience of creation, the one more concerned that nothing shall detract from the autonomy and grandeur of man in the process of creating himself, the other staking everything on the entirely different absolute because they think, with Father Girardi, that man is too great to suffice unto himself.

VIII

What Socialism Is Not

LESZEK KOLAKOWSKI

WE INTEND TO tell you what socialism is. But first we must tell you what it is not, and that is something on which we have had to change our minds very thoroughly.

Here then is what socialism is not:

A society in which someone who has committed no crime sits at home waiting for the police.

A society in which it is a crime to be the brother, sister, son or wife of a criminal.

A society in which a man is unhappy when he says what he thinks and remains happy when he says nothing.

A society in which a man lives better when he has no convictions.

LESZEK KOLAKOWSKI is both the leader and hero of the young Polish critically-minded Marxist intelligentsia. He has been expelled both from the Party and his teaching position on the philosophical faculty at Warsaw University. He wrote this piece in 1967 for the student journal *Po Prostu*. The entire article was censored. Thereafter the journal itself was proscribed. The text was affixed by students to the notice board of Warsaw University, but was soon removed. It has since circulated widely in manuscript form.

A society in which a man is unhappy because he is a judge and another man is happy because he is not.

A state where men do well when they praise their leaders.

A state in which it is possible to be condemned without trial.

A society whose leaders appoint themselves.

A society in which ten people live in one room.

A society which has illiterate men and women.

A state which does not permit everyone to travel abroad.

A state which has more spies than nurses and more people in prison than in hospital.

A state in which civil servants increase at a more rapid rate than workers.

A state in which people have to tell lies.

A state in which people have to steal.

A state in which people have to commit crimes.

A state that possesses colonies.

A state that produces superb jet planes and bad shoes.

A nation that oppresses other nations.

A state that wants its citizens to agree on one philosophy, one foreign policy, one economic theory, one view of literature and morality.

A state whose government determines the rights of its citizens but whose citizens have no say in determining the rights of the government.

A state in which a man is made responsible for his ancestors.

A state in which some of the people earn forty times as much as the rest.

Every government that is opposed by the majority of the governed.

A solitary and isolated state.

A group of underdeveloped countries.

A state that thrives on nationalist slogans.

A state whose government believes that nothing matters more than power.

A state that is in league with crime and then fits its ideology to this pact.

A state which wants its foreign ministry to determine the fate of mankind.

A state which finds it difficult to distinguish between slavery and liberation.

A state which gives free rein to the proponents of racism.

A state in which the means of production are in private hands.

A state that thinks it is socialist because it has put an end to the private ownership of the means of production.

A state that finds it difficult to distinguish between social revolution and armed invasion.

A state that does not believe that people under socialism should be happier than people without it.

A society that is very melancholy.

A caste system.

A state which always knows the will of the people before it asks them.

A state that can punish the people and get away with it.

A state in which it matters which view of history you hold.

A state in which the philosophies and theories always say the same as the Generals and Ministers.

A state in which the road maps of cities are secret documents.

A state in which the results of elections are always predictable.

A state which has slave labor.

A state which has feudal relationships.

A state which maintains a monopoly on scientific progress.

A state in which whole groups of people can be transplanted from one place to another.

A state in which the workers have no way of influencing the government.

A state which believes that it alone can save mankind.

A state which thinks it is always right.

A state in which the historians exist to serve the politicians.

A state whose citizens are not permitted to read the best of contemporary literature, to see the best of contemporary painting and to hear the best contemporary music.

A state that is always satisfied with itself.

A state that claims that the world is a very complicated place, but really believes that it is a very simple one.

A state in which people have to be sick for a long time before they can see a doctor.

A state that has beggars.

A state that believes everyone loves it, although the opposite is true.

A state that is convinced that no one in the world has better ideas than it has.

A state that does not care if people hate it, as long as people fear it.

A state that decides who may criticize it and how they may do it.

A state in which people are required on one day to say the opposite of what they were required to say the day before and are required to believe that they are still saying the same thing.

A state that does not like its citizens to read old newspapers.

A state in which lots of ignoramuses are reckoned to be scholars.

That is the first part.

Now, pay attention, because we want to tell you what socialism is: Here is what it is—socialism is a good thing.

IX

The Pattern of Encounter in Britain

JAMES KLUGMANN

IT SHOULD BE said at once that in a sense "the dialogue" is not new to Britain. Since Chartist days there has always been in one form or another an active, if small, Christian-Socialist movement. In the 1930's there was much common discussion and action not only between Christians and the labor movement in general, but specifically between Christians and Marxists. Christians of most Protestant denominations (but very few Catholics) worked together with Marxists in many of the struggles against war and fascism, including the campaign of solidarity with republican Spain, and on many social issues like unemployment.

Over the last half a century, but deepening profoundly in the last few years, there has been a growing ferment and discussion taking place within most Protestant sections of the Church in Britain. This has involved an ever greater turn away from "other-wordliness," a growing demand that man's duties to man should be accepted in *this* world here and now, that man's faith should be tested in his actions *now*, a spreading doubt

JAMES KLUGMANN is the editor of *Marxism Today*. This essay was originally published in the *World Marxist Review* in March 1968.

in the morality of capitalist society, a movement of rebellion against ritualism and often against what could be called the "religious establishment."

Moreover, and this is very new, the same questioning, rebellion against other-worldliness, growing acceptance of social responsibility in *this* world, along with spreading doubts of the morality of capitalism, is, in the last few years, extending amongst British Catholics.

This profound crisis of ideas within the Church, rebellion against acceptance of the Church as part of the political establishment, acceptance too of responsibility to man in this world, and—amongst many—an acceptance that involves direct participation in struggle now for peace, against poverty, against racialism, and—for some—struggle against colonialism and against capitalism, clearly enough provides fertile ground for a renewed, qualitatively stronger, much wider and deeper dialogue between Christianity and Marxism.

Certainly this renewal of dialogue has been considerably helped and inspired, too, by the reports and influence of the dialogue taking place in countries like Italy, France and Spain, by the reports of various international confrontations and by the publications in English of articles on the dialogue including those in *World Marxist Review*.

DISCUSSION IN "MARXISM TODAY"

In March 1966 a discussion article on "Dialogue between Christianity and Marxism" was published in *Marxism Today*, the theoretical and discussion organ of the Communist Party of Great Britain, by Dr. John Lewis, the Marxist philosopher. It analyzed new trends in the Church and called for an extended dialogue.

Dr. Lewis, calling for this extended dialogue, argued that it could lead to "a widening of the sphere of common action and the breakdown of entirely baseless prejudices and illusions—these being important immediate objectives."

More than this, he argued, the discussion would inevitably involve problems of ethics, it would come to discuss both Christian and Marxist views of the individual, the state, freedom and materialism, and, in the course of it, we should be able to show "that the practice of an accepted moral code can only lead to hypocrisy or futility unless a radical reconstruction of the system of social relations makes it feasible. . . ."

On the publication of Dr. Lewis' article, the Editorial Board of *Marxism Today* invited a number of Christians of different denominations to discuss in its columns their views of the need and possibility of a Christian Marxist dialogue.

The response was immediate and warm, and rather representative of different Christian approaches.

Whilst, as would be expected, the Christian participants in the discussion held a wide diversity of theological (and probably political) views, what was most interesting was that they shared many approaches to the Christian Marxist dialogue.

All, without exception, welcomed the dialogue.

MAN—THE MAIN SUBJECT OF DIALOGUE

Nearly all stressed what they considered to be the deep responsibilities of Christians to life in *this* world. We should all, they felt, be concerned with the improvement of man's life in this world. Here they saw the main basis of dialogue.

"The only proper and possible subject of the dialogue," wrote Reverend Paul Oestreicher, Associate Secretary of the International Department of the British Council of Churches, "is man, the double question: what do men need and how are they to get it!" Theologico-ideological discussion should not be ruled out, but "the necessary philosophic wrestling must remain rooted in human reality. And all the while we need to remember that most people are neither Christians nor Marxists, they are hungry."

Our dialogue should *begin with man,* wrote Reverend Alan Ecclestone, Vicar of Darnell, Sheffield, and a member of the Communist Party—"Man offers possibilities of common ground, God does not . . . unless and until we discover such ground, the talk about changing the world is likely to be left quite unrelated to political and social actions and programmes and plans. . . ."

What common ground can exist, asked Father Corbishley, S.J., between Catholic and Marxist? And himself replied that the answer is surely "a common concern for human well-being."

Above all the significance of the dialogue will be tested by cooperation in the practical work of solving the urgent problems—peace, disarmament, and the alleviation of world hunger.

RESIGNATION OR RESISTANCE?

The revolt against ideas of "acceptance," "resignation," "passivity" in this world, ideas that in one or another form have so often accompanied the teaching of the established Christian Church, was well expressed by Professor D. M. MacKinnon, an eminent Christian lecturer in the philosophy of religion: "I have heard it sug-

gested by one distinguished contemporary Scottish in-
terpreter of Bultmann's thoughts that it is from Christianity that 'men and women must learn how to suffer
aright.' Not, you will notice, how to eleminate the causes
of human suffering, how in a measure to make ourselves
masters of our destiny, but simply how to accept what
it is subtly suggested it would be almost impious to seek
to change!"

"In 1961," he continues, "in a report on the ethical
problems raised by the development and use of nuclear
weapons, a committee set up by the British Council of
Churches, urged Christians to 'learn to live with the
bomb.' Again, what they counseled was not an effort at
radical understanding, aimed at eliminating the appall-
ing distortion of human achievement, seemingly built
into the fabric of our world, but an acceptance of what
it was alleged could not be changed. Christians often
accuse Marxists of determinism: but when the student
of the history of our age contrasts the attitude of mind
advocated in this deplorable document, with the extraordinary resolution displayed by Lenin in his hour of opportunity in the autumn of 1917, he must surely begin to
wonder whether the boot should not be on the other foot."

In the course of the *Marxism Today* discussion Marxists and Christians seemed agreed that the dialogue could
not be of value unless it led to practical cooperation now
on such immediate issues as struggle against war, against
racism, and against poverty. But, whilst there were
differences on what could be achieved by more theoretical, ideologico-philosophical discussion and on the most
fruitful subjects of such discussion, there was general
agreement that it must be pursued. In the first place,
clarity on each other's long-term aims and deeper
approaches, even when there was no agreement, would
make immediate cooperation easier, not more difficult,

and in the second place it was felt that much common ground could be found at least between Marxists and some Christians on many long-term approaches.

William Barton, who participated in the discussion as a Quaker, and who had traveled considerably in socialist countries, called particularly for joint discussion on ethics: "Christians, following the dialogue, should recall the strong ethical content in Marx's attack on capitalism and his vision of the ideal society." And they should study too, he added, the moral approaches of the existing socialist countries noting their interest in ethics such as exemplified in the emphasis put by the Soviet Union on the "New Man" and the "Moral Code of the Builders of Communism."

Two other points should perhaps be drawn from the *Marxism Today* dialogue. One is the mutual insistence on the need for self-criticism on both sides in the course of discussion. The Reverend Paul Oestreicher not only emphasized this, but proceeded to apply it in his view of the history of Christian approaches: "The institutional Church has for centuries managed to deny the essential humanity of its mission. Where that mission has been effectively lived, then it has generally been done in spite of and not because of established religion. I speak, in this context, unhesitatingly of the apostasy of the Church. . . . It is therefore my contention that the Marxist analysis of religion (mainly Christian) based on observed history, is, broadly speaking, right."

The other, and this was accepted by both Marxists and Christians, was that for the dialogue to succeed and be fruitful there must be the utmost frankness on both sides. It was of the greatest importance *not* to attempt to conceal differences, which would on some issues be profound. What was being sought for was not some impossible "synthesis" of Marxism and religion but the breaking down of hostility between Marxists and Christians, the seeking for common ground and common action.

The *Marxism Today* discussion lasted eighteen months. (The contributions are published in book form.) It made a modest contribution to the development of the dialogue which during that period has widened considerably.

In February 1967 the Marx Memorial Library was filled to the brim with Marxists and Christians for an open discussion on Marxism and Religion introduced by the editor of *Marxism Today*.

The next month a discussion conference on "How to Change the World" was held at Coventry, jointly organized by the Young Communist League and the Christian Group for East-West Contact, and in May a most successful discussion on "Marxism and Christianity" was held in the course of the International Youth Festival organized at Skegness by the Young Communist League.

Early in June, under the joint auspices of *Marxism Today* and a group of Quaker Peace and International Relations Committee, a friendly ten-a-side weekend discussion was held on the subject of "Man, Society and Moral Responsibility." In October a follow-up conference was held on "Problems of Power, Force and Social Change." At both conferences there was extremely interesting discussion on conceptions of revolution and political power.

Locally, in all sorts of forms—lectures, seminars, debates—the dialogue has developed in the most diverse places ranging from theological colleges to Communist

Party branches, from university unions to Methodist organizations, from school sixth forms to Roman Catholic teachers' training colleges. The dialogue is spreading to all sorts of areas of Britain—Birmingham and Coventry, Bristol and Leeds, Plymouth and Edinburgh. In November two Communists were invited to participate along with other speakers of different outlooks in an "Encounter Week" at Manchester University which was concerned with the problem of different beliefs (including, of course, Marxism), the external, internal factors that govern the development of man, the nature of commitment and the future of Britain. And during this week the two Marxist speakers spoke at a dozen or so meetings with well over two thousand attending, and in all the various discussions Christian Marxist dialogue played a central role.

Under the title of "The Sacred and the Secular" the Provost and Chapter of Southwark Cathedral in London are presenting, instead of evening services, a year's program of Sunday evening discussions, which opened last October. It is interesting that the prospectus for these "Sunday Nights in Southwark" opens with these words: "A recent Marxist writer has made this criticism of the churches: 'All over the world the religions are languishing and seem quite incapable of self-renewal. . . . Today, all the churches see as their end their own preservation, in other words, their end is no longer man but themselves.' This criticism has much validity, we should be grateful for it." To try to remedy this, subjects of every sort are being introduced at the evening discussions—from alcoholism to immigration, education to art.

It would, of course, be wrong to exaggerate or to claim that what is taking place is more than a beginning, but the extent of the dialogue and the fact that what is being discussed is Marxism and not some vague "socialism," and that it is taking place between really representative Christians and Marxists, indicates that it is already quantitatively and qualitatively greater than ever experienced before.

MARXISTS AND CATHOLICS

Certainly what is most new is the extent of fraternal discussion now developing between Marxists and Roman Catholics, something that even two or three years ago would have seemed unthinkable. It is not only that the Catholic press was for long a regular center of anti-Communism but in the Trade Union movement for example, various Catholic organizations continuously organized against the left and militant trade unionists and shop stewards, and in particular against Communist trade unionists. Catholics tended to look upon Communists as by definition enemies, and it should be added (though not to the same extent) this was often reciprocated.

One interesting development that has helped to foster the dialogue has been the evolution in the last few years of a left-Catholic group around the journal *Slant*, who draw much of their inspiration from the writings of Marx.

About three or four years ago, a group of Cambridge University Catholic students, with the help of some priests, decided to launch a journal committed to a radical examination of the Roman Catholic Church and its ideas. The group was at first confined to students but later broadened and developed on a national footing. Then the publication of *Slant* was taken over by the well-known Catholic publishing firm of Sheed & Ward. Four years before the emergence of *Slant*, another group of people, mainly professional workers, university teachers and some priests, started an annual conference with similar social aims. Meeting in December they became known as the *December Group*. Now the two groups have merged with a membership that is mainly but not uniquely Roman Catholic and unite around the journal *Slant*, the aims of which (as summed up in January 1966) are that, "roughly speaking, the periodical —and the group which supports it—is engaged in the exploration of the idea that Christian commitment at the moment carries with it an obligation to be Socialist."

In September 1966 the group published "The *Slant* Manifesto: Catholics and the Left" and since that date have published a considerable literature.[1]

They are intensely committed to social change and their inspiration is in general terms Marxist. They have come to the conclusion in the words of two of the founder members of the group writing in the *Slant* Manifesto: "That Christians can never be conservatives, or liberals or even right-wing socialists; they must fight capitalism as evil; they must align themselves perhaps with all those traditional enemies of the Church, left-wing socialists and atheistic Marxists."

There have been several informal and friendly discussions between *Marxism Today* and members of the *Slant* group.

But discussions between Marxists and Catholics have not been restricted to the Catholic left or to Catholic intellectual circles.

There is the beginning of a discussion on a far wider basis, and, what is of special interest, the discussion has

[1] See Terence Eagleton, *The New Left Church*, Sheed & Ward; L. Bright, O.P. (editor), *Christians and World Freedom*, Sheed & Ward; L. Bright and Simon Clements (editors), *The Committed Church*, Darton, Longman & Todd.

begun to develop in working-class areas, including areas where there has been in the past a deep Catholic opposition to Marxism and militant trade unionism.

THE MEETING AT LIVERPOOL

Perhaps the most interesting event in the recent Communist-Catholic discussion was the public meeting held in the Liverpool University chaplaincy in June 1967. The discussion was jointly organized by Communists and Catholics in the Liverpool area. Speakers from the Catholic side included Frank Hendry, a teacher and journalist, John Jenning, director of the Simon Community (a voluntary organization concerned particularly with problems of the homeless) and Dr. Markus, a lecturer in Medieval History at Liverpool University, and from the Communist side Roger O'Hara, an engineering worker and Communist municipal candidate, Sheila Kay, a lecturer in Sociology at Liverpool University, and Gerry Cohen, Secretary of the Mersey Area of the Communist Party.

The audience of over three hundred was probably equally divided between Catholics and Communists. It included priests, nuns, trade union officials, shop stewards from factories and building sites, workers straight from the job, housewives and students. The atmosphere was, in the words of the Communist area organizer, "really electric and very enthusiastic; what emerged above all was the tremendous desire all round to seek common ground." This is all the more significant in that in Liverpool, not so long ago, Communists were received by Catholics at best with considerable hostility and sometimes even with violence.

BRITISH COUNCIL OF CHURCHES

Naturally in Britain, where Roman Catholics form a relatively small minority of religious people, the main dialogue has developed with various Protestant denominations.

An important step in the dialogue was the holding in October 1967 of a fifteen-a-side discussion conference on "What Sort of Revolution?" jointly organized by *Marxism Today* and a Committee of the International Department of the British Council of Churches.

The discussion was held in the apt setting of the Royal Foundation of St. Katherine in the dock area of East London. The Christian delegation, which actually exceeded fifteen, contained Protestants and Roman Catholics. Three sessions discussed "Man and His Place in Society," followed by a series of practical discussions on "Change in British Society," "Peace," "Poverty and Justice" and "The Future of the Dialogue." Discussion was intense, polemical, friendly and constructive, ranging over many problems of philosophy, theology, politics and practice. It was agreed that a continuation committee should be formed to carry the dialogue further. The meeting was widely reported in the press and gave rise to a considerable extension of the dialogue including a series of late night television discussions between the organizers of the meeting, the Reverend Paul Oestreicher of the British Council of Churches and James Klugmann, editor of *Marxism Today*, which were held on five consecutive nights under the title of "Communist and Christianity" and treated such subjects as the nature of religion, human nature, revolution, man and society and "Kingdom Come" or the future of society.

THE ILFORD MEETING

One of the dangers of such dialogue is that it should be formal, with both sides making as it were prepared parallel speeches but hardly listening or replying to each other, that it should be confined to "specialists" who almost know their speeches by heart (and those of their opposite numbers) and that there should arise a new ritual of professional "dialoguers" in meeting.

And one of the most important perspectives if the dialogue is to be significant is that it should become more and more informal, popular and mass.

Perhaps the most important, and certainly the most moving, event in the dialogue to date was the public Christian Marxist dialogue held in the Ilford area of Essex (a county in southeast England) at the end of May 1967.

The meeting was jointly organized by the South-Essex Communists and local Church of England and Catholic priests following a number of informal encounters in the area. In the Chair was the (Anglican) bishop of Barking, Dr. William Chadwick. On the platform two Marxists (the South Essex District Secretary of the Communist Party and the editor of *Marxism Today*), the Reverend Paul Oestreicher of the British Council of Churches and Father Lowe, a Roman Catholic parish priest from East London.

The audience of about two hundred included about eighty Marxists and one hundred and twenty Protestants and Catholics, many from Fords and other local engineering works. The atmosphere was excited, expectant, almost intense, many of the audience finding themselves in the *same* meeting in a friendly capacity for the first time in their lives. More important than the speeches from the platform (and I think all the platform would agree on this) was the prolonged discussion from the floor. This was critical; many hard questions were asked on both sides; but throughout it all, throughout all questions and criticisms, there was an overwhelming feeling for the need and possibility of common action against war, against poverty, against racialism. The meeting ended with a considerable collection, not only to cover expenses but for medical aid in Vietnam.

DOUBTS AND PROBLEMS

The great interest aroused in these early stages of the dialogue must not lead us to exaggerate the achievements to date nor to cover up problems and difficulties, and, on both sides, doubts.

It is clear that only a beginning has been made, that those who know of and have participated in the dialogue are a small minority. What has happened is, or at least could be, the prelude to a much wider and popular dialogue.

Moreover, there is a certain resistance to the dialogue —I would say both amongst some Marxists and some Christians. In a discussion on the dialogue that continued over many weeks in the *Morning Star*, the daily paper of the Communist Party, the Reverend Charles observed that on the Christian side "Fundamentalist objections to dialogue recur in the modern Church." It is said "Communists intend to destroy religion and we should oppose them in every way. If we sit down and talk with them, they will use us for their own wicked purposes."

Similar objections were made in the *Morning Star* by

some who consider that for real revolutionaries, no dialogue with Christians is under any circumstances permissible. A correspondent, for instance, wrote: "It is absolute hypocrisy to attempt any dialogue whatsoever . . . the real aims of Communists are known, so also are the real aims of Christians. The one is the pillar and bulwark of the proletarian masses, and the other upholds the absolute rights of the hierarchy and privileged classes of bourgeois society."

DOUBTS ANSWERED

It would seem to me that an important aspect of the dialogue is that these genuine doubts in its possibility or justifiability be answered.

In the first place it is essential that the dialogue be throughout sincere and open with no differences, however profound, concealed. If differences are hidden, dialogue becomes something of a trick, or expedient, subject to abuse. Marxists should at no stage conceal in any way their materialist approaches in philosophy nor their conception of revolutionary change in society and the need for socialist revolution. This is, I am convinced, not only what Marxists want, but what Christians who join in the dialogue want also. There is no contradiction at all between explaining differences and, at the same time, seeking for common ground.

Those who are Marxists, and I would hope Christians also, need to study what Marx and Engels wrote on religion—all of it.

There are some four hundred pages in the English edition of *Marx and Engels on Religion,* not just one short phrase—"The opium of the people."

Conversely, Marxists, insofar as Christians put their

faith in forces outside man, in supernatural forces, consider that this "impoverishes them," limits to an extent their capacity as human beings to appreciate and exercise their own capacities to change the world and themselves.

But this does not mean that the whole phenomenon of religion can be reduced to opium nor that the task of the revolutionary who has a materialist approach to religion is one of simple "militant atheist" propaganda. "Religious distress," writes Marx, "is at the same time the *expression* of real distress and the *protest* against real distress. Religion is the sigh of the oppressed creature, the heart of a heartless world . . . it is the *opium* of the people," and he continues: "The abolition of religion as the *illusory* happiness of the people is required for their *real* happiness. The demand to give up the illusions about its conditions *is the demand to give up a condition which needs illusions.*"

In other words, when man is oppressed, exploited, deprived, and feels powerless to control his environment and society, he projects his lost humanity into a world beyond, into a God or gods, into religion. And for Marxists, the essential way of combating religion is helping man by science to understand nature and to master it, and by knowledge of society and social struggle so to change society that there is no need for him to escape from it.

Marx and Engels, who well understood how often established religion had preached acceptance and resignation and had indeed become an integral part of cruel and exploiting ruling classes, equally understood how often men and women expressed their progressive and even revolutionary aims in religious terms, how peasants in the peasant wars, revolutionaries in the English Revolution in the 1640's, fought out the class war in religious terms. Nothing could make this more dramatically clear than Engel's essay "On the History of Early Christianity."

It would be foolhardy not to understand today how thousands and thousands of sincere Christians in their desire to return to what they see as the human essence of early Christianity are reflecting a genuine desire to improve conditions and often, indeed, radically to change society.

Marxists should not for a moment give up their materialist outlook including their materialist understanding of the origin and nature of religion, but they do need to get rid of a narrow and non-Marxist dogmatic view of religion which is very far from what Marx taught.

Nor does the dialogue with Christians involve in any way the renunciation of *revolutionary* aims, nor the openly expressed determination to struggle in whatever way the situation demands in a particular country for a revolutionary change in the social order.

Indeed it is the Marxist understanding of the outdating of capitalism, of its spiritual as well as economic crisis, of its, if you like, inbuilt immorality, which might frighten off a few Christians and Christian organizations who have embedded themselves in the Establishment, but which for so many Christians constitutes a challenge and a deep force of attraction. In the course of the dialogue there will be much discussion on the nature of revolution, the forms that it must take, questions of violence, its necessity and its abuse, and this will help, not hinder, mutual understanding. It was precisely this for example that underlay many of the discussions that took place between Marxists and Quakers last June and which will will be continued more in detail at our next meeting. It is significant that it was a *Quaker* proposal that further discussion should be held on "Power, Force and Change," and that by mutual agreement the nature and need of revolutionary change will be considered at the coming dialogue with the British Council of Churches.

The argument that the dialogue is a great Jesuit trick is no more worthy than the contention that it is a crafty Communist plot. Marxists are not magicians and should not attempt to be so. They do not believe in instantaneous conversion. They know that people in struggle and through experience as well as through education and debate come to change their outlook and change themselves.

Therefore, when people begin to change we should welcome it not fear it. When people are ready to work with us for causes we believe progressive we should welcome it not fear it. When people are ready sincerely to discuss with us our views and their views and to look for common ground, we should welcome it and not fear it. There are many deep reasons for the great crisis of faith and outlook within Christianity today. One is the growth and spread of science and technique. Another is the fear that this same technique and science can be used in the total destruction of society. Another is the growth and achievement of the socialist sector of the world. Another is the examples that Communists have given of courage and sacrifice in struggle against imperialism, oppression and war, which has made many Christians ask what is the force that thus impels them, motivates them, moves them. Yet another is the achievements of the colonial peoples in their struggle for liberation. And another is the challenge, despite many mistakes and setbacks, of the socialist way of life to the capitalist way of life, of the socialist to the capitalist morality.

Why should we be sad when people find themselves

nearer to us and ready to cooperate with us? Should we not rather, paraphrasing Togliatti's words, welcome, understand and assist it?

It is true that there will always be some who endeavor to stem progressive development by "going along with it," in order to stop it or to divert it, but the fact that they are forced to do so is in itself evidence of advance.

Above all, the conditions in the world virtually shout aloud for the closest and most active cooperation of people of every outlook, religious and non-religious, Marxists and Christians, to fight now to combat war, colonialism, militarism, racialism, poverty and hunger.

X

Christianity and Social Action— Three Hypotheses for Discussion

JOHANNES B. METZ

FIRST HYPOTHESIS

THERE IS HARDLY anything at the present time which is so unclear and yet so surcharged with feeling as the relationship between religion and society, between the Church and the world at large, between the Christian belief in promise and social practice. The historical roots of this situation are to be found in the Enlightenment, and its theological roots in an extremely individualistic tendency within modern theology.

Explanatory Note:

1. In the thinking of the Enlightenment (in France) the automatic unity of and mutual relationship between religion and society, religious and social life, was already broken. In its relationship with the surrounding society the Christian religion came to appear as separate; this meant that its claim to universality was historically conditioned. (This is also, by the way, the root of the question of the so-called "historicity" of Christianity;

JOHANNES METZ is one of the younger generation of radical academic German theologians in the Roman Catholic Church. He teaches theology at the University of Münster. This paper was first read at the 1967 Conference of the Paulusgesellschaft at Marienbad, Czechoslovakia.

without a socio-political dimension this problem cannot arise and remains in essence artificial!)

This problematic situation served as the starting point for the Enlightenment's criticism of religion and later for that of Marxism. The criticism assumed the form in which it still appears today (and to which theology's scheme of apologetics generally does not do justice). This criticism of religion is in fact a criticism of ideology; that is, it tries to unmask religion as a function, as the "ideological superstructure" of certain social relationships and practices; it tries, by means of the slogan "false awareness," to reveal that religion is practiced by a society which is not yet aware of itself. A theology which is trying to counter this criticism must of necessity also work out the socio-political implications of its own concepts and terms. But this "political" form of religious responsibility is the undoing, to state this in a very short-hand form, of classical metaphysical theology, whose concepts and categories are in fact based on a complete harmony in the relationship between religion and society, between theory and practice. As long as this presupposition is justified, a metaphysical interpretation of religion can be very relevant to society—as it was, for example, in the leading figures of medieval theology. But when this unity is destroyed, its position as the theoretical defendant in the on-going case of the Christian message of salvation verus the socio-political reality is threatened by radical crisis. It then appears—to use Kleist's illustration—as the form of religious reason which has not eaten a second time of the tree of knowledge.

2. Modern theology, with its transcendental, existential and personal emphases, has recognized the problematic situation created by the Enlightenment. In a certain sense it has developed as a reaction to this situation. But in general this reaction has been mainly

a matter of treating the social dimension of the Christian conception of salvation, either covertly or openly, as "inessential" or "secondary"; in effect it has individualized the core of the message of salvation and limited the effects of salvation to the unworldly decisions of the individual. In this way it attempted to solve the problem which the Enlightenment had raised by eliminating it; it attempted to be master of the Enlightenment without having really passed through it and its problems.

A religious view influenced by this sort of theology sees the socio-political reality as of passing duration. The predominant anthropological categories in this theology, when interpreting the message of salvation, are those of the personal, the private and the apolitical. Love, like all the phenomena of interpersonal life, is much emphasized but only really finds expression, as is natural, in its personal and, in some sense, non-political forms: as the I-Thou relationship, as the relationship in the meeting of individuals, perhaps as a "neighborhood relationship." The predominant category is that of encounter. And the "essential" form of religious expression is considered to be the personal form of address; the "essential" dimension of religious experience is the climax of the individual's free subjectivity or the intangible, ineffable center of the I-Thou relationship.

3. Such an individualistic tendency in its own theology now, however, exposes the Christian religion to the danger of being claimed and appropriated by modern socio-political ideologies in an uncritical, uncontrolled way. It is also exposed to the danger of missing the very individual to whose life it appeals, because an individual's existence today is bound up with forms of social mobility to a very high degree, and therefore any existential and personal theology which does not see existence as a political problem (in the widest sense)

remains an abstraction from the existential situation of the individual. And finally a religion which is seen and interpreted in this way takes on more and more the characteristics of a non-binding directive which "is binding insofar as no one may touch it and many are impressed by it, but which exists without consequences because it evokes no reactions other than such as are necessary for its own survival."[1]

SECOND HYPOTHESIS

An understanding of historical development and the biblical tradition demand not the re-establishment but rather the re-definition of the relationship between the Christian religion and social practice.

Explanatory Note:

1. The *understanding of history* can also be illustrated by a problem which was expressed by the Enlightenment and has become unavoidable since Marx. According to Kant, the enlightened man is one who has the freedom to openly exercise his reason in all respects. The exercise of this "enlightenment" is therefore never merely an individual or purely theoretical problem; it is in essence a political problem, a problem of practice, that is, it is linked with socio-political conditions without which it cannot be enlightened critical reason. And therefore only those are enlightened who at the same time fight for the establishment of the socio-political conditions on which the possibility of a public exercise of reason depends.

But where reason appears to be dependent on political freedom, where therefore theoretical, transcendental

---

[1] A. Gehlen, citing H. Schelsky, *Auf der Suche nach Wirklichkeit* (Dusseldorf, 1965), p. 271.

reason appears as an aspect of the practical (and not the contrary), a de-individualization of this reason becomes unavoidable and any "pure theory," however dialectically and carefully it may be contrived, represents a reversion to a pre-critical awareness.[2]

The individual's claim to criticism can then be not merely theoretical or a matter of private contemplation. "The conception of the rule of pure reason as something which exists as such, independent of practice, removes the subject's freedom, turns it into an instrument to achieve particular aims. Reason's help in self-reflection would here be the transition to practice: it would see itself as one aspect of it; it would know that, rather than thinking reason itself to be absolute, it is the absolute's way of acting."[3]

This suggests a new relationship between theory and practice, between knowledge and morality, between reflection and revolution, which also must influence theological awareness if it does not want to revert to an earlier, pre-critical stage of awareness. Practical, political reason—in the broadest sense—must henceforth share in all critical theological reflection; it is, increasingly, becoming the focal point of the classical problem of the relationship between *fides* and *ratio,* and it has made the problem of the responsibility of faith much more acute. All of this has nothing to do with a dangerous, power-political involvement of faith, or with some kind of reactionary neo-politics for religion. Quite the contrary. It is only by recognizing its public, critical responsibility that it can become not merely the ideological super-structure above the particular social order

[2] Cf. G. Picht, "Aufkärung und Offenbarung," in *Glauben-Wissen-Bildung* (Freiburg, 1966).

[3] Cf. T. W. Adorno, "Fortschritt," in *Argumentationen* (Festschrift for Josef König) (Göttingen), pp. 1–19.

of the time, nor the function of a particular social status quo, nor merely the Grail guardian of a "false awareness."

2. The *biblical tradition* itself compels a critical re-examination of the relationship between the Christian religion and social practice.

a) The salvation on which the Christian faith is based in hope is, namely, not a private salvation. The preaching of this salvation led Jesus into a fatal battle with the public authorities of his time. His cross is not erected in the most intimate sphere of the individual's personal life, nor in the Holy of Holies of a religious realm; it stands on the other side of the threshold of the carefully guarded private or of the fenced-in "purely religious": it stands "outside," as the theology of the letter to the Hebrews says. The veil of the Temple is rent for good. The scandal and the promise of Christian salvation are public. This publicity cannot be withdrawn, abolished or hushed up. It goes hand in hand with the Christian message of salvation throughout history. In the service of this message the Christian religion is called upon to exercise public responsibility in a critical and liberating way. "All of the New Testament writers were convinced that Christ is not a private individual and the Church is not a club. Therefore, each in his own way, within his own context, related how Jesus Christ and his disciples encountered the political and national world and its authorities. No one so thoroughly understood this encounter as St. John the Evangelist. He already recognized that the story of Jesus in general is a lawsuit which the world, represented by the Jews, is conducting against Jesus—or thinks it is. This lawsuit is brought up for public, legal verdict before Pontius Pilate, the representative of the Roman state who wields political power. . . . So it was necessary then, as it is now, to learn from John the apostle that the case which the world brings against the truth, which Jesus is, in a certain sense, still goes on and that that scene in which Jesus stands before Pilate . . . has typical features."[4] The salvation which Jesus preached may not be cosmologically related to the world, but it is certainly worldly and world-related in a permanent public, social and, in a sense, political way.

b) The promise of peace and justice based on him is not a private promise to the individual, not a partial promise nor an exceptional promise; it is a promise for *all*, a promise which is open to all, especially to the poorest, least important and most distant. If it is not open to all, then no one can claim it for himself. Because of this promise of peace and justice one can no longer speak of "Gentile or Jew, circumcised or uncircumcised, barbarian or Scythian, slave or free man" (Col. 3:11). This promise, based on the cross of Jesus, is not the privileged possession of a group, nor of a religion, nor even of the Church. The Church exists because of the promise and not vice versa; it is there in order to infect all with the hope of universal peace and justice and to combat passionately any form of contempt.

c) The contents of this eschatological promise—freedom, peace, justice, reconciliation—cannot be restricted to the individual; time and again they act as goads to social responsibility. Of course this promise cannot be identified with particular historical social conditions —however, we, for our part, may define them. The history of Christendom shows more than enough such direct identifications and political entanglements of the Christian hope. But in them the "eschatological aspect,"

[4] H. Schlier, *Besinnung auf das Deue Testament* (Freiburg, 1964), p. 193; cf. also H. Schlier, *Die Zeit der Kirche* (Freiburg, 1956), p. 310.

which serves to show that every stage which society may reach in history is provisional, is sacrificed. But I say provisional and not haphazard! Because this "eschatalogical aspect" does not imply a rejection of but a dialectical relationship to the society of the present. The promise of salvation, to which it refers, is not in fact an empty horizon of religious expectation or merely a guideline for one's thinking; it is always also a critical, liberating imperative for the particular present, an encouragement and a challenge to make these promises effective in the historical circumstances of the present, to make them "come true" in this way, because their "truth" has to be "done" (John 3:21). In the Christians' eschatological hope the distinctions between merely examining the world and critically overcoming it, between promise and demand, between expectation and struggle, have already been superseded. (Yes, precisely because our human quest is guided by such a promise it does not stop at examining the world but goes on to make historical demands, and historical disappointment does not condemn it to theoretical scepticism and resignation but spurs it on to new initiatives within history.) Taking the divine promises of peace and justice seriously "estranges" our contemporary historical existence; it continually brings and forces us to look critically at the present conditions of the society around us.

THIRD HYPOTHESIS

In relation to social practice the Christian religion can be defined as an institution of creative social criticism.

Explanatory Note:

1. We start by assuming that there is no longer, and

can and should no longer be, a direct, immediate, in a sense pre-critical, unity of religion and society understood as the theo-political unity of the two. On the basis of this assumption we must ask what is the possible point of contact between religion and social processes and practice.

2. It is clear that social practice can only serve in the development of a free humanity and not its destruction, if it is critical. It is also clear that it is possible to so idolize an abstract conception of progress which results in downright inhumanity that true progress would be found in critical, liberating opposition and not in an uncritical submission because of a belief that this will not be permanent.[5] But where is the source of creative opposition?

3. Let us first look briefly at science and philosophy as instruments for the criticism of society. If a social practice or political decision is simply determined and enforced without there first being a critical examination of the preliminary decisions which it demands, one can call this an irrational or even a purely ideological practice. But this form of irrationalism and of ideology of the "first order," as it were, is not the problem in contemporary criticism of society. Nowadays social practices and political decisions, as well as the institutions related to them, are critically thought out, scientifically informed and technologically rationalized. But although modern decision-making theories, working with mathematical, cybernetic, sociological, economic, etc., models, can rationalize socio-political practice within a certain means-aim relationship, nevertheless their methods cannot determine the so-called preferences among the different aims to be achieved.

[5] T. W. Adorno, *op. cit.*, p. 19.

Here decision faces a new irrationalism beyond its scientific rationalization.

The introduction of scientific method in social practice brings about an "irrationalism of the second order," quite irrespective of the fact that modern science—"project science," big science—can no longer adequately be divided into science and apparatus, theory and instrumental technique; it develops a tendency to domination within itself which cannot even be controlled scientifically. Even the philosophical criticism of social practice, to which one would like to appeal in such situations, is subject to the threat of a similar "irrationalism of the second order": an irrationalism which is not the result of a lack of reflection, but produced by that which the individual philosopher has reflected on and critically worked out, vanishing again in randomness and a lack of general validity. The continual critical reflection, which philosophy is forced into today because it has nothing more immediate than its obvious starting point and content, results time and again in subjectivity and not in something rational and binding. This is probably why there are also modern movements which, tired of this situation, are aiming at the "silencing of critical subjectivity"; I think for example of Heidegger, of Karl Löwith with his flight into archaic naturalism, but also of the view of Levi-Strauss and the French structuralists. Others have tried to preserve the effect of their philosophy on the criticism of society and to combat the random nature of philosophical subjectivity by institutionalizing their own views: they speak a language which "exists" up to a point independently of the individual critical thoughts, which can always be recognized—like a trade mark—and provides some consistency beyond subjective reflection.

This institutionalization of a stunted philosophy

seems to me symptomatic of the fact that we have reached a new phase of history in which institutions are acquiring a quite new significance: they do not appear only and primarily as the objects but as the bearers of critical, responsible social action. The criticism of society initiated by the Enlightenment and provoked by Marx into revolution, which was criticism of the existing institutions and of the distribution of power among them, is today being transformed into a criticism of society which is itself in need of institutions and cannot simply act according to the principles of liberalism of whatever kind.

These institutions are, in a sense, "institutions of the second order," whose purpose is not established before critical reflection on social practice but only becomes clear in the midst of this reflection; they are institutions which are not made superfluous by critical social action: it is this which makes them possible at all, because they save this action from purposelessness. Perhaps, by way of experiment, we should even talk of "ideologies of the second order," of enlightened ideologies which are not immediately obvious to a critical social understanding but which are an essential part of the desire for effective criticism of social practice and of the search for binding social action.

3. These institutions and ideologies of the second order must themselves, as is obvious from what I have already said, be safeguards of or means to freedom; they cannot be opposed to enlightenment or reflection; public life itself must be able to exercise a critical function within them. For a discussion of the religious institution as an institution of freedom I refer you to the lectures of Professor Fries and Professor Moltmann.

4. *This* is where I see the place and task of the Christian religion as an institution for the creative criticism

of society. It takes its directives for this task of social
criticism from its eschatological vision, which is also
a vision of universal brotherhood. (*Cf.* second hypothesis, 2c.) This view may not make possible nor impose
one clear positive social order, but it does supply individual elements of social criticsm. I shall mention
two by way of example.

a) By measuring every conception of progress and
humanism against the "eschatological hope" it protects
the individual man at a particular time from being
seen only as the material and means for the construction of a future conceived exclusively according to
technological reason. It criticizes the attempt to see
individuality merely as a function of the social process
which is governed only by technology. Admittedly,
even utopian conceptions of future society may have
a positive view of the individual. But even in these
is not the individual important only as the first in the
opening up of new possibilities for society, insofar
as he anticipates within himself the revolution in the
social process? Is it not a matter of: "insofar as individuality can be justified in any direction it must be
nothing more than the first, a forerunner in any organic
development of the human as a whole, but which
is open to all men following the natural train of
potential development!" Is it not that "to be the 'only
one' is worthless, a wretched trick of fate for an individual. To be the 'first' is everything! . . . Such a one
knows that the whole of mankind is following him! . . .
True individuality consists of already being what all
must later become!"[6] But then what about the "poor
and oppressed" who are "poor" precisely because they
are not able to be the "first" in this way? At this point

[6] P. Altenberg in T. W. Adorno, *op. cit.*

the "eschatological view" of religion has to protect an individuality which cannot be defined by the value of its contribution to the progress of mankind.

b) Even the central Christian concept of love contains an element of potential social criticism. This love cannot be restricted to the limited personal realm of the I-Thou; it must also not only be seen as charitable "neighborliness"; its social dimension has to be interpreted and made effective: love means an unconditional demand for justice, freedom, peace *for others*.

But the means that love can exercise two types of social criticism: on the one hand it demands clear criticism of sheer force. The credibility and effectiveness of this criticism will depend, not only in the last resort, on the fact that this religion, which claims to be a religion of love, does not give the impression of being a religion of power. It can and may not try to use power in order to prevail. Basically it is not serving its own ends but the goal of salvation in history—for all men. The hope which it proclaims is not the hope of the Church's religion but of the Kingdom of God as the future of the world. And so—rightly understood— it also lives from the proclamation of its own transitoriness. It has no power over and above the power of its promise: that is, the power of peace, of freedom and of justice. But that itself is a sentence which is profoundly critical of society! It compels religion time and again to examine sheer force and it is an indictment if—as has often been the case in the past—it speaks its critical word to the powers that be too softly or too late, or intervenes too hesitantly for all who are threatened "without respect of persons."

On the other hand it is true that, when Christian love becomes active in society as an unconditional desire for justice and freedom for others, circumstances can arise in which this love needs to use revolutionary means. Where the social status quo contains as much injustice as may arise by overthrowing it by revolution, then a revolution—for justice and freedom for "the least of the brethren"—may not be prohibited even in the name of Christian love. This makes Merleau-Ponty's accusation all the more pointed, that one has never seen a church support a revolution simply because it was a just one. Once again it becomes clear that the impetus in Christian love which inspires social criticism always entails an impetus for examining religion. We Christians will only be able to develop the power for social criticism which love contains if—because of our own history—it forces us to undertake a critical self-examination.

5. In what sense and in what way—to ask the last question in this connection—can a form of social criticism based on religious tenets find possibilities for cooperation with social criticism on other bases? Is not social criticism, inspired by a religious institution, condemned to inevitable isolation and hence to being a matter of opinion? The basis for joint social criticism by Christians and non-Christians, by men and groups with a wide variety of ideological views, is not primarily a positive evaluation of the social process, a particular concept of the content of the free future society of mankind. There will always be different views and pluralism in this sort of positivism. Pluralism in positive plans for society cannot be abolished in our historical situation unless complete ideological manipulation takes the place of freedom.

Therefore I see the basis for this joint social criticism primarily in a negative experience: the experience of the threat to humanity, the experience of the threat to freedom, justice and peace. We must not underestimate this negative experience. The "negative mediation" of the peace, freedom and justice which we seek is the only form of a generally binding access to what is positively human. It is this negative experience which creates solidarity. Even though we may not be able to agree directly and straightforwardly on what freedom, peace and justice are positively, we nevertheless have had long and painful experience of what the lack of freedom, peace and justice are. This negative experience offers a possibility for unity—less in a positive plan for freedom and justice than in resistance to the horror and terror of the lack of freedom and justice.

The solidarity which this experience offers, the possibility of a common front for protest, has to be recognized and mobilized. The danger of another threat to peace is still too close. The irrationalism within our own socio-political practices is too clear. The possibility of "collective darkness" has not yet been banished. The danger of a lack of peace, of freedom and of justice is too great for indifference not to constitute a crime.

XI
Dogmatism and Integrity

YLENA MARCULESCU

THE AGONIZING CONTRAST between the relativity of
values at an intellectual and cultural level, and the
need to pinpoint truth at the more practical levels of
life and of social action are probably among the
basic realities of our time. For the ideologies involved
both in the process of creating new values within and
of transforming the world in practical ways, this tension can become almost unbearable. It can lead to
confusion in fundamentals. It makes living with a
paradox a necessity.

Thinkers like Kierkegaard, considered utterly reactionary on political and social grounds by orthodox Marxists,
expressed this tension in the form of an inescapable
alternative: either to submit to ethical norms or to
reject them. It is not a choice between good or evil,
but between ethical and non-ethical criteria. In passing

YLENA MARCULESCU is a young philosopher who teaches
in the Philosophical Institute of the University of Bucharest
and who, almost alone in Rumania, took an early interest
in studying the relevance of Christianity to philosophy.
She first became known to a wider public at the Conferences of the West German Paulusgesellschaft, the most
significant of which was held in Marienbad, Czechoslovakia, in 1967. This paper was read in French at the World
Council of Churches Consultation on Christianity and Marxism, Geneva, April 1968.

from an ethical to a religious stage, a choice appears to exist between martyrdom and something less than martyrdom. Kierkegaard thought in his time that being a mere witness to truth was not enough. Truth called for a total commitment, for nothing less than martyrdom. This alternative, considered by Kierkegaard to present an irreconcilable contradiction, is enormously relevant both for Christians and for Marxists in the present situation. We are faced with the problem of the relativity of knowledge and of science and at the same time with a necessity for immediate action at a political level. The superstructures and ideologies of revolution as hitherto elaborated are completely incapable of preventing the alienation inherent in contemporary power structures and technology, either in their crude or in their more subtle forms.

Unnecessary violence and the misuse of techniques which increase man's capacity for domination, are among the most striking forms of alienation, apart from war and open oppression. Apocalyptic ideologies such as Schwengler's or Berman's have been outlived. There are still ideologies, however, which are concerned with the historical process and with the conscious role of the individual in society. In this category I would put both Marxism and Christianity and perhaps even existentialism in its relation to them both.

In the context of our dialogue, these ideologies are becoming increasingly aware of their respective limitations and of the possibility both of areas of confrontation and of mutual enrichment. Ten years ago even non-dogmatic Marxists were judging other ideologies in terms of their compatibility or incompatibility with a rigid nucleus of laws and principles. The Marxist catechism was still in full force. We have now come to understand better the relative truths of our ideological adversaries who sometimes express our own insights better than we can.

This situation is not without ambiguity. One might well ask whether in the course of ideological discussion and political collaboration in more or less revolutionary situations, our opinions have evolved to the point of congruence, or whether we are taking part in a process of opportunistic synthesis, forgetting our respective norms and ideals. This question has to be faced because it is fundamental to our processes of thought. This is a philosophic problem, but it is bound up with our essential and constant commitment to social change.

The revision of Marxism is surely a proper process since Marxism itself must be seen as a paradigm for scientific knowledge and never as an end in itself. No scientific theory can remain creative without a questioning of its foundations, sometimes with intent to strengthen it, sometimes with intent to produce from it a deeper understanding of truth. The question then becomes, what is left after all the revisions? This is a very important question because our concept of intellectual integrity will depend on the answer we give. There are a few irreversible Marxist tenets. In my opinion they are the materialistic explanation of society and history and the concept of dialectics. These are, however, not fixed points in the sense that they constitute a matrix of explanation, a structure which in itself is neither true nor false, but which serves as an instrument for the analysis of reality. It is up to the thinker to use them creatively and to infuse them with useful scientific contents. It is an ideological problem whether one should preserve one, two or a whole set of principles and this is really an intangible problem for Marxism. There was a time when I thought

that nothing remained but the good intention of transforming the world, an intention expressed in Marx's
eleventh thesis on Feuerbach.

Many Eastern Marxists, disappointed at the inability
of their own ideology to offer satisfactory explanations,
are perhaps willing to accept an almost total revision
of Marxist philosophy, economic theory and of the
whole idea of scientific socialism. The dogmatization of
Marxism and its vain pretension to put itself in the
place of the living natural and social sciences, has led
to a profound distrust in its heuristic power, utterly
oversimplified in the form of Stalinism. Such Marxism
was only able to hinder the progress of thought, never
to accelerate it. For a time both the hermeneutical and
the heuristic functions of Marxist philosophy were lost.

The de-Stalinization of Marxism which necessitated
a return to Lenin produced little in the way of scientific dynamism either. It is perhaps a truism to say
that the revision of Marx began with Lenin but the
rigidity of Lenin's materialism and his own theoretical
confusion in evaluating objective truths (and then the
catechization of every word of his *Filosofikie Tetradi*)
gave rise to a further, much more profound revision
of Marxist-Leninism related both to the understanding
of science and to the newer forms of social life, to the
requirements of the new society. Less so in Russia
and much more profoundly in the Eastern democracies
the discovery of events which were unexpected from
an orthodox Marxist point of view threw up an intellectual challenge.

To the leadership, revisionism became the *bête-noire*.
To contest Lenin's formula of objective truth or to
adopt the principles of non-determination in physics
remained equally capital sins. In 1956–58 a revisionist
elite was formed to discuss freely, honestly and factu-

ally—in a spirit of vindicating socialism—every hitherto uncontested thesis of Marxist orthodoxy. If there were no such people in Russia where even the most non-conformist philosophers had to use compromise formulas in order to be published, and where the boldest of them never were published, there were Kolakowsky and Schaff in Poland and a number of philosophers and economists in Czechoslovakia and Rumania. Yugoslav philosophers and economists were in any case thought to be utterly revisionist.

Scientists were deeply involved in this process. Although a clear directive was given in 1957 by the Communist Party in my country calling for the renunciation of "mitchourinist" and other Soviet agro-biological practices based on so-called dialectical materialism, the inert forces within the scientific establishment maintained the false positions vigorously until 1963. There are still scientists who maintain this position because it is easier not to study either genetics or physiology but simply to apply a strict ideological pattern in discussing natural phenomena. In some scientific circles not directly involved in technological processes dialectics are still illustrated and explained in a most mechanistic way.

As the development of philosophy was almost totally halted some people were tempted to abandon Marxist categories altogether. Allergic reactions to Marxist phraseology have become prevalent, especially among the young who are ready to reject any ideology that cannot express itself in normal human un-stereotyped language. This profound linguistic alienation is an expression of a deep intellectual alienation which goes to the root of the human personality. The reaction is violent and produces a general refusal to take Marxist ideology seriously at all. Problems are de-valued along with the language which is used to express them. This is only one source of the profound scepticism toward ideology and of the tendency toward wholesale revisionism.

A monopoly of power leads to a monopoly of truth. As with the economic and political leadership, the monopoly of scientific research in philosophy is maintained by a small group which is not only believed to represent national philosophic thought abroad, but which leads to the actual physical limitation of liberty at home. Under conditions such as these, no one dares display any worthwhile work that gives evidence of constructive and original thought.

The situation is far from being as simple as it at first appears. Obviously this sort of monopoly needs to be opposed and the right to think freely proclaimed. But having said that, it must be remembered that it must be done within the context of Marxist ideology which we intend to uphold. Why? Why not get rid of the restrictive cadres caught up in apparently fossilized thought pattern? Why not declare Marxism dead? I feel that in many respects it is a dead doctrine but its heart has, for a century, been the lively inspiration not only of a great restructuring of society, but also of the human mind. The heuristic power of Marxism has not, in my opinion, been entirely lost. I can think of no other theory which gives equal scope to both the material and the spiritual in man. Anti-Marxists have often declared a profound incompatibility between materialism and dialectics. They have declared this to be a false and indeed an absurd combination.

It is on account of the rigidity of dogmatism that this truly unexpected synthesis could appear to be sheer eclecticism. Dialectics are in reality a difficult tool to use. They make possible an unlimited capacity for the integration of new findings and theories. But that is not to say that anything can be done with dialectics in any way. There is a principle of inner consequence and coherence within Marxism which must be respected if one is to construct one's philosophy on a Marxist base.

It seems to me that the Marxist ideology, possibly like others, has a chance of survival in history only if it can from now on develop scientifically. The empirical foundation of both historical and dialectical materialism must not be sacrificed to a "theological, transcendental" anthropology.

But to be scientific does not mean merely to resort to physicism. Philosophy is a science in its own right. Like all *Geisteswissenschaften* it has a subjective-objective subject matter. The basic principle in Marxist philosophy should no longer be viewed as materialistic but as objective. This does not mean that we are trying to turn man into an object. To objectify is not to reduce everything to things. But the outstanding trend in psychology, psychoanalysis, the psychology of art and even in morals today is to discover the objective patterns which motivate behavior or contribute to its distortion, which permit adaptation or generate an inability to adapt.

Everything then that contributes to the discovery of truth objectively must, in my opinion, be encouraged, and everything that contributes to maintaining subjectivity and arbitrariness must be rejected. That is not to say that we do not recognize the inevitable subjectivity of the whole human personality, be it in thought or action. It is a natural social tendency to objectify. This does not lead to alienation in any perjorative sense, although it is to some degree an exteriorization, an *Entäusserung*.

In opposing other ideologies such as existentialism

which should be discussed within the context of our dialogue (including phenomenological and structural methods) I believe that the distinctive contribution of Marxism, the one which must be kept alive, is the stress put on human activity, on doing rather than contemplating. But I cannot envisage a valid theory of action (praxiology) which takes no account of the nature of human motivation, or is unwilling to allow for unconscious motivation, be it at the individual or at the corporate level.

Ideology, then, should advance not only in dialogue with theology, which could provide the impetus for its humanization, but in assimilating the patterns of science which could provide it with the tools for further investigation into reality and with a means of objective control. And so both religious and scientific models should be maintained in the fields of philosophy and ideology, providing normative principles and rules derived from philosophy, a kind of sublimation of philosophy for use in the behavioral sphere. At this point we should take up a serious problem: whether politics or ideology should take priority. I shall certainly be accused of philosophical or ideological "imperialism" but for my part, as a Marxist, I should put philosophy at the top of the super-structural pyramid and derive from it my ideology and only then my politics. I believe that political science should rest on ideological principles which are not political in themselves and which are not pragmatically derived from external circumstances. Politics should be philosophically grounded in reflection about the nature of man and of his universe.

XII

A *Marxist View of Dialogue*

KONRAD FARNER

Since 1923 I have been a member of the Communist Party of Switzerland, today known as the Swiss Labour Party. For some years I have been a member of its Central Committee. At the time when the Party was still illegal, I took part in political and social struggles. I do not regard myself, then, as a "parlor Communist" for whom Marxism is merely a theory—if in fact it

KONRAD FARNER was born in 1903 in Lucerne, the son of an old Zurich family. He attended the universities of Frankfurt-on-Main, Cologne, Munich, Basel, specializing in philosophy and theology (as a Marxist and a disciple of Karl Barth), history of art, and history, economics and political science.

In the period of 1926–32 he was a dealer in rare and old books, specializing in old graphic works, arranging exhibitions of various painters, among them Paul Klee. He was chief reader of the Benno Schwabe Publishing house in Basel and editor of the book series "Mensch und Gesellschaft" (Man and Society) for the Franck publishers in Bern, and "Erbe und Gegenwart" (Inheritance and the Present Day) for Mundus Publishers in Basel. Since 1947, he has been a free-lance writer.

Konrad Farner's most important activity consists in carrying on literary polemics with bourgeois philosophers, as well as in having personal discussions (in the ecumenical conferences and the conferences on theory of art). Educational leader of the Labour Party in Switzerland (which succeeded the Communist Party of Switzerland), he has been a memis ever possible for anyone to experience Marxism merely theoretically, which I deny, since Marxism demands the closest unity between theory and practice. Similarly, unless one is a dialectician it is impossible to comprehend the dialectical realism of Marxism—or, as Hegel put it, to understand dialectic, you must be a dialectician yourself.

Again, I hold no brief for eclecticism nor for the sort of global humanism offered for sale cheap in some "moral" emporia nowadays. I am in favor of absolute clarity and clear distinctions. But this itself calls for a quite specific attitude towards one's partner in dialogue; it forces one to take him seriously, to listen to his arguments, but also to expect him to be equally unambiguous. In the case of the Christian Marxist dialogue one must be able to assume that the Christian really lives his Christianity in practice, that his faith is not merely theoretical and passive, not a halfhearted Sunday Christianity, not a conventional church-taxpayer's Christianity, but a real, living Christianity which embraces and engages the whole person and is therefore *lived*. Obviously this already considerably reduces the numbers on both sides. But I am convinced, and nearly forty years of practical experience substantiates this conviction, that for both the Christian and the Marxist a dialogue can be fruitful only if these conditions are fulfilled, only if neither partner can be accused of being halfhearted.

There are many other conditions for genuine dialogue, of course; for example, it cannot be a question of a dialogue between an accuser and an accused; it is not

ber of the Party since 1923 and for the last seven years a member of the Central Committee.

This address was given at the third Study Conference of the European Federation for Catholic Adult Education held at Zurich in September 1967. It was published in *Vorwärts*.

a matter of proving that the other side is completely wrong or even guilty, for both sides are in the wrong. Otherwise the condition of the world today would not be so precarious. Both parties are guilty; the only difference is one of time: Christianity has had nearly two thousand years' history (some of it extremely shameful) whereas Marxism has only one hundred years' history to answer for (some of it equally shameful).

Clearly then, the question is not "which is the guilty party?" but "Where is your brother?" This does not mean the brother in any sentimental, romantic sense, nor does it mean a missionary zeal to save souls; nor should it be understood in the sense of St. Martin sharing his cloak with the leprous beggar. It is rather in the sense of St. Benedict who brought the land under cultivation, or of St. Theresa of Avila who set up her Carmel in the heart of the slums. The time is over now when, in the basis of a social hierarchy backed by natural law, the charity of the rich could be reckoned as a Christian virtue smoothing their path to heaven. The time has come for the Christian to redeem his promissory notes, presented to him for payment today by the exploited and by the colored races. Today the question is not one of giving the beggar half your cloak so that he may no longer freeze; it is rather to end beggary altogether. For the first time in human history this is possible today, and will be tomorrow on a world-wide scale, thanks to modern technology with its new methods of production and distribution. "Charity" is therefore largely obsolete. The Marxist regards charity merely as first aid, not as a cure. Certainly, bleeding wounds must be attended to, but at the same time the whole body must be healed. This is why the Marxist is bound to have reservations about Danilo Dolci or Abbé Pierre and even Tullio Vinay, however much he respects them as genuinely

Christian personalities. The same applies to the new communities like Taizé which are really pioneers in a new Christianity, but which only influence a relatively small field as far as social ethics are concerned.

Genuine dialogue also requires of both partners in the discussion greater modesty about their own point of view and more interest in the other approach. Both should have more courage when they are asked questions which they themselves are unable to answer immediately, and should not resort so readily to ready-made answers. They should also put radical questions to *themselves*, not only to their partner in the dialogue. And they should be far less anxious and afraid. I have never understood how a Christian could ever be anxious, in view of his assurance of salvation. Was St. Francis afraid? Catherine of Siena, Ignatius, Charles de Foucault, Teilhard de Chardin? Christians who betray signs of anxiety as partners in dialogue, or even issue strong warnings against any form of dialogue, remind me of Marxist officials who express their answer not with their brains but with biased simplifications, insinuations and ultimately (if possible) official compulsion. But there are Christian officials of this kind too, so neither side can cast any stones.

Again, genuine dialogue is poles apart from missionary propaganda and proselytizing. Nor is it apologetics, in the sense of traditional Christian catechism or of official Marxist textbooks; only in the sense of complete openness towards the partner in discussion, a readiness to learn from him. Thus it is simultaneously criticism and self-criticism.

Moreover, genuine dialogue demands informed knowledge of both sides, knowledge of one's own position and of the opposite one. It is not absolutely essential for the Marxist to have read the *Summae* of St. Thomas Aquinas or Barth's *Church Dogmatics*, nor for the

Christian to have read Marx's *Das Kapital* or Lenin's *Materialism and Empiriocriticism*. But each should understand the other's ultimate concern and the basis for it, and the reasons for what is real and possible. The Marxist should realize that "the Church *waters down* the message of Christ" (to quote Hans Urs von Balthasar) and that it is obliged to do so because the wine of the Christian message represents far too potent a concentrate for men; how many of them have got as far as loving their neighbor as themselves? The Marxist should not dismiss this dilution of the Christian message with an ironic, superior, complacent smile. Does he not also water down many principles? As a dialectical realist he should try to *understand*. The Christian should realize that (to quote Ladislaus Boros) "the basic insight of Marxism is very close to certain basic truths of Christianity"; he should also realize that (in the words of the Catholic, Albert Massiczek) "the Marxist is one who seeks to realize a purer humanity."

There are other conditions to be fulfilled if fruitful dialogue is to be possible. The Christian, on his side, must not think of Marxism simply as a philosophical system, or even as simply an economic and social system, or simply as a way of regarding and changing the world. He must recognize that Marxism is a world view in which philosophy, anthropology, sociology, politics and economics are all integrated. In addition, Marxism (being subject to its own scientific categories) is constantly developing, changing, expanding, with fresh differentiations; it is not a fixed system of rigid dogmas; although it has sometimes been treated as such, this is (and will always be) contrary to the very essence of Marxism.

On the other hand, the Marxist must note that the Christian message is not identical with the visible

Church; that the Christian faith is not belief in a world view either (this assumption is one of the chief misconceptions of the non-Christian world, as well as of Christendom itself). The Christian faith is faith in justification as the assurance of salvation, and so a matter of divine grace. In this respect there is no theocratic knowledge, since knowledge and faith operate at completely different levels. If Christians had made this heart of the Christian message clearer, it would have been spared centuries of controversy with science (as science became more and more independent)—a controversy in which the Church has been far from successful. Many of our debates today would prove unnecessary if both partners to the dialogue were more aware of this heart of the Christian message.

Again, the Marxist must realize that Christianity is not tied to any specific form of religion and that (as the Protestant Bonhoeffer and the Catholic Balthasar both assert) Christianity can even be lived without religion at all; the Christian message can be proclaimed without traditional "religion." Then, in this respect at least, the criticism of religion in the Marxist classics will become meaningless.

There is another respect in which the Marxist criticism of religion can become meaningless. In the words of Marx, Christianity is "an expression of man's real suffering and a protest against it." Religious life thus has two mutually contradictory aspects: on the one hand, it is a passive, resigned reflection of human suffering; on the other hand, it is an active hope of overcoming human suffering. Thanks to modern means of production, Christianity today is confronted with a concrete choice between passive reflection about social suffering and active conquest of social suffering. If Christianity decides unequivocally in favor of action, comprehensive action, even revolutionary action (please don't be alarmed!), then an important element in the Marxist criticism of religion becomes groundless, since this criticism is directed primarily not against God and His existence (this distinguishes it from the bourgeois free-thinker movement) but against the man whose faith in God (perhaps a mistaken one) leads him to accept social and personal misery, and even to justify it. It should be clearly stated that this justification of misery, backed even by appeal to natural law, has been the great blight which has marred the entire history of the Church from the Epistles to the Ephesians (6:5) down to the encyclical *Quadragesimo Anno* of 1931, where we read: "The worker should accept without complaint the place which Divine Providence has assigned to him." Johannes Baptist Metz rightly says: "Christians have been too ready to console the poor and enslaved with the prospect of heaven." It is up to the Christian to remove this ground for Marxist criticism of religion.

The Marxist must realize that this is now a possibility. But he will only do so, and rightly, when Christianity produces clear proof of this on a wide scale, in other words, when the Marxist transformation of society finds itself in competition with Christian rivalry in the field of social ethics. It is not only the Marxist who must realize that this is possible; above all the Christian himself must do so. The Christian must realize that what is required is a structural change in property relationships, in the ownership of the main means of production, these being the material basis of society. The Christian must realize that the change required means transforming an economy based on personal profit into an economy based on collective need. The encyclical *Populorum Progressio* is a first theoretical step in the Catholic world, a late beginning certainly, nevertheless a beginning, like the Second Vatican Council and the World Conference of Church and Society held in Geneva in 1966 when (to the alarm of bourgeois Christians) the word "revolution" unexpectedly took a central place. It remains true, however, that (as Bishop Hermann Dietzfelbinger of Bavaria, the new president of the Council of the EKD, has said) "Whenever the Church wants to be up-to-date it always arrives five minutes too late!" All the social encyclicals, ever since Leo XIII, have (to put it mildly) arrived "five minutes too late."

The Christian must realize much more acutely that the traditional social reforms change things very little. He must realize that, from the standpoint of world history, we stand at the beginning of a new, deeper, more radical social awareness, one which calls for fundamental changes in economic structure, in ownership relationships. The challenge of the Catholic historian De Rosa, on the occasion of a culture conference of "Democrazia Christiana" at Lucca on April 28, 1967, may still be only an isolated voice in the ranks of that party, but it is nevertheless symptomatic of the present situation: "Christianity must rid itself of reformism because reformism is conservative."

Reforms, by all means! But reforms do not effect a cure, they are only palliatives. The real solution is not reformed capitalism, nor "organized capitalism" (as the new term so beautifully expresses it!); the real solution is *socialism*. If you will forgive me for saying it so bluntly, "organized capitalism" is simply a new form of fascism, i.e., centralized monopoly capitalism with a centralized organization of state power to protect this "organized capitalism." Many economic, social, political and even ideological facts in the sphere of world capitalism today point very clearly to this. We have here the alternative to socialism-Communism. This is the choice also for the Christian, however much he refuses to face it or is tempted to call it an oversimplification or vainly seeks a compromise which is not ultimately anchored in previous social encyclicals. These encyclicals, as we have already remarked, are unfortunately not "avant-garde."

This certainly does not mean that the cause of Christianity is, and always will be, a rearguard action, as many Marxists think and even hope. The ecumenical conference in Geneva last summer is clear proof of the contrary. The slogan "revolution" was, so to speak, in the air, according to Hans ten Doornkaap, a delegate at that conference, whose report appeared in the far from revolutionary *Neue Zürcher Zeitung*:

It is in the first place a clear abandonment of all theological social ethics bent on maintaining the existing traditional social forms. If Christianity still has any chance left it will only be by a resolute revolutionary attitude. . . . The possibility of active participation by Christians in the violent overthrow of existing orders was explicitly reckoned with. . . . In itself this is nothing new. . . . What is new is the attempt to make revolution the main basic principle. . . . One of the tasks of theological social ethics will be to find, not "rules of play" for such revolutions, but a real concept of revolutionary action, and to give this concept concrete form, with or without a situation-ethic.

Therefore the Christian, especially the Christian theologian, of whatever confession, must enter into a thorough confrontation with socialism and Communism. Not with an apologetic intention, in the old sense, in defense of antiquated values, nor as a polemical theology (if I may use this term here) but in the form of active participation and entering into possession. "Socialism brings more justice to the world than the previous social structures have done. The human significance of work, the abolition of class divisions, the building of socialism—we are under an unconditional obligation to examine all this sincerely and frankly" (writes the Jesuit Father, Gonzales Ruiz, one of the courageous leaders of the Young Catholic Workers in Spain).

Theology must enter into discussion with Communist socialism, not with any fear that it may possibly lose something, but in the hope of being able to gain something, even something of supreme Christian importance. Admittedly, it will lose something in the process: bourgeois Christianity which identifies Christian with the "middle-class" or more explicitly with the propertied middle-class. The stupid and often malicious reaction of certain bourgeois capitalist newspapers, parading as Christian, to the encyclical *Populorum Progressio* (this modest first step) is characteristic of the present situation. If the Christian wishes to play a vital part in the future, he will have to cease being bourgeois and become a citizen instead.

The Marxist, for his part, must adjust himself to the historical fact that Communism in the sense of a social system is not a Marxist invention, still less a Marxist monopoly for shaping the future. As an ideal form of society, as the "great hope," Communism is already found in Solon and in Plato; it has also been an important element in Christian history from the days of the early Church via Chrysostom of Byzantium down to the present-day Christian communities, even though pushed to the circumference by the main stream of Church history since Constantine and frequently decried. As we have already said, the Communist idea in the form of a visible Kingdom of God has for the most part been violently persecuted by the official Church as heresy and only tolerated in the monasteries and convents in the form of small communities integrated into the Church under strict safeguards.

Communism is not contrary to the Christian message; it cannot be for, on the one hand, the Christian message is not tied to any particular social order, still less to any particular property system and on the other hand because Communism, like socialism (but unlike Marxism), is not a world view but simply a social order with a particular concept of property. Christianity existed at the time of the slave system in antiquity, in the age of feudal serfdom, under capitalist exploitation; it can also exist in the age of socialism-Communism. Communism can be Marxist, or Christian, or Moslem, or Buddhist; as has been emphasized, it is not tied to any one world view or religion. Indeed, Communism can be explicitly Christian; its concern is anything but non-Christian or anti-Christian. In adopting a hostile attitude to Communism down to the time of Pius XI, the Vatican was expressly attacking a Communism which was atheistic in tendency, not Communism as a property-system. Moreover, the only existing concrete embodiment of the communist property-system is to be found in the Christian and Buddhist monasteries. What is being built up in states ruled by Marxist parties is merely socialism as the prelude to Communism.

Is the Christian afraid of losing his faith, his life as a Christian, because of Communism? Is the Marxist afraid of losing his view of history, his apparent monopoly of communism, because of a renewed Christianity? What strange anxieties, when we consider the world as it is, when we face the enormous tasks involved in changing this world! What has happened to the sovereignty of faith for the Christian? Where is the Marxist's sovereignty of science? What mistaken, timorous, anxious, defensive attitudes!

We must, of course, keep constantly and clearly in mind that Christian eschatology, as represented for example by Leonard Ragaz's idea of the Kingdom of God or Teilhard de Chardin's vision of the future as a communist social order, is supernaturally orientated, whereas the Marxist goal of a classless communist society free from exploitation is directed wholly towards this world, and is entirely *"innerweltlich."* The two perspectives are therefore on different levels, as far as the "Last Things" are concerned. The Christian "hope of heaven" (pardon this expression) does not rule out the "hope of earth" (to use Teilhard de Chardin's term). On the contrary, the question is whether this "hope of earth" is not to be regarded as an indispensable preliminary, an essential indication? I have already suggested that one of the most important, perhaps the most important, task of the Christian today is to demonstrate that this is so.

For it must be recognized that the "great hope" constantly reappearing in human history in the form of the lost Golden Age, or the expectation of Paradise, or the idea of a Kingdom of God, or a theistic or atheist Utopia, is a vital part of Christian as well as of Marxist anthropology, and that neither Christianity nor Marxism is conceivable without "hope." Jurgen Moltmann's "theology of hope" is just as symptomatic of man's yearning today for a better order of society as Ernst Bloch's "principle of hope." The Marxist "principle of hope" (incidentally this is not identical with what Bloch says) contains by logical necessity far more, since in addition to communism it also includes revolution. We have to ask whether the Christian "theology of hope" should not be widened to include a "theology of Communism" and a "theology of revolution." In other words, hope today has Communism as its social goal and revolution as its means of achieving that goal politically and socially. If the Christian wants to continue to play an active role in history, if he wishes to have a real part in shaping the society of the future, then he cannot evade a thorough study of these two phenomena as the theory and practice which are going to determine the shape of the world of the future. Again, if the confrontation is not to be merely a matter of apologetics and defense, then he must seek to integrate these two phenomena.

One of the tasks of the Christian is to look again at his own history and rethink it. That history, from Constantine down to the present day, has been primarily a history of restoration and even of reaction, of alliance with the ruling powers of this world, condemning any rebellion on the part of the oppressed. The Christian must re-examine this very questionable history of the visible Church. Indeed, he must write a completely new history of Christianity, a revolutionary history. He must ask himself whether Christian existence does not in fact mean revolutionary existence, and this not in a merely theoretical sense.

The Marxist too must re-examine more soberly, more closely, these two fundamental elements in his own world view. He must rid himself of the tendency to idealize, idolize and mythologize the revolution and Communism; he must be more sober, more accurate, more "nuancé" in his analyses. He must learn to think in terms of world history, less narrowly, less in terms of today. He must realize that complete revolutions, like the building up of socialism, cannot be established overnight, but require the contribution of generations; that we are not yet on the eve of Communism. He will also need to realize that, while it is not too difficult to restructure the material basis of society, to change the mental superstructure, especially the social conscious-ness, constitutes one of the most difficult and protracted problems of human history.

The Marxist must realize that, while material change and mental change are dialectically closely interrrelated, the former does not automatically produce the latter. Again, the relation between "being" and "consciousness" is anything but mechanical; it is an exceptionally com-plex constant reciprocal process. The Christian must realize that a spiritual change is not enough—the history of Christianity shows this clearly—because such a change presupposes the reconstruction of the material foundations of society. The Marxist must also realize that at the international level he cannot effect the change on his own; in countries hitherto Christian change cannot be brought about without the Christians. The Christian must also realize that, on his own, he cannot bring about a fundamental change, least of all through "healing by the Spirit." Both Christian and Marxist depend on one another wherever Christianity has existed for any length of time. Still more must it be emphasized that what both are concerned for is not simply that people should have a higher standard of living, but that they should *be better*.

To avoid any ideological confusion or illusions, and in order to establish a clear starting point, we must add this. The Marxist cannot be a Christian, since he rejects all forms of supernaturalism; he must continue to be a Communist because it is an essential part of his world view that Communism is the social goal. The Christian, for his part, cannot be a Marxist, since the heart of the Christian message (i.e., the grace of God) is anchored in the supernatural. But he can still be a Communist (although he does not *have* to be) since Communism as an earthly social order is not anti-Christian.

Everything said so far represents simply a first essential preliminary for dialogue between the Christian and the Marxist; no more than a preliminary! Basically it amounts to this: a clear theoretical position making practice possible. For a dialogue without practical consequences is for the Marxist a mirage, something which does not bind him (in view of his principle "no practice without theory, no theory without practice"). The practical consequence means, for the Marxist, cooperation in changing society; it means (don't be alarmed!) revolutionary practice. For the political and social revolution is at the door, indeed has already pushed the door open all over the world. Not in Switzerland and the countries around it, of course, which (as bourgeois capitalist and bourgeois Christian Western Europe) are living today in the back room of history. But Western Europe ceased long ago to constitute the world; the position today is very different. Today revolution no longer stems solely from Moscow; it springs from many different points, from Peking, Havana, Algeria; it has become polycentric. It can take the form of barricade fighting, guerrilla action, or even the form of enlightenment through intellectual discussion, or of political, trade-union and cooperative organization. It can take other forms completely unknown to us today; it can produce new structures in the building up of socialism with which we are still not familiar.

Unquestionably revolution is on the agenda today all over the world. So is counterrevolution, since no ruling propertied class ever voluntarily relinquished its privileges. Whether we live in Greece, in Vietnam, in France or in Argentina, the alternative confronts us: revolution or counterrevolution. The Christian has to make his choice, in the same way that the Marxist has made his choice from the outset, on the basis of his view of history.

To both of us applies the statement made by Fidel Castro a few weeks ago at the Havana Conference of the Organization for Latin American Solidarity: "What distinguishes the true from the pseudo-revolutionary is his decision to take action." This action is not necessarily armed action; it can, as we have seen, be expressed through social and political struggle, through manifestations and demonstrations, through enlightenment and education.

It can therefore be said that many Christians have already decided in favor of revolution, and as far as I can see Christians are increasingly doing so. I recall the speech made by the Nigerian, Bole Ige, in Geneva, on what is happening in Spain and South America. I think of the priest, Camillo Torres, shot by government troops as a guerrilla leader and today the secret saint of the poor, exploited people of Bolivia. I think of the address given by the Nobel prizewinner Dr. Martin Luther King in Riverside Church, New York, on April 4, 1967, in which he said: "All over the globe men are in revolt against the old social system of exploitation and oppression. From the womb of a shattered world order, new orders of justice and equality are being born. The men of earth, barefoot and naked, are rising as never before. . . . If we wish to put ourselves on the right side in this world revolution, then we must as a nation experience a radical reversal of values. This is my firm conviction. We are confronted with the blatant contrast between poverty and wealth . . ." We should also remember the worker priests in France and their letter of June 1964 to the Episcopate. . . . I personally recall discussions with Catholic and Protestant theologians, where com-

munism as the objective was no longer discussed because
it was already taken for granted, and the discussion
concerned joint *action*. Fundamentally, therefore, communism is not an alternative to Christianity, as many
"yesterday Christians" and "yesterday Marxists" (of
whom there are not a few) think. It is one social possibility for Christianity; probably it will soon be the
only possibility (please don't be alarmed!).

Dialogue between Christian and Marxist must accord-
ingly concern itself in the first place with socialism-Communism. In my view, the question of God, the Church,
supernaturalism, transcendence, theism and atheism, is
not our main theme today. That question can indeed
be an escape from the reality of the present world. It
will remain in the discussion, of course, if only so that
we should learn to know one another more intimately,
both as thinkers and as human beings. But it is only
after society has received a new basis, namely socialism,
that this question will become the great intellectual
theme, especially of anthropology, of humanism. When
society has been largely liberated from the material
these great questions may even become the most urgent
and pressing concern of all.

Escape from the world and fear of the world, even
escape into martyrdom, will then become superfluous.
Highly as I esteem Balthasar as a significant theological
thinker, his new "theology of a new martyrdom" (pardon
the term), which amounts to a longing for the martyr-
Church, seems to be an escape of this kind, an escape
into self-centered striving for salvation, as part of late-
bourgeois extreme individualism. History has never been
made by martyrs and pillar-saints; perhaps not even
salvation-history. If I had to choose today between the
attitudes of two great Christians of the past, I would
incline more to the *action* of Theresa of Avila than to

the *contemplation* of John of the Cross. If I had to choose between two great Catholic theologians of our time, I would incline more to Rahner than to Balthasar, although as a pupil of Barth I try to understand them both. But it is no longer possible to go back, because the revolution and the counterrevolution have in great measure already begun; more than ever before man stands in the world, more than ever before he has an obligation to the world; this applies also to the Christian man.

To revert to the martyr-Church. Here Christian and Marxist are faced with new insights, experiences and necessities. The Christian for his part must adopt as his own the view expressed by Cardinal König about atheism, urging the Christian in countries under Communist Party rule to demonstrate that his religious life does not act as a brake but rather gives him more energy to cooperate with others in changing society than atheism can generate. The Marxist for his part must finally rid himself of antiquated and basically un-Marxist ideas. He must stop confronting the Christian with a mere negation and learn to value him in a positive, constructive way. He must stop persecuting religion and churches, and abandon all duplicity. He is not required to become a Christian, but he must not be anti-Christian. He must discard traditional free-thinking, rooted in the bourgeois Enlightenment and for the most part concerned with superficial matters, especially the dubious conditions and reactionary attitude of the visible Church in denying all forms of human liberation in this world. Of course, the Marxist realizes that this Church, bent on restoration only, is still everywhere present, intellectually and concretely; we need only recall in how many countries the Church is still a great landowner with large holdings in capitalist concerns, or how the

policies of certain so-called "Christian" parties (representing the propertied bourgeoisie) make it almost
impossible for the Church to be the standard-bearer of
the world of tomorrow. But the Marxist must also realize
that, despite all internal resistance, Christianity is under-
going a tremendous transformation, a crisis in which it
does not need to disown its message. On the contrary,
after the crisis (which may be regarded as a catharsis)
the Christian message can be lived out more purely
once it has been cleansed of the accretions of a mistaken
world view and an obsolete alliance with the world.

The Marxist must also realize that wherever the
Christian message is really lived out the Communist goal
of the just society, freed from poverty and exploitation
can be understood even better than it perhaps is among
some Marxists. The Christian must realize that, when
it no longer brings material benefit to pursue pseudo-
Christian politics and to be a "Sunday Christian," the
Christian Church will become much smaller numerically
but richer in quality. Both the Christian and the Marxist,
in answer to the ironical or even sincerely held view that
if there were more genuine Christians there would be
fewer Communists, must realize that if there were more
genuine Christians there would be *more* Communists,
i.e., Christian Communists. So much for the present
situation.

It is precisely this present situation which has necessitated such frequent use of the word "must" in my
address, much as I would have preferred to avoid it.
But as I see it, the days of lovely discussions in lovely
places are now over. There is no question of staging
a dialogue here and now, but simply of outlining the
essential conditions for such dialogue. Nor is there any
question of extending the discussions of the "Paulus
Society." I welcome those discussions, of course, if

only because I have friends on both sides. But those discussions are still mainly well-phrased discourses by systematic theologians and casuists. I do not despise theoretical systematics or practical casuistry. But in face of the situation in the world today, the rise of a new fascism, the millions of people dying of famine in the midst of unprecedented abundance, in face of pestilence and disease which decimate entire nations, in face of the monstrous war in Vietnam, the conditions in Spain and Portugal, in Sicily or Greece, in Latin America and Angola, in face of the Negro revolt in the U.S.A. and of the slums in great Christian (but very un-Christian) cities, in face of social insecurity, the threat of atomic warfare, the continuing exploitation of man by man, by tyranny in various forms—in face of all this I take the position of the great Catholic writer Georges Bernanos: "The restoration of a human world is not a theological problem, but a social one. The casuists can give us no help at all." And if Bernanos assumes that this "human world" is a Christian one, then it is primarily the business of Christians to show that this is the case.

The evidence might show, however, that this new "Christian world" is entirely different from the traditional one, and cannot be fitted into the framework of Christianity in the past. The Marxist might cooperate in providing this evidence, not to his own loss but to his advantage. Indeed the outcome might be that both of them, the Christian and the Marxist, would be like St. Christopher bearing this "New Thing" safely through the raging waters.

XIII

Beyond Dialogue

A Letter From Seventeen Roman Catholic Bishops of the Third World Interpreting *Populorum Progressio*

31 August 1967

IN THE FACE of the profound movements which today are arousing the masses of workers and peasants in the Third World, some of their pastoral bishops address this message to their priests, their faithful, and all men of good will.

From Columbia and Brazil to the South Seas and China, in the Sahara, Yugoslavia, and the Middle East, the light of the Gospel illumines those questions which are everywhere almost the same.

At a time when the poor peoples and races are becoming conscious of themselves and of the exploitation of

THIS DOCUMENT, stemming from some of the radical bishops of the Roman Catholic Church and expressing their deep social concern, a concern which recognizes the need for revolutionary changes in the countries whose people they serve, is not concerned with the dialogue as such. Nevertheless, it is through statements such as these, in particular as they arise from the important papal encyclical *Populorum Progressio*, that dialogue becomes possible and can be seen to be practical. For Communists a declaration of this nature is a much more straightforward opening to dialogue than any number of philosophical discourses on the nature of Marxism. (Editor.)

which they are still victims, this message will give courage to all who suffer and struggle for justice—which is the indispensable condition for peace.

(1) As bishops of some of the peoples who are striving and struggling for their development, we unite our voices with the anguished appeal of Pope Paul VI in his letter *Populorum Progressio.* We wish to clarify the responsibilities of our priests and faithful, and to address some words of encouragement to all our brothers of the Third World.

(2) Our churches, in this Third World situation, find themselves embroiled in a conflict which is no longer just a confrontation between East and West. There are now three major groups of people: the Western powers which grew wealthy in the last century, the two large Communist countries which have become great powers, and finally the Third World which is still seeking to escape the hold of the great powers and to develop freely. Even within the developed countries certain social classes, races or peoples have not yet obtained the right to a truly human life. An irresistible pressure moves these poor peoples toward their advancement by liberating them from all forces of oppression. While most nations have succeeded in obtaining political freedom, peoples with economic freedom are still rare. Just as rare are those with social equality, which is an indispensable condition of true brotherhood—there can be no peace without justice. The peoples of the Third World form the proletariat of mankind today. They are exploited by the great and threatened in their very existence by those who, because they are more powerful, assume the right to be the judges and policemen of the less fortunate. Our people are neither less wise nor less just than the great of this world.

I. FREEDOM IN POLITICAL, ECONOMIC
AND SOCIAL SYSTEMS

(3) Revolutions have happened or are happening in the present evolution of the world. All the powers which are now established were born in an era more or less far removed from revolution—and by "revolution" we mean a rupture with a system which did not secure the common good and the inauguration of a new order better able to obtain it. Not all revolutions are necessarily good. Some are only palace coups which do nothing but change the people's oppressors. Some are worse, not better; they "produce(s) new injustices." (*Populorum Progressio.*) Atheism and collectivism, with which certain social movements think they must be bound, are grave dangers for humanity. History shows, however, that some revolutions were necessary, and rose above their temporary anti-religion, producing good fruit. It is no longer contested that the 1789 revolution in France made possible the affirmation of the rights of man (cf., *Pacem in Terris*). Many of our nations have had to effect, or must now effect, these far-reaching changes. How should Christians and churches respond to this situation? Paul VI already has cast light on our way with the encyclical, "On the Development of Peoples" (*Populorum Progressio*).

(4) Doctrinally, the Church knows that the Gospel requires the primary and radical revolution which is called conversion—the complete about-face from sin to grace, from selfishness to love, from pride to humble service. This conversion is not only internal and spiritual; it concerns the whole man, corporeal and social as well as spiritual and personal. It has a communal aspect

of immense consequence for the whole society, not only for men's life here below but especially for the eternal life in Christ who, raised from the earth, draws all humanity to himself. In the eyes of the Christian, this is man's complete fulfillment. Thus for twenty centuries the Gospel has been the most powerful ferment for profound changes in mankind, whether visibly or invisibly, whether within or apart from the Church.

(5) Nevertheless, in its historical pilgrimage the Church is in practice always linked with a political, social and economic system which, for that moment of history, assures the common good or at least a certain social order. Sometimes the churches even find themselves so bound to a certain system that the two seem to be identical, unified in a single flesh as in marriage. But the Church has only one spouse: Christ. It is never married to any system, whatever it be, and especially not to "the international imperialism of money" (*Populorum Progressio*). Likewise it was not married to royalty or to the feudalism of the *ancien régime,* nor will it be married tomorrow to this or that socialism. A glance at history is enough to show that the Church has survived the destruction of powers which once believed they had to protect her or could use her. Today the Church's social doctrine, reaffirmed at Vatican II, has already broken away from this imperialism of money with which it was allied for a time.

(6) Following the Council, voices were raised energetically, demanding an end to this temporary collusion between the Church and money which was denounced from various sides. Some bishops have already provided the example.[1] We must undertake a serious examination of our own situation and liberate our churches from all

---

[1] *Populorum Progressio* cites the example of the late Bishop of Talca (Chile), Manuel Larrain.

servitude to great international finance. "One cannot serve God and money."

(7) In the face of the present development of the imperialism of money, we address to our faithful and restate for ourselves the advice given to the Christians of Rome by the seer of Patmos before the imminent fall of this great city, prostituted in luxury based on the oppression of the people and on the slave trade: "Come out, my people, away from her, so that you do not share in her crimes and have the same plagues to bear" (Rev. 18:4).

(8) In its essential and permanent aspect—that is, its fidelity to and communion with Christ in the Gospel— the Church is never bound to any political, economic and social system. When a system ceases to assure the common good for some, the Church must not only denounce the injustice: it must disengage itself from the inequitable system and be ready to collaborate with another more just system better adapted to the needs of the time.

II. FIDELITY TO THE PEOPLE

(9) The following applies to Christians, as it does to their hierarchies and to the churches. Here below we do not have a permanent city, because our leader, Christ, was willing to suffer outside the city (Heb. 13:12, 14). Therefore, none of us remains in bondage to the privileges of money, but is ready to "[share his] resources, for these are sacrifices that please God" (Heb. 13:16). Even if we have not been able to do so willingly and lovingly, let us at least know how to recognize the hand of God who corrects us like sons in the events which compel us to this sacrifice (Heb. 12:5).

(10) We do not judge or condemn any who, before God, have believed or believe they must go into exile to safeguard their faith or their children's faith. The only ones who must be condemned strongly are those who drive out the population by oppressing them materially or spiritually or by taking their land.

Christians and their pastors desire in their hearts to remain among their people, in the land which is theirs. History shows that only rarely do people remain happily in exile over a long period, seeking refuge in another place. They must either defend their land against unjust foreign aggression or accept the governmental changes imposed on their country. It is wrong for Christians to withdraw from their country and their people in the hour of trial, especially if these Christians are rich and are really fleeing only to save their wealth and privileges. Certainly a family or an individual might be obliged to emigrate to seek work in conformity with the right of emigration (cf., *Pacem in Terris*), but the massive exodus of Christians can cause deplorable situations. Christians are normally called by God in their own land, among their own people, to fulfill their life in solidarity with their brothers of whatever religion in order to witness among them to Christ's love for all.

(11) We bishops and priests have an even more pressing obligation to remain at our place. For we are the vicars of the Good Shepherd who does not desert like a hired servant in time of danger, but remains with his flock, ready to give his life for theirs (John 10:11–18). When Jesus told his disciples to flee from one town to another (Matt. 10:23), it was only in the case of personal persecution for the faith. This is quite different from war or revolution involving a whole people when the pastor must remain in solidarity with them. It is his duty to stay with his people. If all the people decide to go into

exile, the pastor can follow his flock. But he cannot save only himself or a minority of profiteers or cowards.

(12) In addition, Christians and their pastors must know how to recognize the hand of the All Powerful in the events which, form time to time, put down the mighty from their thrones and raise up the humble, turning the rich away with empty hands and satisfying the hungry. Today "the world demands tenaciously and forcefully the recognition of human dignity in all its fullness, the social equality of all classes."[2] Christians and all men of good will cannot but join this movement, even if they must renounce their privileges and personal fortunes for the benefit of the larger human community. In no respect is the Church the protector of the big property owners. With John XXIII, it requires that property be distributed among all, because property has from the beginning a social purpose.[3] Recently, Paul VI recalled the words of St. John: "If someone who has the riches of this world sees his brother in need and closes his heart to him, how does the love of God abide in him?" (I John 3:17), and the words of St. Ambrose: "The world is given to all, and not only to the rich" (*Populorum Progressio*).

(13) All of the Fathers, both Eastern and Western, repeat the Gospel:

Share your harvest with your brothers. Share these crops which tomorrow will be rotten. Abominable avarice which would rather let everything rot than give it to the needy! "Who do I hurt," says the miser, " by keeping what belongs to me?" Where do you get it? You are like the man who goes to the theater and wants to prevent anyone else from coming in so that he can watch the performance alone to which all have the right. These are the rich: they have

[2] Council intervention of Patriarch Maximos, October 27, 1964.
[3] *Mater et Magistra.*

declared themselves masters of the common goods they
have hoarded because they were the first occupants. If
everyone would keep only enough for his immediate needs
and would give what is left over to the needy, wealth and
poverty would be abolished. . . . The bread you save belongs
to the hungry. The coat in your closet, to the naked man.
The shoes which are rotting in your house, to the man
without shoes. The money which you keep to yourself, to
the man in misery. Thus you oppress as many people as you
could help. . . . No, it is not your greed that I condemn
here, but your refusal to share.

(St. Basil, Homily 6, *Against Wealth.*)

(14) Taking account of some necessities for a certain
material progress, the Church for a century has tolerated
capitalism with lending at legal interest and its other
practices which scarcely conform to the morality of the
prophets and the gospel. But it cannot but rejoice to see
the appearance among men of another social system
which is less distant from this morality. The Christians
of tomorrow should, following the initiative of Paul VI,
return the moral values of solidarity and fraternity to
their true Christian source (cf., *Ecclesiam Suam*). Christians have the obligation to demonstrate "that the true
socialism is Christianity completely practiced in the just
sharing of goods and fundamental equality."[4] Far from
remaining cool to socialism, we can adhere to it with
joy as a form of social life better adapted to our time
and conforming more to the spirit of the Gospel. Thus
we can avoid the confusion some make between God
and religion and the oppressors of the poor and the
workers—feudalism, capitalism, imperialism. These
inhuman systems have begotten others which, in the
attempt to liberate the people, oppress individuals when

[4] Council intervention of Patriarch Maximos IV, September 28,
1965.

they fall into totalitarian collectivism and religious persecution. But God and true religion have nothing to do with the various forms of iniquitous Mammon. On the contrary, God and true religion are always with those who seek to further a more equitable and brotherly society among all God's children in the great human family.

(15) With joy and pride, the Church greets a new humanity in which honor no longer goes to money accumulated in a few hands, but to laborers, workers, and peasants. The Church is nothing without him who ceaselessly gives it its being and action, Jesus of Nazareth, who worked with his hands for many years to show the important dignity of workers. "The worker is infinitely superior to all money," as a bishop recalled at the Council.[5] Another bishop, from a socialist country, likewise declared:

If workers do not succeed in some way in becoming owners of their work, every reform of structures will remain ineffective. Even if workers receive higher wages in some economic systems, they will not be content with this wage increase. They really want to be owners and not sellers of their work. Workers are becoming increasingly aware today that work constitutes a part of the human person. But the human person can neither be sold nor sell himself. All sale or purchase of labor is a sort of slavery. . . . Human society is making progress in this matter, certainly even in this system which is said to be less sensitive than we to the dignity of the human person, that is, Marxism.
(F. Franic, *Split*, Yugoslavia, October 4, 1965.)

(16) This is to say that the Church rejoices to see within humanity the development of forms of social life in

[5] Intervention of Msgr. G. Hakim, Archbishop of Galilee, November 10, 1964.

which work finds its true primary place. As Archpriest
Borovoy of the World Council of Churches recognized,
we were wrong to accommodate ourselves to the pagan
legal principles inherited from ancient Rome. Unfortunately, the West has sinned no less in this respect than
the East.

Of all Christian cultures Byzantium is the one which
contributed most of all to the mere sanctification of social
evil. It took over without objection the entire social inheritance of the pagan world and gave it a sacral anointing.
The Civil Law of the pagan Roman Empire was preserved
in the guise of ecclesiastical tradition for thousands of years
in Byzantium and medieval Europe, and for centuries in
Russia from the time (sixteenth century) when our country
began to regard itself as the heir of Byzantium.

But that is radically opposed to the social tradition of
early Christianity and the Greek fathers, the messianic
preaching of our Savior and the whole content of the
Old Testament prophets, which never grows old.

(World Council of Churches, July 12, 1966,
Church and Society Conference, Geneva.)

III. FIDELITY TO THE WORD OF GOD

(17) No one should look for any political inspiration in
our words. Our only source is the Word of him who
spoke by his prophets and apostles. The Bible and the
Gospel denounce as sin against God any violation of the
dignity of man created in his image. In this necessity of
respect for the human person, atheists of good faith
today join believers for common service to mankind in
the search for justice and peace. We therefore address
these words of encouragement to all of these. For all
need much courage and strength to succeed at the

immense and urgent task which alone can save the Third World from misery and hunger and deliver humanity from the catastrophe of a nuclear war: "No more war, down with arms!"[6]

(18) The people of the poor and the poor of the peoples, in whose midst the Merciful One has placed us as the pastors of a small flock, know from experience that they must count more on themselves and their own power than on the help of the rich. Certainly some rich nations or some rich of the nations give considerable aid to our peoples, but it would be illusory to wait passively for a free conversion of all those about whom our Father Abraham warned: "They will not be convinced even if someone should rise from the dead" (Luke 16:31). It belongs primarily to the poor peoples and the poor among the peoples to accomplish themselves their own advancement. That they recover confidence in themselves; that they educate themselves, leaving behind illiteracy; that they work diligently to build their destiny; that they train themselves and utilize all the means that modern society places at their disposal —school, transistors, magazines; that they listen to those who can awaken and form the conscience of the masses and especially to the words of their pastors. That their pastors give them the Word of truth and the Gospel of justice in its entirety. That the militant laity of the apostolic movements understand and put into practice the exhortation of Pope Paul VI:

. . . it belongs to the laymen, without waiting passively for orders and directives, to take the initiative freely and to infuse a Christian spirit into the mentality, customs, laws and structures of the community in which they live.

[6] Paul VI at the United Nations.

Changes are necessary, basic reforms are indispensable: the laymen should strive resolutely to permeate them with the spirit of the Gospel.   (*Populorum Progressio.*)

That, finally, the poor and workers unite because only union creates the power of the poor to demand and promote justice and truth.

(19) The people hunger primarily for truth and justice, and all those charged with their instruction and education should work enthusiastically for it. Certain errors must be dispelled quickly: No, God does not want there to be poor people who are always miserable. Religion is not an opiate for the people. Religion is a force that raises the humble and humbles the proud, which gives bread to the hungry and makes the satisfied hunger. Certainly, Jesus warned us that there will always be poor among us (John 12:8), but that is because there will always be the rich to monopolize this world's goods and also always certain inequalities due to differences of capacities and other inevitable factors. But Jesus taught us that the second commandment is equal to the first because one cannot love God without loving his fellow man. He warns us that we and all men will be judged by a single word: "I was hungry and you gave me food. . . . I was the one who was hungry. . . ." (Matt. 25:31–46). All the great religions and sages of mankind echo this statement. Thus the Koran announces the final trial at which men are submitted to God's judgment: "What is this trial? It is the ransom of the captives, the feeding of the orphan in time of famine . . . or of the poor man sleeping on the cold hard ground . . . and effecting a law of mercy" (Sour. 90:11–18).

(20) We have the obligation to share our bread and all our goods. If some hoard for themselves that which is

necessary for others, public powers must impose the sharing which was not done in good will. Pope Paul VI recalled this in his most recent encyclical:

If certain landed estates impede the general prosperity because they are extensive, unused or poorly used, or because they bring hardship to peoples or are detrimental to the interests of the country, the common good sometimes demands their expropriation. While giving a clear statement on this, the Council recalled no less clearly that the available revenue is not to be used in accordance with mere whim, and that no place must be given to selfish speculation. Consequently, it is unacceptable that citizens with abundant incomes from the resources and activity of their country should transfer a considerable part of this income abroad purely for their own advantage, without care for the manifest wrong they inflict on their country by doing this.

(Populorum Progressio.)

No longer can foreign wealth be allowed to come to exploit our poor people under the pretext of establishing commerce or industry. Neither is it tolerable that some rich exploit their own people. This provokes the exasperation of nationalisms which are always regrettable and opposed to true cooperation among the peoples.

(21) What is true of individuals is also true of nations. Unfortunately, there is today no truly world government which can impose justice among the peoples and distribute goods equally. The economic system now operating permits the rich nations to increase their wealth, while giving bits of aid to the poor nations who are becoming proportionately poorer. The poor must therefore demand, with all the legitimate means at their disposal, the establishment of a world government in which all peoples, without exception, would be represented. This government would be able to demand, indeed even impose, a just distribution of goods, the

indispensable condition of peace (cf. *Pacem in Terris,* and *Populorum Progressio*).

(22) Within each nation, workers have the right and obligation to join in real unions in order to demand and defend their rights: a fair wage, paid vacations, social security, family allocations, participation in the management of the business. It is not enough that these rights be recognized legally on paper. The laws must be applied, and it behooves governments to exercise their powers in this area in the service of workers and the poor. Governments must work to bring an end to the class conflict which, contrary to popular opinion, the rich too often have set in motion and continued to conduct against the workers by exploiting them with insufficient salaries and inhuman working conditions. Money for a long time has slyly conducted a subversive war throughout the world, murdering entire peoples. It is time that the poor people, supported and guided by their legitimate governments, effectively defend their rights to life. God revealed himself to Moses by saying: "I have seen the miserable state of my people . . . I have heard their appeal to be free of their slave-drivers . . . I mean to deliver them" (Ex. 3:7–8). Finally, Jesus took on himself all humanity to lead it to eternal life. Here below, the preparation is social justice, the highest form of brotherly love. When by his resurrection Christ freed mankind from death, he brought all human liberation to its eternal fullness.

(23) To all we also address this word of the Gospel which some of us[7] spoke to our people last year, moved by the same concern and hope which is shared by all the people of the Third World:

[7] Manifesto of the bishops of North-East Brazil, Récife, July 14, 1966.

We exhort you to remain firm and fearless, as evangelical ferment in the world of labor, confident in Christ's words, "Stand erect, hold your heads high, because your liberation is near at hand." (Luke 21:28.)

THE SIGNATORIES:

Helder Camara, Archbishop of Récife, Pernambuco, Brazil

Jean-Baptiste Da Mota e Albuquerque, Archbishop of Vitoria, Espirito Santo, Brazil

Luis Gonzaga Fernandes, Auxiliary Bishop of Vitoria, Espirito Santo, Brazil

Georges Mercier, Bishop of Laghouat, Sahara, Algeria

Michel Darmancier, Bishop of Wallis and Futuna, South Pacific

Armand Hubert, Apostolic Vicar, Héliopolis, Egypt, U.A.R.

Angel Cuniberti, Apostolic Vicar of Florencia, Colombia

Séverino Mariano de Aguiar, Bishop of Pesqueira, Pernambuco, Brazil

Frank Franic, Bishop of Split, Yugoslavia

Francisco Austregesilo de Mesquita, Bishop of Afogados de Ingazeira, Pernambuco, Brazil

Grégoire Haddad, Melchite Auxiliary Bishop of Beirut, Lebanon

Manuel Pereira da Costa, Bishop of Campina Grande, Paraïba, Brazil

Carlo van Melckebeke, Bishop of Ning Hsia, China

Antonio Bastita Fragoso, Bishop of Crateüs, Ceara, Brazil

Etienne Loosdregt, Bishop of Vientiane, Laos

Jacques Greut, Bishop of Tual, Maluku, Indonesia

David Picao, Bishop of Santos, Brazil

XIV
Marxism as a Philosophy of Human Existence

MILAN PRUCHA

As DIMENSIONS OF the creative development of man, historicity and social relations do not, at first glance, seem to present any very great difficulties. In one way or another, we all know what history and society are. The first question that arises is really this: Whether for mankind the historical-social aspect suffices, and what the positive *meaning* is of historicity and social relations.

Our Christian friends have often assured us that they appreciate the efforts within Marxism which are devoted to *a complete renewal of the Marxist concept of mankind*—as a protest both against the reduction of the Marxist philosophy to the abstractions of dialectical materialism and against the reduction of the Marxist view of society to a mere social technique of revolutionary metamorphoses. If such expressions as "practice," "alienation," "total man" meet with sympathy among

MILAN PRUCHA is one of the foremost of young Czech philosophers. In cooperation with Professor Milan Machovec, he pioneered the dialogue at a time when this required considerable courage. His early philosophical training was received in Moscow at a time of Marxist orthodox rigidity, and was continued in Paris where he related his Marxism to existentialism and also to Christianity. Dr. Prucha teaches philosophy in the University of Prague. This paper was first published in German in *Neues Forum, Vienna* (November 1967).

Christians, a reservation, even a contradiction, remains. For, however much these Marxist terms may have proved that they can bear the great weight placed upon them, the question still is: Can the concept of man be confined to them? Are Marxists not pursuing a kind of one-sided view of history, a reduction of all human problems to social and historical problems?

Does Marxism offer ways of *breaking through* this historicism? The difficulty known as "humanist-orientated Marxism" is bound to be revealed in the question: Where is the drama of human life enacted? Are we concerned with the situation of man in the universe? Are the questions at issue those of life and death which are independent of the social formation? Or are they solely historical questions which will find an ultimate solution in harmony between the individual and society as a whole?

Keeping as closely as possible to Marx, I have tried to present a defense of *Marxism as a philosophy of human existence.*

DEBATABLE ALIENATION

My point of departure is the dispute surrounding the nature of the alienation of man. How can it come about that the fruits of human creativity confront their maker in the shape of a blind and often hostile force, and that this force often overpowers him? The answer to this question displays a remarkable unanimity between many prominent Marxists and many Catholic, Protestant and existentialist *critics* of Marxism. The existentialistically inclined Jean Hyppolite voiced their more or less united conviction in a confrontation of the alienation principle in Marx and Hegel: to Hegel, alienation is brought about by the material character of the world, while Marx sees the source of alienation not in the independent existence of material things vis-à-vis mankind, but in private ownership. Therefore, according to Marx, alienation cannot be overcome by removal of the contradiction between subject and object, but by the elimination of capitalism.

The effectual conclusion which existential and Christian philosophy is bound to reach is therefore this: Fundamentally, Marxism takes no cognizance of man's conflict with a suprahuman world; it boxes him up in the historical process and hands him over helpless—although he may be capable of solving historical problems—to his existential predicament.

The "economic-philosophic manuscripts" provide abundant evidence of how far from the truth is the idea that Marx neglected the meta-historical existential difficulties. Can anyone seriously believe that Marx was only concerned with capitalism when he wrote:

To be sensual, that is, truly to exist, is to be an object of the senses, a sentient object, i.e., to possess sensual attributes outside oneself, objects of one's sensuality. To be sensual is to suffer. Man as a tangible sentient being must therefore suffer, and as one who is aware of his suffering he is a passionate being. Passion is the essential human force in energetic pursuit of its object.

It is to be regretted that, for years, the Marxist philosophy allowed many of its inner potentialities to lie untended. This applies, for example, in connection with the problem of *death* as the dissolution of all the human senses, as an absurdity which is not simply lying in wait somewhere at the conclusion, but rather creates in our consciousness owing to its constant presence a sense of the impermanence of all values. What has Marxism to say to this?

Existentialism in its vulgar form interprets finiteness above all as mortality. Marx, on the other hand, allows of no such limitation. He sees finiteness as a passionate urge in man, indispensable to the attainment of effectuality outside himself: he sees it as a longing for the things of the outside world, as sexuality, as a copious amalgam of specifically human needs.

This is man in the eyes of Marx—by no means as a result of moral decision, but through the structure of his *being* in anticipation of any conscious choice whatsoever—the stark antithesis of nihilistic resignation. To Marx, man is freer than vulgar existentialism would have him; man has at his disposal an abundance of positive values, and he himself influences his scale of values, in which the preservation of life need not in all circumstances take first place. Thereby the *tyranny of death* appears to Marx to be to a certain extent canceled out.

COMMUNISM AS A TASK

In an attempt to consider further the historicity and social existence of mankind in Marxism, Marx's celebrated statement is particularly relevant: the nature of man is not an abstraction residing in the individual person. In its reality it is the assemblage of social circumstances.

Marx cannot be "corrected" by naive insistence that the individual is also determined by nature. A narrow, historical, one-sided *social* interpretation of human existence will not do either. We must picture social existence as a reality in which material, moral, intellectual and also aesthetic values are created, in which the individual has his part. Here lies the historical, *concrete* answer to the question: What is man?

The individual existence of man and his social nature cannot be reduced to a common denominator. It is never possible to do more than examine and influence the tension between the two; it adopts various historical forms and is the most general parameter of social development.

In the forever open dialogue between the individual and man as a social animal, there is one question of preeminent importance: To what extent has mankind attained a state of autonomy in the face of nature and been able to deploy his wealth of social contacts? Does the individual live in harmony with the social being? Is this social being an expression of the power of the individual or is its effect that of an alienated and uncontrollable force?

Seen from this angle the Communist idea appears in a rather different light: not as the *result* of a particular transitory historical situation, but as a *task*, the fulfillment of which is not guaranteed by the inevitability of a happy "end of the story." Among the most diverse historical material conditions it will stand open as long as the social and the human nature of man remain in a state of mutual alienation. We have now perhaps cleared away any possible misapprehension according to which Marxism sees the historicity and social relations of man as his sole, exhaustive determining factors.

MATTER AND GOD

Where can further meditation on other human dimensions lead us? To the observation that man has a "nature," has a "soul," that he is a credulous, philosophizing creature? However diverse and profound any such enumeration of the component parts of human nature may be, it at once has to do penance for the error whereby the banal, everyday concept "man" is elevated to a substance of which the meticulously investigated attributes are required to correct the naiveté of the preconception which marked the point of departure.

Would it not be possible to reverse the whole exercise and ask what is the position of mankind as a dimension of the historical, the social. and, for Christians, the divine order? What evidence have we that the abstract examination of existence presupposes some entity to examine the "being"? How do we know that examination of the nature of man is the equivalent of the enquiry: What is man?

When in the course of a dialogue between Christians and Marxists we speak of existence, *das Sein,* ought we not to begin with a discussion of being and existence— or should it be *matter* and *God?* There seems to be no greater divergence of opinion on existence than in the designation "God," or alternatively "matter" for the ultimate essence. In the most commonly accepted view it is precisely "God" which expresses the meaningfulness of that-which-is. I refer in this connection to Friedrich Nietzsche's calamitous "God is dead." On the other hand, in a climate of enlightened materialism today, the concept "matter" also calls for the courage to commit an apparent absurdity.

Materialism mounts in dialectical progression to its culmination in a conscious being, in which matter is cognizant of its own existence—and theology proceeds upwards, sometimes dialectically, from nature to God, and in so doing runs through a dialectical sequence of aspects of existence similar to that of materialism.

Therefore, the materialist and the theologian have now reached a point of propinquity at which they can say: Take your courage in both hands, put the crowning touch to your dialectical view of the world, and renounce God—or vice versa: I dare you to take the dialecticians's final step, and forego materialism!

It goes without saying that conclusions of this kind, inspired on the one hand by Engels' dialectic of nature, and on the other by Teilhard de Chardin's vision of the universe, would be a caricature and would give rise to justifiable objections. All the same, in the appearance of their outer form, the thought processes of materialists and theologians possess a certain stylistic unity: both sides think of existence as something which is not only known, but also perceived.

The quest for the absolute involves definition of the absolute; it requires that its essence be determined. Whether we regard matter or God as the principle of all principles, this "basis" is in either case of the same nature as the remaining being: it is a transparently lucid, assimilable being that can be controlled.

It is possible to say in respect of this basis, just as with the other elements, *what* it is. This way of taking our bearings from the *Quidditas* is a *Weltanschauung*. Man lives as one who is aware of the nature of the absolute.

Within this *Weltanschauung*—this applies both to theologians and to materialists—the sense or non-sense of man, his historicity and temporality are *known;* man, historicity, temporality, have their ultimate meaning. This kind of view of existence logically means complete freedom to manipulate it at will. God, says Kierkegaard, can be listed together with things like water, roads, lighting, paving and so on; the state uses God to keep its citizens content on the cheap and with the minimum of effort; Christianity, says Mounier, is one vast company selling insurance policies against *lebensangst*.

Seen in this light the style of philosophy possessed in

common by materialists and theologians—that is to say the subordination of social life, historicity and the entire immanent sphere to the presupposition of a cognizable essence of the absolute—is *more important* than the difference between God and matter.

This also casts a new light on the *dialogue* between Christians and Marxists. The likelihood is that the world is not very concerned in the conflicting nature of our principles and dogmas. It is probably far more interested to know how we turn these principles and dogmas into practice. The dialogue cannot exist on the discrepancies or even on the concordance between our abstractions. It will only come to fruition on the basis of a common reality which we apostrophize in our abstractions and express in a new form.

AN END TO THEOLOGY?

Do not expressions such as "cognizable essence of the absolute," "God the highest being," obscure the difference between the philosophy of secularity and theology? There has been heavily emphasized criticism in the Paulus Society of the philosophy of immanence. Does this not show that in the context of immanence God cannot be apprehended as the highest being, as the one and only true transcendence?

If, however, theology is to profit in this way from an emphasis on the necessity for *real* transcendence—i.e., a getting away from the secular, traditionally metaphysical conception of existence as proceeding from the highest being—then a new, very significant question arises. Has theology not adopted an unjustifiably favorable position in relation to Marxism? A position, that is to say, to which it might only lay claim once it had solved the following difficulty: If modern philosophy with its new conception of existence is to be accepted by theology, *in what terms will theology then speak of God, how can it still remain theology?*

In all its branches, contemporary philosophy is becoming conscious of the crisis in metaphysics. On all sides the objection is being raised that metaphysics is confusing existence with each relevant concrete being when it takes matter, energy, life, etc., as its primary principle. Existence does not permit of being grasped in this way. It is a somewhat questionable adventure to call "Zero" by those names, because here it is not the definable which is the point at issue, but rather the fact that the development of all definitions has to start somewhere. Every first step—in life, in philosophy, in the sciences—proceeds from nonreflection and leads back to it.

At the frontier of all knowledge no concept exists which, as in a vise, holds the world together in total unity and as one universal order; there is no all-inclusive meaning to be found there in which all knowledge could rest, nor is there a total suspension of meaning, so that any particular rendering could be actively disputed. Existence, as understood by contemporary philosophy, does not mean empty negativity, otherwise it would remain a mere aspect, to be abstracted in any given case from the ultimate being, a kind of negative ontological dialectic of the transitory. This existence is, rather, a positive "space" to contain the presence of the being at any given time, but it is a far too "capacious" space for the being issuing from it to be able clearly to unveil its countenance, to betray its true character.

It is without a doubt a conception of existence of this kind which also inspires Christian philosophy today. It would surprise no one if in this connection I were to quote Gabriel Marcel. It is of greater significance, however, that prominent interpreters of Thomas Aquinas also follow this trend, because Thomas enjoys the highest official recognition of the Church. In this I am attempting no disloyal interpretation of theological attitudes; Etienne Gilson is far more intransigent in this respect.

Gilson's attempt to equate the teaching of Thomas Aquinas with contemporary philosophy, approaches, in my opinion, the boundary where valid exegesis ends. He joins Thomas in invoking the words from Exodus: *"Si dixerint ad me filii Israel: Quod est nomen ejus? Quid dicam eis? Dominus respondit: Ego sum qui sum."* It follows therefore: *"Dei essentia est suum esse"*; therein, precisely, would lie the distinction between God as existence and any being which is restricted by that which it is, i.e., by a particular being. The philosophical consequences are obvious: *"Non possumus scire esse Dei, sicut nec essentiam,"* *"Esse Dei est ignotum."* According to Gilson, existence cannot be conceived as being, that is to say as something about which it is simultanously declared *that* it is and *what* it is.

Let us leave on one side the question whether or not Gilson's interpretation of Thomas Aquinas is authentic. I can well imagine that the theologians of the Paulus Society could bring up a number of objections. Also, one of the most recent texts on this problem contains the statement that the ideas which Gilson emphasizes are certainly present in Thomas Aquinas, but Meister Eckhart was the first to expand them. The important thing is the primitive but fundamental question: *Then why go on using the word "God"?* Because faith demands it? But then theology cannot use this word *beyond* the boundaries of philosophy, as Gilson believes, but exclusively in opposition to philosophy. For if philosophy considers it necessary now to point to existence and now to preserve silence on the subject, it is not abstaining from using the word "God" because it does not know, or know for certain, whether that which it does not know might become an object of belief. On the contrary, philosophy's silence is a *necessity*, and theology's talk of God takes no account of this philosophical necessity.

BRAVING TRANSCENDENCE

In my opinion faith encounters obstacles which are hard to overcome when it compares its own potentialities to breach confinement within the immanent sphere with the potentialities possessed by philosophy. This has often been observed in discussion between Christians and Marxists. At any rate, it is an unsatisfactory generalization to maintain that we are concerned in both cases, in theology and in philosophy, with the expression of infinity in the language of finiteness. When modern philosophy makes propositions in connection with existence, it is not trying to establish a concept, but to demonstrate, clarify and postulate that which is *not* capable of being reduced to a concept. By contrast, in speaking of God, faith at once betrays the difficulty of its access to the contemporary philosophic conception of transcendence.

Terms such as the "incomprehensibility" of God, on the other hand, are more at home in theological tradition than in contemporary philosophy, for which the irreducibility of existence possesses a considerably deeper meaning. If philosophy is taken as a projection of transcendence into immanence, it is never seen as more than *one* possible version of this projection, whereas faith claims to be the last, ultimate and only true version of transcendence. Philosophy recognizes that it has no ultimate sovereignty; the presence of existence within it is made manifest from time to time by the creation of philosophical thought within historicity; this is a never-ending process. But faith sees the "communication *ex esse*" as a unique act of divine revelation, as a paradox, that eternal truth was incorporated into us at a particular moment in history.

In this connection the reserved but biting criticism of religion voiced by Karl Jaspers at the conclusion of his book, *The Philosophy of Existence*, should be quoted:

As far as it is possible for a philosopher to judge, religion appears to show a characteristic tendency to encounter transcendence as a sensual particularity—that is, as specific holiness—in this world. In philosophical terms, on the other hand, apperception of transcendence can occur in any form of sensuality and empirical reality. This originates in historical diversity of freedom as the abode of this power of perception. Basically, everything can become holy and nothing of general validity is exclusively holy for all.

Our Christian friends in the Paulus Society have given us courage in regard to transcendence. All the same, we have to return the challenge. The sanctification of the status quo, the conservatism, the rigidity which still often characterize Christianity have their self-evident social roots. But beyond this have they not also their deep philosophical source? Does not the insufficiency of Christian transcendence lie in adherence to the immanence of that particular "sanctity," in the reduction of transcendence to that "sensual particularity," as Jaspers critically describes it? For a long time we Marxists have been making efforts to criticize and to put a brake on the Christian urge towards transcendence. Should we not consider ourselves obliged to point out to Christians that religion hampers them in their pursuit of transcendence? Ought we not to spur them on to greater radicalism in this pursuit?

Denial of existence in the name of being is connected up with a state of confinement within the immanent sphere, with the pursuit of each respective "content" as the one and only fact or the fact *per se*. The degradation of the respective being in the name of existence leads to nihilism. Sin is then no longer an act of a particular kind, but any kind of engagement in the sphere of the being. In the religious conception of transcendence the existence of man is not so much an expression of an ontological distinction between existence and being, as the connection between two beings, God and man. Transcendence then has a divided role to perform: It is simultaneously absolute and concrete, i.e., concreteness raised to the degree of the absolute. The danger is that this may easily lead on to fanaticism, even to criminality: "Sacrifice thy son unto me!"—or at least conservatism: adherence to "order" at any price.

NO METAPHYSICAL GUARANTEES

By contrast, it follows from the philosophical conception of existence that no human deeds of any kind can be insured by metaphysical guarantees. Human deeds are done for human reasons; the existential horizon remains unobscured. Finiteness is the only sphere in which transcendence is present; transcendence is the only form or condition in which things can have their being. "To be human" does not mean a role which we take upon ourselves as humans to enact; through the dialectic of engagement and withdrawal it offers indications as to the structure of reality.

From this point it could seem as though it would be

easy to draw concrete social-political conclusions from philosophical premises. But this attempt is always problematical and may, of course, arouse hostility. We might at this juncture discuss the question whether certain philosophical conceptions do bring about certain social-political attitudes. Going further, we could ask to what extent there is a connection between the thought of Heidegger, Gilson, Jaspers and Marcel on the problems of transcendence, and the thought of Marx. Are similar ideas to be found in Marx? Are we justified in employing such ideas in a dialogue between Christians and Marxists?

Every convinced socialist who is interested in philosophy must ask himself this, because he cannot overlook the significance of developments in philosophy outside of Marxism which are taking place both in socialist countries and on the political left in capitalist countries. Today, names like Wittgenstein, Husserl, Carnap, Heidegger, Russell, Merleau-Ponty, Teilhard de Chardin have international weight. For Marxists, confrontation with these philosophies is an act of intellectual honesty, because for Marxist philosophy they often represent something much more than an ideological opponent.

Here too, the catch-word for many hopes and desires is "dialogue." But what possibilities do such a dialogue present? In a lecture in Paris, Gustav Wetter willingly left to Marxism the initiative and responsibility for the theory on the necessity for an ideological conflict between Marxism and religion, but he accepted this thesis himself. Here "dialogue" was merely mounted upon a lame horse. Will it remain a life and death duel? Why not? After all, even a mortal duel can have its rules. But there are various points of view on this today both among Christians and Marxists. An unavoidable technical struggle between Marxism and religion can be carried out either in the form of mutual polemics, of propagandist brow-beating of the opponent, as a psychological war or alternatively as a serious confrontation between ideologies in full awareness of their essential irreconcilibility and without forfeiting the intention to prevail over the opponent, to overcome and put an end to conflicting viewpoints.

In the same terms, a fundamental objection can be raised against the use by Christians of a conception of dialogue formulated in Marxist terminology: Is it fully justifiable to speak of an ideological struggle between Marxism and religion if ideology is to be considered as an expression of class interest and the ideological struggle as a form of the class war? In other words: Can we, without any further ado, *identify* the contraposition Marxism-Christianity with the contrariety between proletarian and bourgeois ideology, as the Marxist thesis on the ideological conflict wishes to see it expressed at the present time?

Roger Garaudy has assembled a series of very pertinent arguments on this dilemma in his text, *From Anathema to Dialogue.* He distinguishes flexibility between religion and clerical institution, between Christian principles and ideological myth. He examines the historically evolving social role of Christianity and the most recent trends towards the freeing of Christianity from the ideology and institutions of the ruling classes. In so doing he by no means underestimates the reactionary ideological trends in Christianity. But his question is whether Christianity has to be *reduced* to these trends, or whether on the contrary a possibility exists to *release* it from these connections with all their weighty consequences. Marxism does not set out to weaken by metaphysical quarrels a living political community which is engaged in the pursuit of concrete and practical ends. I nevertheless believe that it is only possible to come to the necessary practical political conclusions if the validity of the same general principles is accepted. The perennial "logic" of the workers' movement certainly followed a different path. The basis was the community of economic interests, whereupon the search began for forms of actual political participation, while dogmatic ideological regimentation was decisively rejected.

The principal theme in Marxism is its progressive effort to bring about liberation of the working class and thereby of the whole of humanity. This striking idea places it within the reality of the social process where it exerts its influence over the other spheres of culture.

IS ATHEISM UNIMPORTANT?

Marxist philosophy is not meant to extract its directional system from the agglomeration of its creator's ideological concepts, but from the material situation of the working class in society and the struggle for emancipation arising out of this situation. It is unnecessary to differentiate here between what was of "primary" or "secondary" importance in the eyes of the founders of Marxism, as is done by some Christians with a knowledge of the subject, in that they look upon Marx's atheism as a purely fortuitous element in his theory. However original the Marxian philosophy may be, its intermingling with social reality is certainly not the same thing as the sociologically definable connection between Marxism and the working class in general.

Contemporary philosophy is decidedly not impartial toward class or political tenets. Therefore, for modern socialism neither the well-known indifference of the Second International toward philosophy nor the demand that philosophy should cast off its ideological functions, carry validity. Any sociologist would laugh at the very idea today. Philosophy has social ties of a specific kind: a stream of philosophy may run parallel with the material aims of a particular political movement or it may oppose them. A philosophy of absurdity or passivity is, for example, incompatible with socialist changes in the social structure.

A far more subtle and important question for Marxism is the connection between philosophy and science, in particular to sociology; every retrogressive step or even mere stimulation of methodological backwardness or weakness condemns philosophy to carry out reactionary tasks in contemporary social conflicts.

Social engagement as a function of philosophy does not mean that a particular social and class-conditioned basis leaves no room for a variety of philosophical positions. It is hardly possible definitely to legitimate philosophical creativity in terms of class interest, and therefore it deserves no *a priori* guarantees from politics or the state.

Before the question of philosophy's obligations toward society can be answered it would seem to be necessary first to define what philosophy actually is. Only then should its relation to social reality be examined. And yet the essence of the matter rules out such a procedure. A precise explanation of the concept "philosophy" immediately calls for representation of a particular school of philosophy. If, for instance, according to Marx philosophy is the expression of reason in history and therefore it is always a question of the *realization* of philosophy, it at once becomes clear that the historic role of the proletariat, the socialist revolution, the abolition of class, etc., are eminently philosophical subjects and that such a philosophy is logically bound to be political. If, however, we follow the line adopted by many textbooks and see philosophy as the "theoretical foundation of the scientific policy of the party," then its link with public affairs is certainly still powerful, but quite different. Its operative sphere then no longer includes the historical movement as such, but only consists in laying down a few general principles to permit the integration of this movement by means of concrete social-scentific disciplines.

But philosophy is not merely a historical dialectic or a political basis, it is also ontology and anthropology; scientific methodology, also, leads on to philosophical conclusions; and finally there is existential analysis. Thus philosophy may often signify less, and often more, than the idea of the liberation of the working classes and all humanity—the fundamental mission of Marxism.

A MEGALOMANIAC SYSTEMATIC STRUCTURE?

Philosophy covers less ground when it confines itself to the search for theoretical principles and leaves material reality to the special social sciences, but more ground when it oversteps the historical movement and launches out toward the cosmos, the sphere of being, and to the intimity of inimitable human existence.

Should the socialist movement take the megalomaniac path of systematization and, as a result, take on meta-social responsibility—aims which do not inherently belong to its nature? Should it stray so far from its basic elements, from its own initiative, thereby laying itself open to attacks which such extravagant demands are bound to call forth? Ought it to proclaim an artificial integration of the social movement with cosmic-onto-logical events, and as it were "politicize" them? It may be objected that the relationship between philosophy and socialism, or with the whole realm of politics, is not as unequivocal as definitions on the old pattern maintain. And yet why must the coexistence of historical dialectic, methodology of science, philosophical anthropology and ontology disprove the concept of one single philosophy which is acceptable as a whole to socialism? So far as these disciplines are compatible with one another, this means nothing more than a kind of division of duties. But if they are mutually exclusive, how can it then be said that *philosophical* trends which reject the historical dialectic of the liberation of the proletariat as a philosophy, are *politically* viable?

The roots of the misunderstanding lie in the fact that such a rejection does not relate to the *actual* historical process or a particular historical perspective, but is a *philosophical* rejection, that is to say a rejection of the claim to be a philosophy when sociology, economics, political science, etc., are involved.

Identical social foundations and a certain division of work do not exclude the possibility of a conflict of philosophical opinions or a dialogue. Philosophical trends have various points of departure, they link up with a variety of traditions and aim to move forward from there until they embrace the world in its entirety. For this reason philosophical disputes have not necessarily the character of an ideological struggle, if we mean by this a form of the class war.

A confrontation in principle of the philosophical trends with Marxism cannot be exhausted in a comparison of these trends with the historically derived philosophy which speaks in the name of Marxism. A confrontation in principle will not be a *battle* of one philosophical thesis against others, but an examination of the relationship of certain *Weltanschauungen* to the working classes, to the conception of their liberation, to socialism.

That a state which is attempting to realize Marxist socialism and is engaged in conflict with the bourgeois ideology will emphasize those ideas which are associated with the birth of Marxism, goes without saying. It will devote its attention to those currents in philosophy which are associated with the origins of Marxism and are related to historical dialectic of the birth and development of socialism, to the theoretical consolidation of social criterions. Ideological preferences, however—which incidentally are not the sole prerogative of the socialist countries—offer *no* justification for the elevation of a school of philosophy to an official state philosophy, for launching a *kulturkampf* against other ideologies, or for the establishment of a monopoly which is not only damaging to philosophy but also to the interests of the State.

XV

Revolutionary Violence
and the Dictatorship of Consumption

JOSEF SMOLIK

MAN WITHIN INSTITUTIONS

INSTITUTIONAL STRUCTURES CREATED by human society have a marked tendency to harden and solidify, a fact which may be corrobated by merely taking a look at the political and economic institutions around us. What are the roots of this inertia, not to say sclerosis, or in any case this propensity for becoming inflexible?

It is clear that in feudal society institutions were sacralized because they were included in a metaphysical vision of the world. In the present day, ideologies and dogmatisms are the factors responsible for this process, for a new mythology endeavors to maintain the status quo and to present it as a necessity without which the world would plunge back into chaos. Moreover, struc-

JOSEF SMOLIK teaches practical theology at the Comenius Faculty of Protestant Theology, in Prague. As a member of the Theological Commission of the Christian Peace Conference, he has closely followed the problems of revolution and law, and has published numerous articles in the periodical, *Communio Viatorum*. Dr. Smolik is also a member of the Faith and Order Commission of the World Council of Churches and contributes regularly to the Czech philosophical and theological journal, *Krestanska Revue* (Christian Review). This paper was delivered as the tenth annual "Foyer John Knox Lecture," Geneva, November 1967.

tures are formed in such a way as to impede everything
—including democratic criticism—which would call
them in question.

The Judeo-Christian tradition, on the other hand, is
completely opposed to this conception, since it refuses to
accord an absolute value to the status quo, and has a
dynamic vision of reality. For this reason, it is possible
to develop the concept of history within the framework
of the Christian tradition: since the world is a created
reality, it can no longer be sacralized. While ideological
institutions relativize the future and consider it to be of
little importance, in the Judeo-Christian tradition the
whole of history points towards the future, to the moment when the promise of God, which alone can give
meaning to our present existence, is to be fulfilled. Thus
man is in some way set free to be fully human, instead
of being alienated in an institutional structure and
deprived of his authenticity.

My immediate purpose is therefore to attempt to
demonstrate how hierarchical and sacral structures on
the one hand lead to the negation of the liberty of man
and, on the other, engender revolutionary ideas and
movements. In order to do this, I shall draw upon a
few examples from the history of my country.

INTERMEZZO ON CZECH HISTORY

The Desacralization of Institutions

The first person to attempt to relativize the sacral
understanding of papal authority which prevailed in the
fourteenth century was Jan Hus. With the doctrine of
predestination as his starting point, he demonstrates that
the fact of holding a particular office in the ecclesiastical
hierarchy does not automatically sanctify the holder

of that authority. Authority depends solely on the manifestation of God's election in the life of that particular man.

Jan Hus's revolutionary attitude rocked the foundations of the sacral structures of feudal society, and consequently the Church was forced to oppose Hus and his disciples in Bohemia and Moravia. The Hussites, against whom a crusade was declared, took up arms to defend their master's teaching. It is true that, in a certain number of cases, they also had a social revolution in mind, for they wanted not only to destroy the power of the Church, but also to overthrow that of the lords in order to establish the people's rule. The first stage of their revolutionary activities led to the creation of a model Communist society in the Tabor settlement.

Questions Raised by the Use of Violence

In the following century a small group, inspired by the hope that God's judgment would bring the ruin of feudal structures, established itself, convinced that it constituted the new people called to survive the eschatological holocaust. One of the leaders of this group, the Moravian Union of Brothers, was Peter Chelcicki. Although he was as critical of feudal society as was Jan Hus, if not more so, he rejected all forms of violence. The Brethren very soon became the object of all kinds of persecution, yet they reacted without violence, striving by both written and spoken word to convince the king, the archbishop and the whole nation of the justice and truth of their cause. Since they understood their mission in messianic terms, they were also convinced that the future of the Czech kingdom depended directly on the truth which they proclaimed.

Thus a violent revolution was followed by a pacifist

revolutionary movement, which laid the foundations of the Czech democratic tradition.

The Function of Utopia

Just as it had crushed the Hussites, the establishment succeeded in bringing to an end the movement started by Chelcicki: yet despite continual persecution, the Czech revolution, far from being stifled, entered into a new phase at the beginning of the Thirty Years' War, under the leadership of J. A. Comenius.

It was from exile that Comenius organized the resistance against the Hapsburgs, a task praiseworthy in itself. However, his most important contribution to the revolutionary issue was to give the function of utopia its full value, for he considered faith in a new, open future to be essential. Nearly thirty years of his life were devoted to a work entitled *De Rerum Humanum Renovatione Consultatio*, the manuscript of which has just been discovered. In this work he explains how he sees the future of humanity after the fall of the Hapsburgs, and proposes that the three universal institutions (politics, science and theology) should design a new future. He relies on education to achieve this aim and to effect a permanent renewal of society.

The Rejection of Revolutionary Violence— A Christian Position?

The principal figure in the new revolutionary movement of the late nineteenth century was T. G. Masaryk, who, like Chelcicki, was a pacifist. He voiced his convictions many times, amongst others in an analysis of Karl

Marx's *Das Kapital*, in 1898. At the beginning of the First World War, Masaryk decided that he could not identify himself with the Austrian Empire and took refuge in Switzerland, where, on the anniversary of the death of Jan Hus in 1915, he declared the Czech national revolution against Austria.

On his election as President of the Republic after the First World War, Masaryk devoted his efforts to opposing all violent forms of social revolution. This explains his constant refusal to recognize the new Soviet government. For him the use of violence in a national war was justifiable, but not in a civil war. His whole program, to which he attributed a Christian inspiration, was contained in the phrase "Jesus, not Caesar," or in other words, "Our example must be Christ's gentleness rather than Caesar's violence." I am certain that it is because of this ideology which condemns violent revolution on principle that Christians have lost the confidence of revolutionaries, who have been forced to become atheists.

ENCOUNTER IN THE MARXIST REVOLUTION

Masaryk's slogan soon became the target for attacks by the Marxists, who effected a successful revolution in 1948. They considered it to be *the* Christian attitude towards revolution and accused it of being a justification of social repression, rejecting it on the grounds that it was both idealistic and reactionary. However, in spite of much criticism, particularly from J. L. Hromádka, Masaryk's thought continued to widely influence Czech Protestantism.

The question which the Marxists then put to the Christians was the following: Is the Christian faith capable of giving a positive meaning to a violent social

revolution? During the course of history the reply has
been resolutely negative, and it is only in most recent
years that Christians have begun to reconsider their
position and to admit that they should give a more
dialectic answer with finer distinctions. Of course the
answer can only be given in terms of the historical context, but it must also be admitted that it was under the
influence of Marxism that Christians rediscovered the
essentially historical character of their faith, whose
Hebraic origins had been denied by the Middle Ages
and by orthordoxy.

However, Marxists and Christians have something
even more important in common than their relation to
the historical situation: both take the greatest interest
in the burning question of today, namely the presence of
suffering. It is here that the central theme of the gospels
is to be found, rather than in traditional christological
dogmas, for only when they are applied to the suffering
of Jesus of Nazareth do the terms "hope," "kingdom
of God," and "resurrection" take on a concrete meaning,
and lose their mythological significance. Here we find
the potential substance of a dialogue with the Marxists
and with secular man.

The more we study the history of Jesus of Nazareth,
the more we discover clear analogies with the situation
of suffering man today. Poor nations suffer because of
the hardness of heart of rich nations, who give violent
expression to this callousness by exerting organized pressure which the poor are unable to withstand.

Today we must therefore raise the following question:
Since the majority of Christians come from rich countries, can they claim to have any right to say "no" to
those who are trying to liberate themselves by force
from the pressure which the rich countries are exerting
on them? Must we not recognize all such objections as

mere manifestations of our own concept of justice and of a certain paternalism, not to say an absence of humanity? It would seem that the rejection of revolutionary violence in the name of the Christian faith in fact betrays the hypocrisy of those who fear that too fundamental a change might force them to make personal sacrifices and to modify their way of life. Not only do they give a false interpretation to the Christian message, but they also seize it for their own benefit.

Is not the acceptance of revolutionary violence therefore truer to the Gospel message than its rejection? A Christian can never accept violence in principle, but neither can he reject it in principle: he must be dialectically open to every situation. If we want to express our solidarity with the poor, and our disapproval of the injustices which weigh upon them, then we can accept violence, for if we admit that it is unjust to use violence in the defense of a just cause, we can equally say that it is just to use violence in combatting an unjust cause.

It is only by accepting revolutionary violence that a dialogue between rich and poor can be established, and that the latter can take part in the discussion on an equal footing. But if the rich nations admit that the poor nations have the right to embark on a violent revolution, they owe it to themselves to engage in the struggle against the powers which are exploiting other continents.

To declare our sincere adherence to the possibility of revolutionary violence is, in the same breath, to criticize and transcend all the rational arguments which try to justify the status quo. Yet—paradoxically—it is to hope that violence will not be necessary. For revolutionary violence seems to be engendered by the violence of the status quo and of sacral structures.

The problem of violence will always be the ultimate question for the Christian. We know well that Jesus of

Nazareth never chose that road even though several people tried to recommend it to him. Each time he deliberately rejected it as though it were a matter of principle, and it is for this reason that pacifism has always held an important place in the Christian tradition as a constant challenge to violence. We might well ask whether it is not precisely the rejection of violence which constitutes the essential difference between Jesus and ourselves, between he who never knew sin and those who cannot avoid sinning.

REVOLUTION AFTER THE REVOLUTION

The change in social and economic conditions brought about by a social revolution can in no way be considered to be the end of the revolution. It is only in exceptional circumstances that revolution can be identified with a violent military upheaval, for there are several types of revolution: in Czechoslovakia, for example, scientific and technological change is still the main concern of the present government. Here, therefore, revolution signifies a permanent process aimed at ridding social structures of their sacral and ideological elements and at relativizing them in the name of a true humanity and of an open future.[1]

Moreover, if our hope for the future is limited to the realization of the "Great Society," or of Marx's classless society, or of the kingdom of God seen as a social program, we are immediately imprisoning the future in ideologies and sacral structures, and rejecting the dynamic revolutionary aspect of history. We are denying

[1] Written, hopefully, before the Czech peaceful "revolution" of spring 1968 which embraced this "open future." (Editor.)

biblical history only to fall back into myth, which is the absence of history.

I would now like to demonstrate why I think revolution is still necessary.

Today socialist societies are ready to introduce cybernetic models into economics, models which obviously have numerous advantages over the mechanistic patterns of Stalinism. But they are not without their dangers either, for they can only be applied in so far as the computers are supplied with information of a mathematical nature, and such information can never take into account all the dimensions of man. Cybernetics involves the risk of depriving man of the fundamental dimensions of his humanity, and of being left with a single type of man having only one dimension. We must therefore question this tendency to reduce everything to cybernetics, and never lose our critical attitude if we are to safeguard man's humanity.

There is a further danger to beware of. All institutions, whether political, cultural, or ecclesiastical, national or international, are inclined to succumb to the pressures of egoism, and to lose sight of their true mission. This is certainly connected with the reality of evil and of sin, expressed in the struggle for power, even in societies which have already accomplished their social revolution.

The dictatorship of consumption is at once the cause and the result of both the aforementioned dangers, for when the transcendental dimensions of life are forgotten, and ontocratic structures cloud the horizon, then the cult of the standard of living inevitably takes control and leads to the idolatry of production. This eventually results in the total disintegration of the human personality, as it finds itself deprived of its freedom. At this point man abandons his struggle for justice, truth and love, thus proving that he has become enslaved to structures petrified by ideology. Moreover, he is compelled to renounce all forms of transcendence and, in so doing, loses the possibility of understanding existentially the fundamental concepts of the Christian faith: grace, forgiveness, sin.

Today one of the most difficult tasks facing those of a revolutionary mentality is to find the ground on which they can fight the invasion of consumption. Of course the problem will not be solved by withdrawing from the world and preaching asceticism. The only possible solution seems to be for those who are like-minded to work together to relativize the structures of society and the ideologies which they refuse to passively accept. Such an effort, carried out in the name of freedom, would already be a revolutionary struggle.

For Christians the most difficult task lies in operating both religious and secular man to the idea of transcendance, which alone can liberate them from the dictatorship of consumption. Whereas in the past revolutionary movements were able to use the hope of a utopia to achieve this, today the future has to be expressed in a new language, which will open man to his future. This is, perhaps, the main task facing contemporary theology.

One cannot help wondering in this respect whether the appeal of the Chinese position amongst Western intellectuals is not due, in the last analysis, to the extremely critical attitude the Chinese Communists have adopted toward the idolatry of consumption.

Finally, although no society could exist today without contact with other nations, there is always the danger that a given society will lose its international and world perspective on its problems and become isolationist

and nationalistic. In such a case it might well happen
that the international differences and tensions caused by
them will replace revolutionary pressures: but it is
obviously far better if revolutionary voices can make
themselves heard within their society and if they can
continually challenge their leaders to never lose sight
of the international dimensions of their task.

REVOLUTION IN THE GOSPEL

The tendency which we all have to restrict reality
to an ideology or dogma seems on the surface to be
motivated merely by a self-protective instinct and by
a need for security. Yet if we delve deeper we discover a "metaphysical" fear of all forms of change,
and it is doubtless this fear which motivates men to
maintain the status quo by every possible means. We
must be fair and admit that a certain sense of responsibility may also explain such efforts; yet it remains true
that in moments of crisis all means, including military
force, seem to be justified in maintaining the status quo,
and at such times fear is much more evident than a
sense of responsibility. As Christians we believe that this
fear will never be suppressed either by force or by
democratic methods, for its roots are to be found in
man's inherent sinfulness, and we can only be freed
from it through the power of faith and hope.

It is precisely this liberation from fear, together with
a strong hope in the eventual success of the enterprise,
which causes a man to become a revolutionary. What
struck me most in Régis Debray's book, *Révolution
dans la Révolution?*, was the author's absolute certitude
that the revolution would succeed: there is no shadow
of doubt. Moreover, this is the focal dogma around

which his whole thought is built. We might well wonder from where Ché Guevara, Régis Debray, the people of Vietnam or of China draw their hope of victory and of ultimate success. We have no idea, and it is evident that only a dialogue at the deepest human level could give us an indication of the answer. But in order to enter into dialogue with them, we must begin by identifying ourselves with the just cause for which they are fighting.

Revolution is therefore primarily a question of freedom, faith, and hope. If we are to achieve a successful revolution we must first be freed from the dictatorship of consumption and from our fear of change, and secondly know how to hope in the victory of truth and justice. It is for this reason, incidentally, that revolution includes a cultural and anthropological dimension. The experience of the Christian Church during the last centuries shows that in fact there have always been groups of Christians who are freed from fear and who have been capable of transcending the status quo in order to embrace a revolutionary task.

Faith in Jesus Christ, far from making life easier, leads us into costly involvement in the struggle against injustice. Yet it also opens up new horizons, where we can discover the transcendental character of the truth and justice which have been revealed to us through the resurrection of Jesus Christ.

XVI

God and Man in the Marxist Christian Dialogue

A. O. DYSON

SOME YEARS AGO I heard an Anglican priest discussing the ecumenical trends in the newly independent African country where he had been working. He took the view that such politically, socially and theologically troubled times as ours were most unsatisfactory for unity negotiations. The best course was to wait until the participating denominations were clearer about their respective positions.

This attitude could be defended on the grounds that negotiations in a time of general unrest might treat as irrelevant to the immediate situation certain issues which, in a more settled period when theologians have time to read their church-history books, could turn out to be of great moment for the long-term future of institutional Christianity. Our priest's attitude could be opposed, albeit rather wanly, on the grounds that the world of the mid-twentieth-century hardly allows us to expect in the foreseeable future a time of political, social and theological equilibrium, and that in

ANTHONY O. DYSON is an Anglican theologian teaching at Ripon Hall Seminary, Oxford. He has made a special study of the relationship of Marxism to the thought of Teilhard de Chardin. This chapter has not previously been published.

consequence the present is as good a time as any for the Churches to seek organic unity. My own defense of the propriety of ecumenical activity would be quite different. I should argue that *precisely because* of the current intellectual and religious ferment we should embark confidently on the path towards Christian unity. And, as I shall try to explain with illustrations from recent literature, I regard the present time, when no general Christian consensus is available, as precisely the moment for prosecuting the Marxist Christian dialogue with all possible vigor.

The sudden emergence in recent years of a new phase in the Marxist Christian dialogue coincides with a slackening of momentum in the ecumenical movement. It is profitable to ask whether these contrary motions are not connected, and whether the scope and presuppositions of the ecumenical movement do not stand in need of careful re-examination. I suggest that among other things the growth in Marxist Christian dialogue reflects, on the Christian side, a legitimate anxiety about the trends of current ecumenism. I sense that while many Christians remain active in the ecumenical movement, they have lost a good measure of existential attachment to it.[1] This does not arise through pessimism or through a new hardening of denominationalism but from a realistic appraisal of the state of the world today. When for centuries the major Christian confessions had ignored and grossly misunderstood one another, it was something of a Galilean springtime for them to come together under the auspices of the World Council of Churches and devote time and labor to understanding and comparing their different attitudes on

[1] *Cf.* Stephen Neill, "The Church of the Future, Reunion and the Ecumenical Movement," *The Modern Churchman*, X, 1966, esp. p. 85f.

Church, ministry, sacraments, etc. But an ecumenical endeavor conducted along such lines is oriented mainly towards the past and for the greater part handles *secondary* theological issues. Over the last decade, however, the feeling has grown that the Churches should above all be concerned with the problems which confront the *world's* existence, problems of peace and war, of famine and the population explosion, and of international cooperation. The Churches' fresh realization of their responsibilities in these directions has had two connected effects. First, it has brought home the fact that, as a matter of pressing urgency, ecumenism should be seen in a much wider perspective, namely at the level of the major competing ideologies of which Christianity is but one. Second, the compelling need for this broader horizon has made Christians far more aware of the *primary* challenges to the legitimacy of their faith coming from other widely held interpretations of human existence. These two issues are connected in that it is wildly unrealistic to expect a serious degree of cooperation on the great problems which confront men as citizens of the world, without there being also a far higher measure of mutual understanding, respect and self-criticism about their different philosophies, ideologies and faiths. It is on this large-scale map that the current Marxist Christian dialogue must be located, and accorded the status of a significant landmark.

However, in this and other contemporary dialogues within a wider ecumenism (e.g., with scientific humanism and with the Oriental religions), a greater degree of mutual understanding and respect does not exhaust the task that lies ahead. Just as in the Christian ecumenical movement one partner discovers that his faith can be enriched and even transformed by the different outlooks and emphases of another, so too with the

wider ecumenism. But the situation is different with the
wider ecumenism in that other faiths such as Marxism
challenge the Christian not simply on secondary issues
but on the main tenets of his faith. Marxism, for example, poses a fundamental and inescapable question to
Christianity about its belief in God.

Here the Christian faces a choice. He must at a very
early stage decide whether to treat this challenge as
of "divine" or "diabolical" origin. We must either see
the challenge of contemporary Marxist existence as a
simple threat to Christianity from the forces of "Anti-
Christ," calling him to cling desperately and aggressively
to the faith that he holds and to the form in which
he holds it, or he must at least allow that it could be
a call to inspect his own faith, to reckon for himself
with the possibility that "to cast down the statues of
the gods is not always an act of unbelief—it is usually
the proclamation of a higher conception of divinity"
(Sabatier). This second alternative does not of course
ask the Christian simply to substitute for his own doctrines others taken over from different forms of contemporary existence, but rather that through a complex and
often painful dialectic with other ways of faith he
should attend to the development of his belief.

I use the word "development" well aware that it
constitutes a thorny theological problem on its own
account. However, I am not so much concerned with
a theory of the indigenous development of theology
as with a development which takes place through
encounter with other interpretations of existence. I take
it as axiomatic that at any one point in history Christian thology will always be underdeveloped in that
it is a phenomenon which is always understanding
itself anew, as human consciousness passes into new
modes of existence in new environments. Moreover, to
say that theology must continually understand itself

anew is quite different from saying that it must adjust
the way it expresses its "truth" to meet the needs of
every new age. This kind of "translation" envisages a
"coated-pill theory" of Christian truth, where one bitter-
tasting coat can be removed and replaced by another
sufficiently attractive for Jones to feel disposed to
swallow. This approach, the separation of an ideal truth
from its form of expression, seems superficially progressive, but it does not treat theology as a living organ-
ism, and means that the encounter with other faiths
can never be whole-hearted but is hindered from imagi-
natively experiencing their thought and praxis. I believe
—and I return here to my earlier discussion about the
right juncture at which to embark on this wider ecumenism—that Christian theology is at present suffering
from notable underdevelopment, not least in relation
to its central doctrine of God. There is a long tradition
of atheism, dating back to the collapse of the Hegelian
synthesis, which mainstream Christian theology has
hardly begun to take into account. Theology has either
thrown in the towel to this tradition and so lost any
distinctive identity, or it has espoused a fideism which
can in fact say very little about God, or it has simply
rested content with an outdated scholastic or natural
theology. There are of course notable exceptions to this
rather sweeping judgment, but that they are only exceptions is demonstrated by the fact that in the second
half of the 1960's we are faced, from within the Church
and from outside it, with a many-sided onslaught on
Christian theism. It is therefore not surprising that the
cures being suggested for this organic underdevelopment
sometimes appear extreme and even threaten to kill
the patient.

It is in this situation that the Marxist Christian dialogue is under way. And it is an especially important
dialogue because the Marxist partners, for the most part,

are no longer interested in anti-theism for its own sake but in atheism for the sake of certain human values. There is consequently all the more reason for the Christian to attend to these Marxist voices in the hope that he may hear noises that speak positively to him as he undertakes the precarious task of developing his theism. The likelihood of such influence is even greater when we consider that on the Marxist side the last few years have witnessed an intense debate about the nature and scope of a new Marxist humanism.[2] It is not my role to ask whether the transcendentalist perspectives of Christianity can help this debate along. But as a Christian I am *a priori* interested in the Marxist vision of man, both in its classical form and in its more recent manifestations, since in Christian theology the doctrine of God and man are always closely connected. As the history of theology shows, the nature of our discourse about man materially affects the nature of our discourse about God. As Leslie Dewart writes:

It would not be unreasonable to suppose, therefore, that if a Christian should wish to understand, appreciate and develop the truth of his own theistic belief, he might usefully approach the subject through a consideration of atheism. Or does not the very existence of atheism in the midst of a culture which is historically theistic . . . tell us something about the nature of Christian theism?[3]

The underdevelopment of Christian theism can undoubtedly be traced in part to its having foregone the taxing demands of a "conditional" theism in favor of an absolute theism. An absolute theism is strangely

[2] See the *Gespräche der Paulus-Gesellschaft* in recent years, especially *Christentum und Marxismus—Heute* (at Salzburg, 1965) and *Christliche Humanität und Marxistischer Humanismus* (at Herrenchiemsee, 1966), published by Europa Verlag.

[3] Leslie Dewart, *The Future of Belief* (Herder and Herder, New York, 1966), p. 52f.

unself-critical and easily concurs with the judgment
that "anything is apt to be God," whereas conditional
theism is "painstakingly self-critical," is insistent that
"*which* God we believe in is of the utmost importance,"
is *both* belief and disbelief.[4] This conditional disbelief
in God reflects a genuine and lived concern with truth.
I think that Dewart's analysis of disbelief rightly leads
him to conclude that therein "we have discovered the
foundation of the Christian tolerance of Marxist atheism,
namely, that it is both a reasonable and a moral possibility."[5] At the same time I want to suggest that
we can go further than this to ask how far Marxist
atheism can help us to discern what about God we
ought to believe and what we ought to disbelieve. I
say "help us to discern" because there can be no living
Christian theology that is not continuously measuring
itself against a *number* of sources, which must of course
include those of the Christian tradition both in the
Bible and in the history of the Church. But to compare those domestic sources with what may be called
the "secular sources of reality" at any one time is, in
my way of thinking, an essential procedure for check-
ing the authenticity and maturity of a dogmatic tradition within the Church. This is, of course, nothing
so perverse, it goes without saying, as to claim that
Christian theism is an atheism *d'intention* any more than
Marxist atheism is a theism *d'intention,* though such
accusations are made about this procedure by those
who claim to defend "orthodoxy."

If we turn to Roger Garaudy's recent book[6] we see

4 *Ibid.*, p. 64f.
5 *Ibid.*, p. 75.
6Roger Garaudy, *De l'Anathème au Dialogue,* Plon, Paris,
1965. *Cf.* also "Lepère Teilhard, le Concile et les Marxistes,"
Europe, March–April 1965, p. 186.

expressed in succinct form something of one theologically literate Marxist's objections to Christian theism.
His criticism is that the Christian God is "above," i.e.,
outside and beyond, human history, and that this same
God is, in the Christian schema, committed to bringing
the march of human history to an end at some arbitrary point in the future. Garaudy objects that divine
transcendence of this kind pretends to solve man's problems from without and puts a brake on the Promethean
soaring of the human adventure. Without at all attribut-
ing to Garaudy a theism *d'intention*, it must be said
that by and large he is concerned to criticize some
traits of theism which seem to run counter to man's sense
of autonomy, to his capacity for coping with the problems which confront him, to his power to shape and
utilize the world around him for the construction of
a *cité humaine* where men might live out their characteristically human dimensions to the full. In other
words, his rejection of theism is relative to his affirma-
tions about man, I have not, of course, performed a
worthy or detailed exegesis of Garaudy's views, for I
am anxious only to indicate the way in which his
rejection of theism occurs. To fill in the picture more
completely I will quote a summarizing paragraph by
Theodore Steeman which I think does reasonable justice to the position of many Marxists in the contemporary debate.

In reality behind modern atheism lies what Bonhoeffer
called the adulthood of man, man's awareness that in this
life he has to create without divine help and intervention
and on his own responsibility whatever must become of
this world. As a "stand-by," a final explanatory hypothesis,
a miracle worker, a last refuge, God disappears. Man has
become autonomous, is aware of his ability to explore, control and know this world constantly better and more pro-

foundly. For all this he does not need God and prefers to do without a God who would merely explain the suffering of this world without abolishing it, and who would hamper his urge to find out and his efforts to improve life in this world. Modern man no longer feels himself to be actually under threat, and where there *is* a real threat he wants to face it courageously, with a will to make this life more secure and with a manly acceptance of what happens to be man's lot: death, illness and weakness. God cannot take this weakness away or make it lighter. Man should be strong enough to accept this as part of his task in life.[7]

Do such attitudes require their proponents to profess atheism in some absolute sense? Or could a person holding this world view properly profess faith in God, and, if so, would it make any difference to him? If the two professions are somehow compatible, what difference would it make propositionally to our God-talk? These are the difficult but apposite questions. Since it is not my place to discuss what the Marxist should or should not believe, I will confine myself to some observations about the implications of these questions for Christian theism. On the whole I would accept Steeman's summary as representing, in what it says if not in what it omits to say, a point of view which I as a Christian feel constrained to accept since the evidence of lived experience so strongly supports it. I think that the "secularization" debate within Christianity has already made it quite clear that on man's shoulders lies the responsibility of bringing this world to greater fulfillment, and that if he neglects to do so, or if he is unable to do so, there are no signs that God is going to step in and do it for him. I feel sure that whatever else being a Christian may involve, it

[7] Theodore Steeman, "Psychological and Sociological Aspects of Modern Atheism," *Concilium*, March 1967, p. 28.

certainly involves an affirmation of the full autonomy and significance of the secular order and of man's total responsibilities within it. Granted this, what of the Christian proclamation of God? Does "assent to it require . . . one to accept a particular metaphysical outlook for which all our experience and thought as contemporary men is negative evidence?" Is it that "this world of time and real relations must then be regarded as but the moving image of the timeless and utterly nonsocial eternity of God, for which the whole natural-historical process is in the nature of the case indifferent"?[8]

It might be objected that this picture of God which Ogden calls "classical theism" is a parody of what Christians in fact believe. It is very difficult to know what Christians do believe. But I am sure that his account is nearer the truth than we may be inclined to admit. Only half a century ago a great many intelligent Christians accepted the scheme of salvation which J. S. Bezzant has so brilliantly summarized in his contribution to *Objections to Christian Belief*.[9] Admittedly "this outline has been so shattered that the bare recital of it has the aspect of a malicious travesty." "But," he continues, "though it can no longer be taken seriously, certain doctrines vital in the Christian gospel of salvation are still taught *in forms which derive from the vanished scheme and from nothing else*"[10] [my italics]. I conclude therefore that the attitude summarized by Steeman stands in legitimate opposition to much of the prevalent Christian proclamation of God, and not least to the presentation of divine salvation as being *from* this world rather than *for* this world.

[8] Schubert M. Ogden, "The Christian Proclamation of God to Men of the So-called 'Atheistic Age,'" *Concilium*, June 1966, p. 48.
[9] Constable, London, 1963, pp. 82–84.
[10] *Ibid.*, p. 84.

The second half of my essay will consider, at different lengths, certain current contributions to the development of Christian theism which take into account some of the Marxist insights about man. I believe that these contributions bear out Ogden's contention that "what distinguishes Western humanity today is not a greater degree of existential distrust of God, but an ever more widespread theoretical dissent from the assertions of classical theism." I am aware that "the formulations in which this dissent is conceptually explicated typically claim to be the rejection of *all* theism." If, however, Marxists and Christians can discuss together some of the working explorations of which I will cite examples, then I suggest that we may discover this claim to reject all theism "is actually the negative echo of the claim of classical theism itself to be the *only* form of theism there is."[11] The working explorations which I cite are also intended to indicate how Christian theology, in the perspective of the wider ecumenism, is attending (as yet uncertainly) to the development of its theism for the sake of its better self-understanding. I hope that Christians are going to move more and more into the heart of current Marxist reflections on man so that this development may be provoked even further.

1. I should regard the "death of God" theology as a somewhat raw, but nonetheless germane instance of these working explorations. Perhaps the main question to address to these theologians is not whether and how God is dead, though Altizer and Hamilton wish to affirm this. What is more important is to ask why they are affirming God's death. In both cases we are concerned, whatever else may be the case, with a protest in the most extreme form possible against the inadequacies of traditional transcendentalism. Thus for

[11] Ogden, *op. cit.*

Altizer, to will the death of God is to free oneself from the Gnostic resentment of reality and from the illusory hope of a future in which the defects of reality will be corrected. The fact that Altizer lays such stress on the Incarnation leads me to conclude that he is not far from a conditional theism, in Dewart's use of that phrase. The Christ or Word,

because it is always incarnate, is historical, moving through history in a series of dialectical self-negations, leading, through the death of God, to the present advent, or epiphany, of the Word on the horizon of our faith, now offering us total redemption in history through a new mode of participation in the sacred.[12]

It may be that Alitzer's work is too arcane to make any long-term contribution to the debate. All the same it is worth noting that what he calls his atheism represents in part a long-neglected attempt with an immanentism not entirely different from that of Teilhard de Chardin, to understand the Incarnation not as an isolated incursion of the divine history but as a perpetual and working self-involvement of the divine in history, a history whose fulfillment is essential to the consummation of all things. This feature emerges in the report of a recent newspaper interview and bids us treat Altizer's atheism with care even if his language here and in his books often seems intractable.

ALITZER: . . . In the cosmic process, it's a kind of dynamic pantheism—God ever becoming other than he was in the past—but nevertheless pantheism in that God eventually will be all in all. Call it a dynamic process pantheism. . . .

12 William Nicholls, "The Death of God Theologies Today," *The Modern Churchman*, X, 1967, p. 216.

BRADEN: Would you call yourself an atheist?
ALITZER: Yes. I do.[13]

Pantheism and atheism are not usually synonymous, so that we must go on to ask to what kind of theism his atheism is relative.

In the case of William Hamilton I should simply wish to observe that, in spelling out his grounds for belief in the death of God, he usually seems to refer to aspects of theistic belief which seem to him to minimize the full reality of the secular order and the full measure of human responsibility towards the world. Thus, "we trust the world, not God, to be our need fulfiller and problem solver, and God, if he is to be for us at all, must come in some other role."[14] Again, ". . . there is something special about the twentieth century that has destroyed the capacity to talk about providence."[15] I think there is value in inspecting these theologians carefully and in being pressed thereby to examine our own theistic stories to see how far they should undergo surgery from the knives of such cultural critiques. Or, as William Nicholls puts it, "the right question might be, what can be said about the being of God if he is such that the event called the death of God can or must happen in our time?"[16]

2. Leslie Dewart, in the book already mentioned, offers some tentative formulations of a more constructive kind. This volume is of particular interest in that it springs out of a painstakingly honest encounter with Garaudy's *De l'Anathème au Dialogue*. Dewart's final

[13] "No Requiem Yet for Theothanasia," *Herder Correspondence*, May 1967, p. 148.
[14] T. Altizer and W. Hamilton, *Radical Theology and the Death of God* (New York: Bobbs-Merrill, 1966), p. 40.
[15] *Herder Correspondence*, May 1967, p. 150.
[16] Nicholls, *op. cit.*, p. 213.

chapter on "The Development of Christian Theism" is, not surprisingly, the most sketchy part of the book; I sometimes have the feeling that his conclusions there do not follow organically from the earlier arguments. Nevertheless his treatment of the "being," "personality," "eternity" and "supernatural nature" of God deserve careful analysis and expansion. For example, discussing the notion of God's omnipotence, Dewart writes:

. . . the reality of God, implying the real possibility of a world totally open to God, implies therefore a world totally open to *future creation by man.* The case is not that God can do the impossible (that is, that God has power to do that which nature cannot do), but that for God all things are possible—and that therefore with God all things are possible to man.[17]

This means that the Christian can no longer fall back upon God, and that he is called on to take a mature initiative in restoring all things in Christ, for "unless we make it be, the Kingdom of God shall never come."[18]

3. I can do no more than allude in passing to the use being made of Process philosophy by some Christian theologians. I believe that this philosophy can serve as a useful platform in the Marxist Christian dialogue, in that it requires the Marxist to consider anew his materialist presumptions and enables the Christian to ground more surely an existentialist conception of God in a way that avoids some of the legitimate objections raised against the God of classical theism. As Colin Wilson has put it, Whitehead "was his own Hegel and Kierkegaard rolled into one."[19] In particular there is much work to be done by theologians in considering

[17] *Dewart, op. cit.,* p. 193.
[18] *Ibid.,* p. 194.
[19] Quoted in Cobb, p. 17 (see note 20).

the relevance for theology of Whitehead's double insistence on the primordiality and consequent nature of
God, where the temporality of the world is never denied
and a real becoming in God affirmed, without his ever
being treated as temporal.[20]

4. Perhaps the conceptual scheme which best deserves
the title of working exploration is that of Teilhard de
Chardin, in his sense that he is already receiving close
attention within the Marxist Christian dialogue. While
I am convinced that Teilhard has some extremely important insights to convey to this dialogue, not least on
the theistic question, there is a great danger that his
thought may be espoused by eclectics on both sides
to produce a hybrid Marxist Teilhardism or Teilhardian
Marxism whose life and influence will undoubtedly be
short. It is quite clear from Teilhard's writings that
where he spoke of a synthesis between the "God above"
and the "God beyond" he did not mean a simple con-
junction of the Marxist infrastructure and the Christian
superstructure. He was talking about a synthesis which
could result if Marxism and Christianity, developing
their potentialities to the full, converged to form a
new entity whose outlines we can at present only
guess.[21] We should not expect from Teilhard a plan
of this future phenomenon but rather hints about the
directions in which Christianity and Marxism should
move if this synthesis is to be realized. This is why a
lot of the discussion about Teihard's orthodoxy *or*

[20] *Cf.* John B. Cobb, *A Christian Natural Theology* (London:
Lutterworth, 1966); Schubert Ogden, *The Reality of God*
(London: SCM, 1967); P. N. Hamilton, "The Theological
Importance of A. N. Whitehead," *Theology*, LXVIII, 1965,
pp. 187ff; W. Richard Comstock, "Naturalism and Theology,"
The Heythrop Journal, VIII, 1967, pp. 181ff.
[21] *Cf.* Claude Cuénot, "Teilhard: Democracy and Dialogue,"
Pax Romana Journal, February 1967, p. 15.

heterodoxy is not likely to lead to valuable conclusions
about his merits. We might indeed ask whether his
starting points are rooted in characteristically Christian ground, but we must then recognize that the
Christianity of the future which he envisages will be
a radical, though not discontinuous, development from
what has gone before. I could therefore broadly assent
to Altizer's rather quixotic estimate of Teilhard as
long as the disappearance or transformation of Christian belief of which he speaks is seen as part and
parcel of a positive evolutionary thrust emerging coher-
ently and dialectically out of the past and present,
not as a negation of the past and the present. Altizer
writes:

We have only to observe the work of Teilhard de Chardin
to grasp the revolutionary consequences for a faith that
would engage in a real encounter with our world. It is
true that Teilhard occasionally and inconsistently intro-
duces traditional Christian language into the pages of
The Phenomenon of Man, but this fact scarcely obviates
the truth that virtually the whole body of Christian belief
either disappears or is transformed in Teilhard's evolutionary vision of the cosmos.[22]

Altizer has seized upon the central point when he
speaks of a "faith that would engage in a real encounter
with our world." For in Teilhard, as in the other working explorations, the chief stimulant to theological transformation derives from an affirmation of the secularity
of the world and of man's proper autonomy. Garaudy
notes this as the most suggestive and novel aspect of
Teilhard's work. From the affirmation of the autonomy
of science and from a radical moral optimism there
flow "major practical consequences: a constant appeal

22 T. Altizer, "Word and History," *Theology Today*, XXII,
1965, p. 383.

to research and work, an exaltation of human power and energy in all man's undertakings to transform nature, society and himself."[23]

What is theologically significant about Teilhard is that these insights, though of course they reflect and cohere with his personal experience of the world, are integrated into a vast over-all perspective incorporating God, man and the world which probably owes its origin in the first place to reflection upon the cosmic Christ motifs of the New Testament than to an inspection of the world. Thus, while on the one hand we can hardly overestimate the revolutionary implications of Teilhard's thought for theology, on the other hand we have to recognize that he began not by rejecting the Christian theological tradition but by trying to understand it anew, and by extending it, in a universe seen as "cosmogenesis." It is not my concern here to attack or defend the validity of this over-all perspective, but only to note something of its relevance for the problems of Christian theism. For Teilhard the focus and fulcrum of the whole picture is the person of Christ. This christological, and therefore theistic, principle is such as positively to license men to set about the construction of the world in order that the cosmos may be brought to its divine-human telos. For,

by His incarnation [Christ] inserted himself not only into humanity, but into the universe which bears humanity— not only by way of being an associated element, but with the dignity and function of being a directing principle, a centre to which all love and affinity converge.[24]

If we then ask about the relation of this Christ to the world of men, we must say that as He is the

---

[23] Garaudy, "Europe," March–April 1965, p. 186.
[24] *Ecrits du temps de la guerre* (Paris: Grasset, 1961), p. 47.

motor of cosmogenesis, so He is the evolver and human-
izer of anthropogenesis. Thus, because

> the cosmos is centered upon Jesus, it should be clear that
> in one way or another collaboration in the future of the
> cosmos is an essential and primary part of Christian responsi-
> bility. Nature grows towards fulfillment and the Body of
> Christ reaches its complete development in one and the
> same movement.[25]

Teilhard clearly regards love as the main motive force
of this collaboration in the future of the cosmos, not
as an abstract virtue but as informing the processes
of change.

> Because everything in the universe is in fact ultimately
> moving towards Christ-Omega; because cosmogenesis, mov-
> ing in its totality through anthropogenesis, ultimately shows
> itself to be a Christogenesis; because of this, I say, it fol-
> lows that the real is charged with a divine presence in
> the authority of its tangible layers . . . I repeat, if the
> whole movement of the world is in the service of a Christo-
> genesis (which is another way of saying that Christ is
> attainable in his fullness only at the end and summit of
> cosmic evolution), then clearly we can draw near to him
> and possess him only in and through the effort to bring
> all to fulfillment and synthesis in him. And this is the
> reason that life's general ascent towards higher conscious-
> ness as well as the whole of human endeavor enter organi-
> cally and by right into the preoccupations and aspirations
> of charity . . . At first the Christian aspired only to be
> able to love . . . *while* acting. Now he is aware that he
> can love *in* acting, that is to say, he can unite himself
> directly to the divine Center through action itself, no
> matter what form such action takes.[26]

25 *Ibid.*, p. 51f.
26 *Oeuvres*, Seuil, Paris, IX, 1965, p. 213f., quoted in Christopher F. Mooney, *Teilhard de Chardin and the Mystery of
Christ* (London: Collins, 1966), p. 161f.

The future of theology seen in this perspective must therefore involve for the Christian what Teilhard in one place describes as "a radical incorporation of terrestrial values in the most fundamental concepts of his Faith."[27] Such a theology has yet to be worked out, though I have tried to hint, from a passing survey of these four working explorations, what kind of form this theological program might take. But the point that I want to emphasize from Teilhard is that the structure which he has outlined for theology takes into its heart the considerations raised by Steeman's paragraph. This does not mean that there are not a number of important things concerning the transcendental nature of God (which Teilhard affirms), sin and redemption that Christians will want to persist saying in one form or another, and which Steeman's average atheist will find unacceptable. Nor am I denying that there is a *skandalon* about the Christian Gospel at which Christians and Marxists balk not because it is untrue or incomprehensible, but because it hurts our pride. "Pull down thy vanity, I say pull down" (Ezra Pound). But at the crucial points of respect for the world, of the possibilities of its development, and of the solemn human responsibility to change the world in the direction of a common human city where man is not deprived of his human dimensions, Teilhard has issued a challenge to Christian theology in the name of Christian faith which differs but little in substance from the challenge issued to theology by the humanist forces within Marxist atheism.

Of necessity I have had to put all this in very abstract terms, whereas the issues which confront us are concrete and practical, involving all manner of

[27] *The Future of Man* (London: Collins, 1964), p. 79.

political, social and other decision-making. To some extent the Marxist Christian dialogue itself merits such a charge at present, namely its lack of specificity. At the same time I cannot regard these theological matters as peripheral since they closely affect the orientation and tenacity of our human action. I believe moreover that the kind of theistic explorations which I have reported themselves raise an intensely practical question for the Christian engaged in the Marxist Christian dialogue.

I refer to the question of how far these recent (and I believe necessary and legitimate) excursions in theism affect our ideas of the nature of Christian existence in respect of prayer, worship, morality, political action, etc. If God is not to be understood as a transcendental need fulfiller and problem solver, but as one who allows us a future in which to bring the cosmos more and more to its fulfillment, in what way can we go on talking of an active personal relationship with Him? In fact can we say that believing in Him makes any practical difference? For the logic of our new theistic explorations seems to require us to say either that, having set us a task to do, He is personally absent (a position not so far removed from the death of God theology), or that He is permanently present in a form and manner difficult to specify (or unspecifiable). As Dewart puts it in a discussion of the meaning of the simultaneous presence and absence of God,

. . . what requires a "demonstration," for it is not immediately obvious, is God's *presence*: whether, in what sense, in what way, and with what consequences, God is present. . . . Present . . . to being, present to world, present to man, present to man's faith, present to the Church, present to history, and present to the future that we create.[28]

28 Dewart, *op cit.*, p. 185.

I suspect that our theological transformation is so much in its infancy that we can hardly begin to formulate approaches to this question. Steeman concludes his article by saying, "But we may expect that God will become present again as the God who enjoins man to take his own task in life and his own responsibility seriously as a holy obligation."[29] Harvey Cox faces the same problem when he asks where the transcendent God meets us in the secular city. He continues:

We have already suggested that God comes to us today in events of social change . . . But how? God is free and hidden. He cannot be expected to appear when we designate the place and time. This means that God is neither close nor far *as such*, but is able to be present in a situation without identifying with it, and He is always present to liberate man . . . God frees us by supplying that framework of limitation within which alone freedom has any meaning.[30]

Cuénot talks of the experience of true transcendence as "participating in God's creative liberty."[31] Ogden speaks of God as "the eminently relative One whom Jesus calls Father."[32] Moltmann would seem to deny that we can know God's divinity between the times. Man can *obey* the *will* of God "by leaving the 'safe fortress' of his social shell and, on the horizon of the future allowed by God, he devotes himself to the alteration of the world and thus enters into history itself." But God's divinity is declared only with the coming of his kingdom: and that will be the kingdom of freedom and justice, of the human creature who is no longer

---

[29] Steeman, *op. cit.*, p. 29.
[30] Harvey Cox, *The Secular City* (London: SCM, 1965), p. 261.
[31] Cuénot, *op. cit.*, p. 15.
[32] Ogden, *Concilium*, June 1966, p. 49.

estranged, but redeemed and transfigured."[33] I cite these different voices merely as pointers to ways in which we shall perhaps start to articulate a language for the affirmation of God's presence in a framework such as Teilhard's. I see this as a project of great importance, for it concerns how the "conditional" nature of our theism at the speculative level is also to be manifestly "conditional" at the level of Christian existence. Even if the defects of the God of classical theism are banished from our minds, they can easily persist as household gods at the level of prayer, conscience, worship, etc. These are surely questions calling for a sustained reflection that will absorb the efforts of a generation or more.

I have tried to outline in a very limited and provisional way some orientations to one of the major problems of Marxist Christian dialogue, namely the God who is both believed and disbelieved for the sake of man. I emphasize the word "provisional," for I fully take Johannes Metz' point that the dialogue must be accompanied by "an awareness of the inadequacy of the theological response." He continues:

Theological discussion with unbelievers should not and need not betray ideological bias, or feign knowledge and presume to supply answers it does not in fact possess. Theology should not and need not, through its supposed surplus of answers and lack of really embarrassing questions, expose itself to the accusation of being merely a mythology in modern dress.[34]

I see the theologian guided by two paradigms in the present situation. The language of "resurrection" affirms that the cry of Jesus on the Cross, when he thought

[33] Jürgen Moltmann, "Hope without Faith: an Eschatological Humanism without God," *Concilium*, June 1966, p. 19.

[34] *Concilium*, June 1966, p. 3.

himself, and others thought him, abandoned, was not the final word, and thus evokes from us the affirmation of God's universal presence despite the appearances. But the Abrahamic resolve reminds us that such an affirmation is not an excuse to sit on our haunches, but a call to "go out, not knowing where we are to go."

This twofold affirmation and resolve stands at the heart of Teilhard's theory of convergence. Only when, and if, Christian theism exposes itself patiently, openly and expectantly to Marxist anthropology, and vice versa, dare we begin to think of the possibility of a synthesis which would develop and transform both, and which could delineate at least one path of further advance for man in a world at once deeply troubled and rich with promise.[35]

[35] I have tried to address a theme similar to that of this essay in a contribution to the symposium *Marxism, Evolution and Christianity*, published by the Garnstone Press, 1967.

Oestreicher, Paul, comp.
   The Christian Marxist dialogue: an international symposium.
[New York] Macmillan [1969]

   xiv, 301 p.   19 cm.

Bibliographical footnotes.

1. Communism and Christianity—Addresses, essays, lectures.   I. Title.

HX536.O3   335.43'8'2   68-23638
                                                        MARC

Library of Congress   [72]